The African Union

D1559380

Fully revised and updated, the second edition of *The African Union* continues to offer the most comprehensive overview of the work of the African Union (AU), with special emphasis on its capacity to meet the challenges of building and sustaining governance institutions and security mechanisms. This new edition:

- Re-examines the AU at the historic moment of the golden jubilee of the OAU (Organization of African Unity), its predecessor. It examines the AU's efforts in its first decade, points out some of the organization's weaknesses, and posits options for addressing more effectively the challenges of peace, security, and governance in coming years.
- Critically reviews several arrangements and initiatives, including the African Peace and Security Architecture (APSA) and the African Peer Review Mechanism (APRM).
- Analyzes performance of key institutions and programs of the AU, including the Commission, the Executive Council, the Assembly, and the Pan-African Parliament (PAP) as well as the New Partnership for Africa's Development (NEPAD).
- Discusses how far instability and insecurity on the continent are consequences of bad governance and the lack of strategic leadership.
- Considers how the absence of a clearly articulated ideology may undermine the implementation of the AU agenda.

In addition to offering revised and updated chapters throughout, this edition includes one new chapter, which critically discusses the AU's new international partnerships. With an emphasis on the current work of the AU and a view to the future of the organization, this book is essential reading for students and scholars researching African Politics and international organizations.

Samuel M. Makinda is Professor of International Relations and Security Studies at Murdoch University, Australia.

F. Wafula Okumu is the Executive Director of The Borders Institute (TBI) in Nairobi, Kenya.

David Mickler is Assistant Professor in Foreign Policy and International Relations at the University of Western Australia, Perth.

Routledge Global Institutions Series
Edited by Thomas G. Weiss
The CUNY Graduate Center, New York, USA
and Rorden Wilkinson
University of Sussex, Brighton, UK

About the series

The "Global Institutions Series" provides cutting-edge books about many aspects of what we know as "global governance." It emerges from our shared frustrations with the state of available knowledge – electronic and print-wise, for research and teaching – in the area. The series is designed as a resource for those interested in exploring issues of international organization and global governance. And since the first volumes appeared in 2005, we have taken significant strides toward filling conceptual gaps.

The series consists of three related "streams" distinguished by their blue, red, and green covers. The blue volumes, comprising the majority of the books in the series, provide user-friendly and short (usually no more than 50,000 words) but authoritative guides to major global and regional organizations, as well as key issues in the global governance of security, the environment, human rights, poverty, and humanitarian action, among others. The books with red covers are designed to present original research and serve as extended and more specialized treatments of issues pertinent for advancing understanding about global governance. And the volumes with green covers – the most recent departure in the series – are comprehensive and accessible accounts of the major theoretical approaches to global governance and international organization.

The books in each of the streams are written by experts in the field, ranging from the most senior and respected authors to first-rate scholars at the beginning of their careers. In combination, the three components of the series – blue, red, and green – serve as key resources for faculty, students, and practitioners alike. The works in the blue and green streams have value as core and complementary readings in courses on, among other things, international organization, global governance, international law, international relations, and international political economy; the red volumes allow further reflection and investigation in these and related areas.

The books in the series also provide a segue-way to the foundation volume that offers the most comprehensive textbook treatment available dealing with all the major issues, approaches, institutions, and actors in contemporary global governance – our edited work *International Organization and Global Governance* (2014) – a volume to which many of the authors in the series have contributed essays.

Understanding global governance – past, present, and future – is far from a finished journey. The books in this series nonetheless represent significant steps toward a better way of conceiving contemporary problems and issues as well as, hopefully, doing something to improve world order. We value the feedback from our readers and their role in helping shape the ongoing development of the series.

A complete list of titles appears at the end of this book. The most recent titles in the series are:

Governing Climate Change (2nd edition, 2015)
Harriet Bulkeley and Peter Newell

Representing Islam in International Relations (2015)
Turan Kayaoglu

Contemporary Human Rights Ideas (2nd edition, 2015)
Bertrand G. Ramcharan

The Politics of International Organizations (2015)
Edited by Patrick Weller and Xu Yi-chong

Global Poverty (2nd edition, 2015)
David Hulme

Global Corporations and Global Governance (2015)
Christopher May

The United Nations Centre on Transnational Corporations (2015)
Khalil Hamdani and Lorraine Ruffing

Praise for the previous edition

This book, authored by two eminent African scholars, is timely and analyses the African continental movement from the OAU in 1963 to the AU. The authors make an honest and sobering assessment of the performance of the AU. Few books have been written on the AU, and this one fills a big gap by providing researchers and lay people with an analysis of this important organization at a time when African leaders are debating the establishment of the United States of Africa.

Ambassador Ahmed Haggag,
Former OAU Assistant Secretary General

The dream of a United Africa is over 100 years old. It crystallized among Black people in the Diaspora, and its founders included the legendary African American intellectual, W.G.B. DuBois. The creation of the AU is the most ambitious stage of Pan-Africanism so far. This book gives us an insight into both the scale of Africa's ambition and the formidable challenges facing such a vision of regional integration. The authors are in command of the facts and are sensitive to the vision.

Professor Ali A. Mazrui, Former Director,
Institute of Global Cultural Studies,
Binghamton University, State University of New York

The African Union
Addressing the challenges of peace, security, and governance
Second edition

Samuel M. Makinda,
F. Wafula Okumu,
and David Mickler

Routledge
Taylor & Francis Group
LONDON AND NEW YORK

Second edition published 2016
by Routledge
2 Park Square, Milton Park, Abingdon, Oxon OX14 4RN

and by Routledge
711 Third Avenue, New York, NY 10017

Routledge is an imprint of the Taylor & Francis Group, an informa business

© 2016 Samuel M. Makinda, F. Wafula Okumu, and David Mickler

First edition published by Routledge 2008

British Library Cataloguing in Publication Data
A catalogue record for this book is available from the British Library

Library of Congress Cataloguing in Publication data
Makinda, Samuel M.
 The African Union : addressing the challenges of peace, security, and governance / by
Samuel M. Makinda, F. Wafula Okumu and David Mickler. – Second edition.
  pages cm. – (Global institutions series)
 Previous edition has subtitle: challenges of globalization, security, and governance.
 1. African Union. 2. Globalization–Africa. 3. National security–Africa.
 4. Africa–Politics and government–1960– I. Okumu, F. Wafula. II. Mickler,
David. III. Title.
 DT30.5.M257 2015
 341.24'9–dc23
 2015001190

ISBN: 978-1-138-79039-1 (hbk)
ISBN: 978-1-138-79040-7 (pbk)
ISBN: 978-1-315-68815-2 (ebk)

Typeset in Times New Roman
by Out of House Publishing

In memory of Professor Ali A. Mazrui (1933–2014)
A public intellectual, great teacher, and mentor

Contents

x *Contents*

Figures

Tables

Contributors

Samuel M. Makinda is Professor of International Relations and Security Studies at Murdoch University, Perth, Australia. He was awarded the medal of Elder of the Order of the Burning Spear by Kenya's former president, Mwai Kibaki, in 2011, for his "distinguished service to the nation." He served on the Australian Foreign Minister's National Consultative Committee for International Security Issues 2001–08. He was also the 2001 Distinguished Lecturer for the United Nations Institute for Natural Resources in Africa, and has held visiting positions at the University of Oxford, the University of Cambridge, the International Institute for Strategic Studies, the Brookings Institution, and the Australian National University. He has published extensively on international relations, international organization, Africa in the world, human rights, and security.

F. Wafula Okumu is the Executive Director of The Borders Institute (TBI) in Nairobi, Kenya. He has previously worked at the African Union and brings that first-hand knowledge with him to this book. He has also held faculty positions at McMaster University, the United Nations University, Prescott College, Mississippi University for Women, and Chapman University. He has published widely on African borders, democracy, human rights, humanitarian assistance, international organization, and security.

David Mickler is Assistant Professor in Foreign Policy and International Relations at the University of Western Australia, Perth, Australia. He previously lectured in International Relations at the University of Melbourne and was a visiting scholar at the Institute for Peace and Security Studies at Addis Ababa University in 2013. He is co-editor of *New Engagement: Contemporary Australian Foreign Policy Towards Africa* (Melbourne University Press, 2013).

Acknowledgments

In the course of writing this book, we incurred substantial debts to several people. We are particularly grateful to the series editors, Thomas G. Weiss and Rorden Wilkinson, for their encouragement, support, and patience. We were delighted that they trusted us to provide a successor to *The African Union: Challenges of globalization, security, and governance* (2008). We were also privileged to work with a very cheerful and supportive commissioning editor at Routledge, Nicola Parkin. The editorial assistant for politics and international studies at Routledge, Peter Harris, was friendly and always handled our requests promptly and with a sense of humour. We would also like to express our gratitude to our respective employers, Murdoch University, The Borders Institute (Nairobi), and the University of Western Australia, for supporting this book project. Finally, we are grateful to our spouses – Isabella, Caroline, and Laura – for their love, understanding, and encouragement. Needless to say, any errors are our own.

Abbreviations

ACCORD	African Centre for the Constructive Resolution of Disputes
ACERWC	African Committee of Experts on the Rights and Welfare of the Child
ACHPR	African Commission on Human and Peoples' Rights
ACIRC	African Capacity for Immediate Response to Crisis
ACJHR	African Court of Justice and Human Rights
ACOTA	African Contingency Operations Training and Assistance
ACRI	Africa Crisis Response Initiative
ACSRT	African Centre on the Study and Research on Terrorism
AfDB	African Development Bank
AFISMA	African-led International Support Mission in Mali
AFRICOM	(United States) Africa Command
AGA	African Governance Architecture
AMIB	African Union Mission in Burundi
AMIS	African Union Mission in Sudan
AMISOM	African Union Mission in Somalia
ANC	African National Congress
APA	African Peace Academy
APF	African Peace Facility
APRM	African Peer Review Mechanism
APSA	African Peace and Security Architecture
ASF	African Standby Force
AU	African Union
AUC	African Union Commission
AUCIL	African Union Commission on International Law

BRICS	Brazil, Russia, India, China, and South Africa
CAAU	Constitutive Act of the African Union
CADSP	Common African Defence and Security Policy
CAR	Central African Republic
CEN-SAD	*Communauté des États Sahelo-Sahariens* [Community of Sahel-Saharan States]
CEWARN	Conflict Early Warning and Response Mechanism
CEWS	Continental Early Warning System
CISSA	Committee of Intelligence and Security Services in Africa
COMESA	Common Market for Eastern and Southern Africa
CSO	Civil Society Organization
CSSDCA	Conference on Security, Stability, Development, and Cooperation in Africa
DRC	Democratic Republic of the Congo
EAC	East African Community
EC	Executive Council
ECA	(UN) Economic Commission for Africa
ECCAS	Economic Community of Central African States
ECOSOCC	Economic, Social, and Cultural Council
ECOWARN	ECOWAS Early Warning and Response Network
ECOWAS	Economic Community of Western African States
EP	European Parliament
EU	European Union
EWS	Early Warning System
FOC	Full operational capability
FOCAC	Forum on China–Africa Cooperation
G8	Group of Eight
G20	Group of Twenty
GDP	Gross Domestic Product
GNP	Gross National Product
GPOI	Global Peace Operations Initiative
HIV/AIDS	Human Immunodeficiency Virus/Acquired Immune Deficiency Syndrome
IANSA	International Action Network on Small Arms
ICC	International Criminal Court
ICGLR	International Conference of the Great Lakes Region
ICT	Information and Communications Technology
IGAD	Intergovernmental Authority on Development

IMF	International Monetary Fund
IOC	Indian Ocean Commission
JAES	Joint Africa-European Union Strategy
LO	Liaison Officer
MINUSMA	UN Multidimensional Integrated Stabilization Mission in Mali
MoU	Memorandum of Understanding
MSC	Military Staff Committee
NATO	North Atlantic Treaty Organization
NEPAD	New Partnership for Africa's Development
NGO	Non-Governmental Organization
NPT	Non-Proliferation Treaty
OAU	Organization of African Unity
OECD	Organisation for Economic Cooperation and Development
OIF	*Organisation Internationale de la Francophonie*
PAP	Pan-African Parliament
PAU	Pan-African University
PCRD	Policy on Post-conflict Reconstruction and Development
PKO	Peace Keeping Operation
PMCD	Partnerships Management and Coordination Division
PoW	Panel of the Wise
PRC	Permanent Representative Committee
PSC	Peace and Security Council
PSD	Peace and Security Department (of the AU Commission)
PSO	Peace Support Operation
RDC	Rapid Deployment Capability
RECs	Regional Economic Communities
RM	Regional Mechanism
SADC	Southern African Development Community
STCs	Specialized Technical Committees
STCDSS	Specialized Technical Committee on Defence Safety and Security
UDHR	Universal Declaration of Human Rights
UK	United Kingdom
UMA	Union of Arab Maghreb

UN	United Nations
UNAMID	African Union-United Nations Hybrid Operation in Darfur
UNDP	United Nations Development Programme
UNEP	United Nations Environment Programme
UNESCO	United Nations Educational, Scientific, and Cultural Organization
UNMISS	United Nations Mission in the Republic of South Sudan
UNOAU	United Nations Office to the African Union
UNSOA	United Nations Support Office for AMISOM
US	United States of America

Introduction

As we were completing this second edition of the book, the international community was debating how it would protect itself from Ebola by addressing the epidemic at its source in West Africa. As of this writing there was no cure for Ebola, but at the request of the Bill and Melinda Gates Foundation, an Australian-based drug company, CSL, announced in early October 2014 that it would look into the possibility of designing a prophylaxis.[1] Besides the Ebola epidemic, Africa has been continuously in the news for other reasons, including: political uncertainty in Burkina Faso after the long-time dictator, Blaise Compaore, fled the country on October 31, 2014; the kidnapping of over 200 Nigerian schoolgirls by the Muslim militant group, Boko Haram,[2] in April 2014; the breakdown in law and order in Libya; and the continuing conflicts in Mali, South Sudan, Somalia, and the Central African Republic (CAR).[3] Thus, there were many issues that suggested themselves for inclusion in our analysis.

The first edition of this book examined the African Union (AU) when it was only five years old. Its main argument was that the AU was established to deal with various global challenges with a view to improving the livelihoods of the African people through the promotion of several common goods, such as peace and security, good governance, respect for human rights and the rule of law, environmental sustainability, and gender equality. The book was organized around the understanding that globalization, security, and governance were symbiotically connected, and that the failure to realize one of them would compromise the opportunities for achieving the other two. It claimed that the lack of a clear African approach to building and sustaining institutions had resulted in the creation of structures that impeded, rather than accelerated, vital public goods, including healthcare, development, democracy, and justice.

In the past decade the AU has undertaken a range of activities with various degrees of success and failure. The performance of the African Union Commission (AUC), the Executive Council (EC), and the Assembly has varied, and, in some cases, has fallen short of expectations. As a result, the AU's accomplishment in some areas, such as the promotion of peace, integration, good governance, and respect for human rights, has been weak. In addition, the AU has taken questionable positions on the International Criminal Court (ICC)[4] and other international issues and processes. It was also noticeable during the golden jubilee anniversary of the founding of the Organisation of African Unity (OAU) in May 2013 that the AU was experiencing what could be described as a lack of ideology and a framework to drive and guide its objectives and missions.

This second edition – *The African Union: Addressing the Challenges of Peace, Security, and Governance* – is designed to re-examine the AU in the aftermath of the historic moment of the golden jubilee of the establishment of the OAU, its predecessor. It examines the AU's efforts in its first dozen years, points out some of the organization's weaknesses, and posits options for addressing more effectively the challenges of establishing and maintaining peace, security, and good governance in the coming years. It critically reviews several key arrangements and initiatives, including the African Peace and Security Architecture (APSA), the African Governance Architecture (AGA), and the African Peer Review Mechanism (APRM). It also critically reviews the performance of key structures, organs, and programs of the AU, including the Commission, the EC, the Assembly, the Pan-African Parliament (PAP), and the New Partnership for Africa's Development (NEPAD). This has entailed revising and updating all of the chapters. However, this revised edition is not simply an update of the earlier book. It features one new chapter on the establishment and management of the AU's emerging international partnerships that shape Africa's widening peace, security, and governance agendas. Moreover, the argument for this new edition revolves around two hypotheses. The first is that the key to most of Africa's problems rests with having the right paradigm and generating appropriate knowledge. The second hypothesis is that the lack of a clearly articulated ideology has undermined, and might continue to hinder, the implementation of a large part of the AU agenda.[5]

The principal assumption of the first edition of this book was that the AU could fulfil its broad mandate only if it capitalized on the dynamic tension between globalization, security, and good governance. This new edition recognizes the vitality of this dynamic tension, but moves beyond it and adds the challenges of peace – broadly defined. The fall of some of Africa's long-serving political leaders in

Egypt, Libya, and Tunisia in the wake of the so-called "Arab Spring" brings into focus the relationship between peace, security, and good governance. Moreover, the crises in the CAR, South Sudan, and the Democratic Republic of Congo (DRC) raise questions about the AU's capacity to help forge and maintain peace, security, and good governance on the continent.

The AU has been in existence for 12 years following its launch in July 2002. Although it was built on the infrastructure of the OAU, which was infamous for turning a blind eye to bad governance, its mandate is different and has been expected to deliver public benefits to the African people. Before examining in detail the AU's achievements and challenges, it is important that we explain the key variables defining the tasks that the organization has been expected to perform: peace, security, and good governance. We are conscious of the fact that each of these factors would look different if viewed through various theoretical lenses, such as constructivism, critical social theory, feminism, liberalism, Marxism, realism or post-colonialism. In this book we take an eclectic approach, which allows us to utilize insights from any theoretical framework to illuminate the issues in question.[6]

The peace imperative

As already indicated, this book is concerned with examining the challenges of peace, security, and good governance on the continent; and whether the AU has the capacity to deal with them effectively or not. Albert Einstein argued that peace was "a moral duty which no conscientious [person] [could] shirk."[7] Underlining the imperative for peace in international society, Johan Galtung, the founder of peace studies, argued: "If we begin with the need to survive, we immediately see that peace is a primary requirement of the human condition itself."[8] Thus, peace, sometimes defined as a period of political tranquility or the absence of war, plays an important role in society. Peace is the foundation for human solidarity, survival, and progress.

Writing in sixteenth century England, Thomas Hobbes argued that without peace, there would be "no place for industry, because the fruit thereof is uncertain."[9] He concluded that "worst of all, [there would be] continual fear, and danger of violent death."[10] Without peace, Hobbes observed, human life would be "solitary, poor, nasty, brutish, and short."[11] Hobbes' observations have relevance for twenty-first century Africa. It is peace that makes development, democracy, healthcare, and education possible. Without peace, other important public goods, such as state sovereignty, security, governance structures, and institutions would be undermined. Hence the need to interrogate the AU's contribution to peace on the continent.

The eruption of crises in Egypt, Libya, and Tunisia between 2011 and 2014 demonstrated not only the fragility of peace, but also the close relationship between peace, security, and good governance. Moreover, democracy, human rights, peace, and security, in any part of the world, are the shared responsibility of all states and other global agents. A former Ghanaian leader, Kwame Nkrumah, underlined this connection in the 1960s. Whenever Nkrumah talked of the "African personality" playing a role on the world stage, he argued that freedom, human rights, and peace were global entitlements that were indivisible. Having declared in the early 1960s that the liberation of the remaining colonial territories in Africa was the responsibility of every African person, Nkrumah insisted that freedom anywhere could be meaningful only if the whole world was free and at peace. Thus, Nkrumah could be credited with advancing the idea that peace and freedom were universal, global, and indivisible. Nkrumah asserted: "World peace is not possible without the complete liquidation of colonialism and the total liberation of peoples everywhere. The indivisibility of peace is staked upon the indivisibility of freedom."[12] In doing so, Nkrumah postulated that it was the responsibility of every state in the world to champion the causes of peace and freedom. It was for this reason that one of us claimed in 1976 that through the African personality, Nkrumah attempted the "globalization of the liberation strategy."[13]

One of our aims in this book is to explore how the AU might utilize the interrelationships among peace, globalization, security, and good governance as a catalyst to pursue the objectives and principles stipulated in its Constitutive Act.

Addressing security

In one sense, security implies boundaries, both real and metaphorical, and these boundaries are, in turn, about identity and interests. Analysts differ over what identity issues and interests are to be secured. Should they be individuals, nations, socio-economic classes, states, or ethnic communities? What should African states and people aim to secure? What role does the AU play in securing these objects? What roles do peace and governance structures play in the construction and management of security in Africa?

In the twenty-first century, good governance – propelled by globalization – has evolved to the point at which public policies are increasingly becoming people-centered. This implies that security policies have to be defined in terms of the aspirations, needs, and dignity of the people.

Accordingly, security should be viewed as people-centered, and whether states achieve, undermine, or are irrelevant to security is an open question, depending on time and place.[14] Therefore, security in Africa, viewed in terms of identity and interests, should be regarded as the protection of people and the preservation of their norms, rules, institutions, and resources in the face of military and non-military threats. The latter may include natural disasters, ecological and environmental degradation, lack of access to affordable healthcare, poverty, severe economic problems, human rights abuses, and the erosion of democratic rule. Ken Booth goes further and equates security with emancipation.[15]

Our definition avoids the binary division between national security and human security. It is broad enough to include the preservation of states and the structures, principles, and institutions on which states are anchored – but only to the extent that protection of state boundaries and the governing structures and elites is not privileged over people. This definition also assumes that people are prior to states, and, therefore, the security of the state is derived from that of the people. However, defining security in terms of people also raises significant questions about gender, which space does not allow us to explore here.

This book is partly concerned with how the AU can "promote peace, security and stability on the continent" (Article 3[f] of the Constitutive Act of the AU) by using globalization and good governance. The interrelationship between peace, security, and good governance dictates that we occasionally isolate particular security issues and explore how peace and governance affect them. For example, providing solutions to the Darfur crisis – which is a security problem – would require negotiations among various parties such as the United Nations (UN), the AU, the Sudanese government, and representatives of the parties within Darfur which are governance entities and structures. It would also require the support of various international actors, such as the European Union (EU). Furthermore, the issues over which the parties negotiate – such as human rights, self-determination, autonomy, and access to food, shelter, education, and health facilities – are interests that are continually recast by globalization. If some of the parties were found to have committed war crimes or crimes against humanity, they would probably be prosecuted through the ICC – which is a governance structure. Good governance appears to be so essential that it is plausible to argue that security is achievable in Africa only where governance structures are stable, effective, and are designed to meet the people's needs, rights, and hopes.

The governance issue

Governance occurs at various levels of social activity, from the village or local council, to the state and the global system. Whenever human beings or social groups interact for extended periods, they establish a set of rules, norms, and institutions. These values constitute governance and may perform diverse functions, but they are particularly significant for providing peace, order, certainty, and stability as perceived by the most powerful agents. In Africa, governance stretches from villages and local councils in such places as Ghana, Namibia, and Tunisia, to Regional Economic Communities (RECs) and the AU, and it involves states as well as non-state agents. This is why the Commission on Global Governance, which comprised a cross section of people from around the world – including five Africans – defined governance as "the sum of the many ways individuals and institutions, public and private, manage their common affairs."[16]

The challenge for African states and the AU is how to work out a formula for deconstructing the norms, rules, and institutions that underpin peace, security, and good governance so that they accurately reflect the intentions of those who drafted the Constitutive Act of the African Union (CAAU). Article 1 of the CAAU provides some definitions, but it appears to take for granted the meanings of important institutions and issues – such as sovereignty and self-determination. Although the CAAU recognizes the importance of good governance, and lists it in its objectives and guiding principles, it was not until 2007 that the AU Assembly adopted the *African Charter on Democracy, Elections and Governance*. As this book partly explores how globalization, peace, security, and good governance impact on the capacity of the AU to fulfil its mandate, it is imperative that we redefine the institutions[17] that constitute good governance and security.

So, what are institutions? Many people – including journalists, academics, and policy makers – have used the term "institution" to refer to two different phenomena: enduring and shared practices; and international organizations. For example, in his annual report to the UN General Assembly on September 19, 2006, Kofi Annan referred to the UN as an "institution."[18] Annan used the term "institution" to mean an international organization with its own Charter, mission, personnel, and budget. Six decades earlier, US Senator Arthur Vandenberg – in his report to the Senate on the San Francisco Conference that established the UN – used the term "institution" to describe two phenomena. He described the UN as an "institution which can promise some element of orderly correction" in a world ruined by war.[19] However, in the same report he defined international law as an institution when he referred to "the new emphasis which is put upon international law as an institution for human service."[20]

To provide a basis for consistency in the way this book employs the term "institution," it is important that we explain its different meanings at the outset. Robert Keohane defines institutions as "related complexes of rules and norms, identifiable in space and time."[21] He argues that institutions are "persistent sets of rules that constrain activity, shape expectations, and prescribe roles."[22] Similarly, Hedley Bull defines an institution as "a set of habits and practices shaped towards the realization of common goals."[23] He views institutions as "an expression of the element of collaboration among states in discharging their political functions – and at the same time a means of sustaining this collaboration."[24] According to Bull, institutions include the balance of power, international law, diplomacy, war, and the managerial system of the great powers. John Mearsheimer also claims that an institution is "a set of rules that stipulate the ways in which states should cooperate or compete with each other."[25] However, he differs with Bull when he argues: "These rules are typically formalized in international agreements, and are usually embodied in organizations with their own personnel and budgets."[26]

The above authors define institutions in two senses. In the first sense, institutions are "stable sets of norms, rules, and principles" that "constitute actors as knowledgeable social agents" and "regulate behavior."[27] Thus, several variables that underpin the AU – such as state sovereignty, diplomacy, international law, and multilateralism – are institutions. These habits and practices have been described as primary institutions.[28]

In the second sense, the term "institution" refers to formal organizations like the AU, the East African Community (EAC), the Economic Community of Western African States (ECOWAS), the Economic Community of Central African States (ECCAS), the Intergovernmental Authority on Development (IGAD), the Southern African Development Community (SADC), and the Union of Arab Maghreb (UMA). However, Bull excludes these organizations, arguing: "By an institution we do not necessarily imply an organization or administrative machinery."[29] These organizations have been described as secondary institutions.[30]

In this book the AU is discussed mainly as an organization and not as an institution. Similarly, entities such as the UN, the EU, the World Bank, the OAU, and ECOWAS are called international organizations, not institutions. Furthermore, entities internal to the AU – such as the Assembly, the EC, the Peace and Security Council, the Commission, and the PAP – are referred to as organs. The term "institution" is used in a limited sense to refer to established practices such as constitutionalism,[31] democracy, diplomacy, international law, multilateralism, religion, the law, and sovereignty. These institutions, in turn, shape the identities and interests of individuals, societies, states, and organizations.

While these institutions are often described as shared understandings among states and other international agents, grasping their true character calls for several qualifications. First, there is no unanimity in the way that states and other international agents – including African countries – interpret institutions such as sovereignty and international law. Instead, there is continuous contestation about their meanings, status, and roles. Second, power and interests play important roles in generating, shaping, and implementing institutions. It is the preferences of hegemonic states, especially Western powers in the current international order, which determine the shape of institutions. This is why Samuel Huntington claimed: "The West in effect is using international institutions, military power and economic resources to run the world in ways that will maintain Western predominance, protect Western interests and promote Western political and economic values."[32] At the continental level it is regional powers, such as Nigeria and South Africa, which dominate the debates on how institutions should be interpreted and implemented at a particular time.

The role of power in the interpretation of institutions implies that existing global institutions may not accurately reflect the values, preferences, and standards of African states and people. Even international law is, to some extent, culturally biased. Both the structures of international law-making, and the content of the rules of international law, privilege Westerners and reflect the interests and identities of Western societies. Whether these institutions can be reinterpreted to reflect African values and norms will partly depend on how African states and the AU control or influence the fountains of knowledge.

The structure of the book

To elaborate the principal claims stated earlier, this book explores various themes – including the impact of colonialism, the imperative for liberation, the fascination with pan-Africanism, the needs for effective and transparent governance, the role of identity, the nature of war and insecurity, and the debates on knowledge, gender, and development. These themes are examined through seven chapters. In doing so, the book does not seek to analyze all aspects of the multitude of activities undertaken by, or involving, the AU that have proliferated over the past 12 years.

Chapter 1 examines the aspirations, power struggles, and fears that surrounded the emergence of the OAU, the AU's predecessor. To provide context and enable comparison it looks at how the establishment of the OAU was driven by the imperative of liberation and the desire for integration. This chapter also explains how the power struggles and fears, in turn, transformed the organization into a mutual protection club for political leaders and states that was unsuitable for the post-Cold War and post-liberation climate. Chapter 2 focuses on the post-Cold War conditions that led to the establishment of the AU – which was driven by a particular set of factors and values, including: globalization, the imperative for peace, neo-liberal economic ideology, the changing perspectives on security, and good governance. Most importantly, this chapter examines the structures, organs, and processes of the AU and the extent to which they reflect the spirit and letter of the CAAU.

Chapter 3 analyzes the challenges of good governance, democracy, and the rule of law. It also examines the effects of corruption on governance and discusses options for overcoming the constraints that African leaders face. Chapter 4 focuses on the AU's capacity for conflict management, peace building, and security. As security in Africa has been internationalized, and as the AU is heavily dependent on international society to fund its activities, this chapter explores the extent to which the AU is in control of its own peace and security agenda.

Chapter 5 examines Africa's international partnerships and how the AU seeks to balance the idea of "African solutions to African problems" with these partnerships. Chapter 6 explores the way knowledge could assist the AU in its efforts to enhance peace, security, and good governance. It examines the measures that the AU could undertake in order to promote the generation of appropriate knowledge. Chapter 7 – the conclusion – discusses the AU's options for addressing the challenges that Africa faces in building and sustaining peace, security, and good governance.

Notes

1 See "CSL Answers Bill Gates Appeal on Ebola Treatment," *The Australian*, October 17, 2014. Available at: www.theaustralian.com.au/business /news/csl-answers-bill-gates-appeal-on-ebola-treatment/story-e6frg906-1227093446160.
2 For a brief analysis of Boko Haram's emergence, see Femi Owolade, "Boko Haram: How a Militant Islamist Group Emerged in Nigeria," Gatestone Institute, March 27, 2014. Available at: www.gatestoneinstitute.org/4232/ boko-haram-nigeria.
3 See, for example, the International Institute for Strategic Studies, *Strategic Survey 2014: The Annual Review of World Affairs* (London: Routledge), Chapter 10 (2014).

4 For example, see Susanne D. Mueller, "Kenya and the International Criminal Court (ICC): Politics, the Election and the Law," *Journal of Eastern African Studies*, vol. 8, no. 1 (2014): 25–42; Martin Welz, "The African Union Beyond Africa: Explaining the Limited Impact of Africa's Continental Organization on Global Governance," *Global Governance*, vol. 19, no. 3 (2013): 425–41.

5 For a recent analysis of the AU's lack of progress towards meaningful integration, see Martin Welz, *Integrating Africa: Decolonization's Legacies, Sovereignty and the African Union* (London: Routledge) (2013).

6 Eclecticism is a reflexive process that enables scholars to construct coherent analytical approaches by utilizing insights from different theories. It can also be described as "an ethic of pluralism," which has the potential to liberate scholars from their paradigmatic constraints. See, Samuel M. Makinda, "International Society and Eclecticism in International Relations Theory," *Cooperation and Conflict*, vol. 35, no. 2 (2000): 205–16; Rudra Sil, "The Foundations of Eclecticism: The Epistemological Status of Agency, Culture, and Structure in Social Theory," *Journal of Theoretical Politics*, vol. 12, no. 3 (2000): 353–87; and Samuel M. Makinda, "Reading and Writing International Relations," *Australian Journal of International Affairs*, vol. 54, no. 3 (2000): 389–401.

7 Albert Einstein, *The World As I See It* (Secausus, NJ: Citadel Press) (1984): 43.

8 Johan Galtung and Daisaku Ikeda, *Choose Peace: A Dialogue between Johan Galtung and Daisaku Ikeda* (translated and edited by R. L. Gage) (London: Pluto Press) (1995): 110.

9 Thomas Hobbes, *Leviathan* (edited by C. B. Macpherson) (London: Penguin) (1968): 186.

10 Hobbes, *Leviathan*: 186.

11 Hobbes, *Leviathan*: 186.

12 Kwame Nkrumah, *Africa Must Unite* (London: Panaf Books) (1963): 203.

13 Samuel M. Makinda, "Kwame Nkrumah's Theory of the African Personality," B.A. thesis, University of Nairobi (1976): 163.

14 This definition is derived from Samuel M. Makinda, "Security in International Society: A Comment on Alex J. Bellamy and Mat McDonald," *Australian Journal of Political Science*, vol. 40, no. 2 (2005): 275–87.

15 Ken Booth, "Security and Emancipation," *Review of International Studies*, vol. 17, no. 4 (1991): 313–26. Booth defines emancipation as "freeing people, as individuals and groups, from the social, physical, economic, political and other constraints that stop them from carrying out what they would freely choose to do."

16 *Our Global Neighbourhood*, The Report of the Commission on Global Governance (Oxford: Oxford University Press) (1995): 2.

17 An additional incentive for defining institutions here is the fact that this book is published in the series on Global Institutions.

18 UN Secretary-General, "Address to the General Assembly," (2004): 4.

19 Senator Arthur Vandenberg, "Senator Vandenberg's Report to the Senate on the San Francisco Conference," *New York Times* (June 29, 1945): 5. Paper located at: www.ibiblio.org/pha/policy/1945/1945-06-29a.html.

20 Vandenberg, "Senate Vandenberg's Report to the Senate": 8.

21 Robert O. Keohane, "International Institutions: Two Approaches," *International Studies Quarterly*, vol. 32, no. 4 (1988): 383.
22 Keohane, "International Institutions": 483.
23 Hedley Bull, *The Anarchical Society: A Study of Order in World Politics* (London: Macmillan) (1995 [1977]): 71.
24 Bull, *The Anarchical Society*: 71.
25 John J. Mearsheimer, "The False Promise of International Institutions," *International Security*, vol. 19, no. 3 (1994–95): 8.
26 Mearsheimer, "The False Promise of International Institutions": 8.
27 Christian Reus-Smit, *The Moral Purpose of the State: Culture, Social Identity, and Institutional Rationality* (Princeton: Princeton University Press) (1999): 12–13.
28 Samuel M. Makinda, "Hedley Bull and Global Governance: A Note on IR Theory," *Australian Journal of International Affairs*, vol. 56, no. 3 (2002): 366.
29 Bull, *The Anarchical Society*: 71.
30 Makinda, "Hedley Bull and Global Governance": 366.
31 For an excellent analysis of constitutionalism in Africa, see, for example, Abdullahi Ahmed An-Na'im, *African Constitutionalism and the Role of Islam* (Philadelphia: University of Pennsylvania Press) (2006): 1–62.
32 Samuel P. Huntington, "The Clash of Civilizations?" *Foreign Affairs*, vol. 72, no. 3 (1993): 40.

1 The Organisation of African Unity
Liberation, integration, and mutual preservation

The Organisation of African Unity (OAU) was established in Addis Ababa, Ethiopia, on May 25, 1963, by the political leaders of 31 African countries. Identity issues and interests, namely liberation and integration, drove the organization's primary goals. Its main interest was the liberation of white-ruled Africa, especially southern Africa. The creation of the organization was a major achievement in terms of identity. One of the foremost advocates of African unity on the basis of identity – that is, with a view to promoting pan-Africanism and the African personality – was Kwame Nkrumah. Nkrumah told the All-African People's Conference in Accra, in 1958, that pan-Africanism could be considered to have four main stages: national independence, national consolidation, transnational unity and community, and economic and social reconstruction. However, owing to the emerging ideological and power struggles between newly independent African states in the early 1960s, the OAU did not embrace much of what Nkrumah articulated.

Another important development that helped to shape the political atmosphere during the launching of the OAU was the military coup in Togo and the subsequent death of the country's first president, Sylvanus Olympio, in January 1963. Some African leaders and the Western press blamed Olympio's death on Nkrumah. Olympio's death had the effect not only of slowing down Nkrumah's campaign, but also of focusing attention on the fear of political assassinations.

So, at the creation of the OAU, two issues exercised the minds of its founders: power struggles and the fear of political uncertainty. There were power struggles between Nigeria and Ghana, which were transformed into competing sub-regional blocs. Over the years power struggles within the OAU took various forms and involved different countries. The issue of fear was turned into an obsession for regime protection. The OAU subsequently sought to preserve at least three issues: state boundaries that had been established by colonialism; the territorial integrity and sovereignty of each state, which meant non-interference in the internal affairs of other states even when their leaders butchered their own people; and heads of state who felt threatened not just by internal insurgencies, but also by legitimate opposition groups.

Thus, the OAU often behaved like a mutual preservation club for African governments – which inhibited it from taking a more proactive role in managing Africa's problems. The only instances where the OAU authorized interference in the internal affairs of other states was in respect to the white minority regimes in southern Africa: Angola and Mozambique until 1975; Zimbabwe (Rhodesia) until 1980; Namibia until 1989; and South Africa until the early 1990s. As South Africa was the most powerful of these countries, its destabilization and diplomatic overtures towards independent Africa in the 1970s and 1980s were monitored closely. The shadow of apartheid South Africa was behind most of the OAU's activities in relation to the strategy of liberation. In an indirect way, apartheid South Africa appeared like an uninvited guest at the OAU dinner table, helping to initiate and shape the debates within the OAU.

How did the OAU utilize the interrelationships among globalization, peace, security, and governance? The term "globalization" was not in vogue until the 1980s. However, Nkrumah debated the issues of liberation, freedom, and peace within a global context. The majority of African political leaders did not embrace Nkrumah's globalist schemes because they feared that he had an ambition to rule the entire continent. Nkrumah insisted that he was "prepared to serve in a political union of free African states under any African leader who [was] able to offer the proper guidance," but his peers did not believe he was genuine.[1]

Security was a major concern for the founders of the OAU, but they viewed it primarily in terms of state interests – especially territorial integrity, state sovereignty, protection of the ruling elite, and the preservation of state boundaries. For this reason they rejected Nkrumah's assertion that there was "no security for African states unless African leaders ... realized beyond all doubt that salvation for Africa [lay] in unity."[2] Moreover, the OAU, like the rest of the world, did not draw a link between the lack of peace, insecurity, and bad governance until the 1990s. In some cases, the security that African leaders sought for themselves merely contributed to poverty, political violence, and the insecurity of their people.

Governance in Africa was also viewed in statist terms, with the assumption that it was an internal matter in which outside intervention was unwelcome. Without modern communications technologies, including the internet, oppression took place largely unnoticed by outsiders.

Moreover, no distinction was made between the interests of the political leader, the ruling party, and the state. Parliaments served merely as rubber stamps of the policies of despotic leaders. Sovereignty was assumed to reside with the ruler rather than with the people. In these circumstances governments routinely violated human rights, political leaders frequently ignored the rule of law, and the OAU often defended them.

This chapter provides an important context for the later creation of the AU, as well as enabling comparative analysis of the two continental organizations. It is divided into three parts. The first looks briefly at the colonial setting and explains why and how colonial policies indirectly gave rise to pan-Africanism. The second discusses briefly the pan-Africanist movement and its twin goals of liberation and integration. The third explains the statist nature of the OAU – especially with regard to state boundaries, sovereignty and non-interference, and the neglect of human rights.

The colonial setting

This section is concerned not with colonialism per se, but with the role that the colonial policies played in the generation of pan-Africanism, which, in turn, led to the creation of the OAU and continues to inform the work of the African Union (AU). There were three key processes or activities through which colonialism helped the pan-African cause: collective humiliation, the foundation for modern political communities, and the universalization of European values.

Collective humiliation

Colonialism's humiliation of black people and its attempts to undermine their cultures helped to give them an identity. This identity, in turn, demanded that they unite if they were to have any chance of getting rid of foreign occupation. Therefore, the interests in liberation and integration were closely tied to identity.

The humiliation of Africans took various forms. In some parts of Africa, the taking away of land and its appropriation for use by white settlers was a humiliation and an insult. It dislocated many Africans, some of whom abandoned ancestral burial grounds in order to make way for Europeans and their projects. Land dispossession was felt most deeply in settler colonies like Kenya, South Africa, and Zimbabwe.

The introduction of European systems of education brought enormous benefits to Africans. However, education was part of the effort to transplant European cultures into Africa. This was accompanied by colonial attempts to discourage certain African cultural practices, with the result that Africans were alienated from some of their roots. Colonial education was also used to deny Africans a history, but not a past. For example, the Regius Professor of History at Oxford, Hugh Trevor-Roper – whose word carried weight in the British colonial office – argued in the early 1960s that there was no such thing as African history except "the unedifying gyrations of barbarous tribes."[3] He claimed: "There is only the history of Europeans in Africa. The rest is darkness and darkness is not a subject of history."[4] These efforts to deny Africans a history cut across ethnic boundaries and made Africans aware of themselves as victims because of their color. In the end, colonialism constructed the consciousness of "Africanness." The subsequent search for identity and the invention of concepts such as the African personality, negritude, and African renaissance emanated from this sense of cultural humiliation. These concepts were designed to restore dignity to black Africans and provided the intellectual base of pan-Africanism.

Edward Blyden made the earliest recorded efforts in this search for an African identity in a speech at Freetown, Sierra Leone, in 1893:

> Honour and love your race. Be yourselves … If you are not yourself, if you surrender your personality, you have nothing to give the world. You have no pleasure, no use, nothing which can attract and charm men, for by the suppression of your individuality, you lose your distinctive character.[5]

The African personality, negritude, and African renaissance were, in part, based on the consciousness of possessing a commonly shared historical experience. African leaders used them in an attempt to assert the resilience of traditional African values.

However, African researchers have explained the cultural influence of colonialism from different angles. For example, Ali Mazrui's concept of Africa's triple heritage does not just focus on the humiliating aspects of colonialism. Instead, it suggests that colonialism added another dimension to Africa's identity. Mazrui claims that the present day Africa is a product of three cultures: indigenous African, Islamic, and Western.[6] Through the concept of the triple heritage, Mazrui sought to express three types of relationships. These were the relationships between: African civilizations and Western cultures; Islamic values and African civilizations; and Islamic and Western civilizations. He believed that these three-dimensional relationships were crucial to understanding much of the African story. By exploring Africa's triple heritage, Mazrui hoped to broaden the understanding of Africa's colonial past.

Foundation for modern political communities

Colonialism also established the foundation for the formation of modern nation states out of various African ethnic groups. A former Tanzanian president, Julius Nyerere, argued that Africans – as a self-conscious group – were constructed by colonialism. Mazrui cites Nyerere, who claimed that the "sentiment of Africa" is "something which came from outside." Nyerere posited: "One need not go into the history of colonisation of Africa, but that colonisation had one significant result. A sentiment was created on the African continent – a sentiment of oneness."[7] Without colonialism, the Ewe, Yoruba, Kikuyu, and Chagga – among others – would have maintained their ethnic identities but would not have become Ghanaians, Nigerians, Kenyans, or Tanzanians, respectively. Adu Boahen has acknowledged that the construction of the modern state to replace "the existing innumerable lineage and clan groups, city-states, kingdoms and empires without any fixed boundaries," was a positive development.[8] Therefore, state-based nationalism – which is a form of identity – was also constructed by colonialism. State-based nationalism was both an aid and a hindrance to continental unity.

Colonialism did not just construct the modern African state out of disparate ethnic groups. It went further and inverted the structures of some traditional societies so that some ethnic groups that had a higher status were relegated to the bottom while those previously with lower status were elevated to the top.[9] In some cases it split ethnic groups into several states. For example, Somalis were split into four countries: Djibouti, Ethiopia, Kenya, and Somalia. The Sisotho speakers are found in Lesotho and South Africa, just as the Setswana speakers are found in Botswana and South Africa. In one case, colonialism created a smaller state within a bigger one: Lesotho, an independent state, is completely surrounded by South Africa. One of the fears that helped to shape the OAU was based on these "artificial" boundaries.

Universalization of European values

One of the achievements of colonialism was the universalization of European values. It partly did this by transplanting various European ideas, concepts, and norms – such as territorial integrity and state sovereignty – into Africa and other parts of the non-European world. Indeed, by constructing modern states colonialism transplanted the neo-Westphalian institution of state sovereignty into Africa. We use the term "neo-Westphalian" to underline the fact that state sovereignty has evolved and thereby acquired different characteristics since it was formalized through the treaties of Westphalia in 1648.[10]

By claiming that colonialism transplanted this form of sovereignty into Africa, we do not imply that Africa had no sense of sovereignty before colonialism.[11] The point here is that the type of sovereignty that accompanied the transition of African colonies into independent entities was an outmoded understanding of sovereignty that was shaped by the values and conditions of absolutist Europe. In the Europe that emerged after the 1648 treaties of Westphalia, political leaders commanded a lot of power because they were thought to have been ordained by God.

While African states achieved independence on the basis of the self-determination of peoples, the form of sovereignty that was promoted was designed to make African leaders behave as if God had ordained them. It was an exclusive and indivisible sovereignty vested in the political leaders, not the citizenry. It was this type of sovereignty that shaped the African leaders' negative views towards liberal democracy and human rights. Indeed, it was this sovereignty that the OAU was determined to preserve at the expense of human rights. Neo-Westphalian sovereignty helped African leaders to bond in a mutual protection club; but it also betrayed the aspirations for self-determination, which had animated pan-Africanism. There are different interpretations of sovereignty, but in an attempt to demystify it we would like to delineate three types. The first, juridical sovereignty, is based on the notion that the state has no other authority over it except that of international law. African states are members of the United Nations (UN) and other international organizations by virtue of their juridical sovereignty. Juridical sovereignty is conferred on the states by international society. If, for any reason, international society decides that a particular state should not remain sovereign, it can take away that state's juridical sovereignty. Taiwan lost its juridical sovereignty in 1971 because hegemonic powers decided that it was not in the interest of global security to have Taiwan as a member of the UN while China remained outside the organization. Juridical sovereignty is not without irony. For example, Taiwan is not a member of the UN; while Somalia, which did not have the capability to govern itself for about two decades after 1991, retained its juridical sovereignty and a seat in the UN.

The second type of sovereignty, empirical sovereignty, is based on the understanding that states have the right and ability to control the people, resources, and all activities within their borders. Empirical sovereignty is not conferred on states by international society. It is demonstrated through a country's capacity to manage its affairs. Somalia lost its empirical sovereignty in the early 1990s. Whenever government representatives talk of their "state sovereignty," they refer to juridical or empirical sovereignty, or both. Robert Jackson has referred to state sovereignty in Africa as "negative" or quasi sovereignty because many African countries lack the empirical dimension to sovereignty.[12]

The third type of sovereignty, popular sovereignty, is predicated on the claim that all people are equal and entitled to fundamental freedoms; and that governments control them only with their consent.[13] Former UN Secretary-General Kofi Annan told the General Assembly in September 1999 that by popular sovereignty he meant "the fundamental freedom of each individual, enshrined in the Charter of the UN and subsequent international treaties."[14] Thus, popular sovereignty rests on the recognition of human rights. This suggests that human rights and state sovereignty need not be in antagonism: they are two sides of the same coin. As popular sovereignty is exercised only by citizens in their relationship with their rulers, it is dependent on the level of civil society and the nature of governmental structures that exist in a particular state. Popular sovereignty is about the ability of citizens to hold their governments accountable. It means that the people have the rights and the structures through which they limit the power and arbitrariness of governments. As African states achieved independence on the basis of self-determination, which is universally recognized as a collective right, it was popular sovereignty that produced African independence. However, many African leaders did not respect this side of the equation. More recently, some African policy makers and analysts have redefined this as "responsible sovereignty," which suggests that political leaders have to be accountable to the populace.[15]

Colonialism, globalization, and governance

How did the colonial structures in Africa utilize the complex relations among peace, globalization, security, and governance? While the term "globalization" was not used at the time, to many Africans there are similarities between colonialism and globalization. Like colonialism, globalization has transmitted Western values to Africa – but Africa has so far had very little impact on its direction. Again, as was the situation under colonialism, the values, standards, and institutions that are promoted under globalization are considered universal. However, while the Europeans were responsible for implementing colonial programs in Africa, African states are expected to embrace globalization, tame it, and utilize it to transform their own societies.

As a governance tool, colonialism provided a terrible role model for future African leaders. It laid the infrastructure for dictatorship and authoritarianism in post-colonial Africa. In all respects the colonial system of governance was undemocratic and racially biased, and demonstrated that political leaders did not have to be accountable to those they ruled. The colonial system of governance went against most of what is promoted under good governance. It was, therefore, not surprising that the immediate post-independence African leaders saw little value in establishing democratic and accountable systems of government. Moreover, most of the immediate post-independence peace and security problems – including border disputes, ethnic tensions, squalid living conditions, and the marginalization of some groups – emanated from the structures that colonialism had established. Some African political leaders sought to deal with these problems at the pan-African level, but that was not to be.

Pan-Africanism: liberation and integration

The establishment of the AU may be regarded as an important step in efforts to return pan-Africanism to its roots. Pan-Africanism started in the early 1900s as a movement of people of African descent. In the second half of the twentieth century African governments dominated the movement and the people were excluded. Thanks to the Constitutive Act of the AU (CAAU), the people are slowly being rehabilitated and pan-Africanism is increasingly becoming a movement in which both governments and people participate to shape the continent's future.

But what is pan-Africanism? Like most social science concepts, pan-Africanism defies any precise definition. Colin Legum calls it "a belief in the uniqueness and spiritual unity of black people; and acknowledgment of their right to self-determination in Africa, and to be treated with dignity as equals in all parts of the world."[16] Legum's explanation suggests that pan-Africanism may be seen at three levels: as part of the reconstruction of identity; as a search for human dignity and equality, globally; and as a movement that would lead to self-government. In this context pan-Africanism was largely about the interests and identity issues that underpinned the OAU: liberation and integration.

Liberation was tied up with the norms of self-determination and human dignity. It would also lead to sovereign statehood. This is why Nkrumah linked pan-Africanism to identity and freedom through the concept of the African personality. He argued: "The spirit of a people can only flourish in freedom. When the liberation and unification of Africa is completed, the African personality will find full expression and be meaningfully projected."[17] Nkrumah also viewed pan-Africanism as a road to global power. He claimed that a divided Africa would remain weak, while a "united Africa could become one of the greatest forces for good in the world."[18]

Pan-Africanism can be traced back to the struggles for racial equality and human dignity by African-Americans and the black people of the Caribbean. West Indies like George Padmore and Marcus Garvey, and African-Americans such as W. E. B. DuBois, were the founders of pan-Africanism. The primary goal of these early pan-Africanists was the dignity, respect, and emancipation of the people of African descent. For example, in a series of studies such as *The Negro* (1915), *Black Reconstruction in America* (1935), and *The World and Africa* (1947), DuBois sought to achieve at least two objectives. The first was to establish historical and cultural connections between Africa and the African diaspora. The second was to draw the world's attention to the fact that Africans had a history, culture, and values that were equal to those of other races and must, therefore, be respected. These and similar issues were later taken up by other African, Caribbean, and African-American writers, including: Frantz Fanon, Aime Cesaire, Cheik Anta Diop, C. L. R. James, Alioune Diop, and Leopold Senghor (who later became president of Senegal).

However, the liberation of Africans on the continent separated pan-Africanism from its roots in the Caribbean and the United States. Mazrui attributes several factors to this separation. First, liberation transformed pan-Africanism from a movement of peoples to a movement of governments. Second, as African states became active in world politics they found themselves increasingly dealing with the American government rather than their black compatriots within the United States. Third, African states were preoccupied with the need to create a continent-wide organization. Hence, the pan-Africanist strategy of integration, which aimed to achieve continental unity, helped alienate pan-Africanism from its Caribbean and American roots. In the course of time the independent African states increasingly alienated pan-Africanism from the people of Africa as well.

According to Nkrumah, identity – which was expressed in various guises – underpinned the ideas, aspirations, and ambitions that animated pan-Africanism. Nkrumah used the term "African personality" not just to assert the resilience of African traditional values, but also to demonstrate to the world that Africa was committed to global peace and freedom. He argued, for instance:

> For too long in our history, Africa has spoken through the voices of others. Now what I have called the African personality in international affairs will have a chance of making its proper impact and will let the world know it through the voices of Africa's own sons.[19]

In an attempt to globalize the African liberation strategy, Nkrumah called on all countries around the world to participate in the liberation of southern Africa. He argued that as long as there were people in any part of the world who had not been liberated, there could be no genuine freedom and peace in the world. He posited that the "indivisibility of peace [was] staked on the indivisibility of freedom."[20] This pan-Africanist strategy of liberation was pursued by the OAU long after Nkrumah had left the political scene. Moreover, by focusing on southern Africa, the OAU ensured that South Africa in particular remained on its agenda. By virtue of its apartheid policies and enormous military and economic power, South Africa (or its shadow) had a permanent presence in OAU discussions from the 1960s. The OAU's anti-apartheid stance became the glue that held the organization together.

As will be demonstrated below, the OAU was a product of compromises among African nationalists who wanted to establish a "united states of Africa", and those who did not want to give up their newly acquired sovereignty.[21] Nkrumah expressed fear that Africa's capacity for self-rule and self-pacification would be undermined by foreign interventions. Self-pacification stems from the desire to see Africans find African solutions to their problems. The idea of self-pacification is a way of arguing that the responsibility to protect the people and states of Africa primarily rests with African states and communities. That is what lay behind the creation of the OAU.

The OAU: statist agenda

As it has been indicated above, the OAU Charter was a compromise between the African leaders who supported a union and those who sought a loose association. By blocking efforts to establish a union, those who sought a loose association won the day. The debate between the two groups demonstrated that the OAU was born out of power struggles among independent African states. In its 39-year history the organization was driven by the same concerns that had led to the power struggles in the early 1960s, and which had strong implications for state boundaries, territorial integrity, and state sovereignty. In much of its existence, the organization behaved like a protection club for the same statist values.

Initial divisions

Prior to the creation of the OAU in 1963, independent Africa was divided into three political groups: Brazzaville, Casablanca, and

Monrovia. The Brazzaville group comprised 12 French-speaking states that first met in Abidjan, Côte d'Ivoire (Ivory Coast) in October 1960: Benin (formerly Dahomey), Burkina Faso (formerly Upper Volta), Cameroon, Central African Republic, Chad, Congo (Brazzaville), Côte d'Ivoire, Gabon, Madagascar (formerly Malagasy Republic), Mauritania, Niger, and Senegal. This meeting was convened by Côte d'Ivoire president Felix Houphouet-Boigny, who wanted the French-speaking states to mediate in the Algerian war of independence without alienating France. Guinea, under Sekou Toure, denounced the meeting and Togo declined to attend. The same group met again in Brazzaville in December 1960. The Brazzaville group sided with France on the Algerian conflict, opposed communist intrusions into Africa, and vowed to remain on the best of terms with France. It also supported the UN policy on Congo-Kinshasa (now the Democratic Republic of Congo), at the time. This group gave the impression that it believed that African unity needed to be approached through economic cooperation, not political integration.

The Casablanca group, however, comprised seven countries that first met in the Moroccan city of Casablanca in January 1961: the Algerian provisional government, Egypt, Ghana, Guinea, Libya, Mali, and Morocco. Seven other countries were invited to the meeting but they declined, namely: Ethiopia, Gambia, Liberia, Nigeria, Togo, Tunisia, and Sudan. None of the "Brazzaville Twelve" were invited to this gathering. The group adopted the "African Charter of Casablanca," which affirmed their determination "to promote the triumph of liberty all over Africa and to achieve its unity."[22] The Casablanca group disapproved of the UN policy on Congo – especially because of the way its prime minister, Patrice Lumumba, was treated. The group supported the Algerian independence struggle and advocated political unity for Africa as a prerequisite for economic cooperation. This group also supported Morocco, which had laid territorial claims on Mauritania.

The type of entity envisaged by the Casablanca group was a federal government based on the mobilization of resources along socialist lines. Nkrumah insisted that for "economic unity to be effective, [it] must be accompanied by political unity." He posited that the "two are inseparable, each necessary for the future greatness of [the] continent, and the full development of [its] resources."[23] Nkrumah repeatedly emphasized the socialist approach to Africa's development:

> Full economic and social development in Africa can only be accomplished within the optimum zone of development, which

is the entire African continent, and under the direction of an All-African Union government pursuing policies of scientific socialism. Until then, the forces of reaction will continue to block progress which threatens the basic pillars of their positions of privilege.[24]

Nkrumah proposed practical ways for how a united states of Africa government would operate. He argued that the sovereignty of individual states would not be entirely relinquished, but that some of their duties – such as foreign policy – would fall under the jurisdiction of a continental government. Some African leaders saw this as a threat to the independence and territorial integrity of their states.

The Monrovia group, which included all Brazzaville group members, consisted of 20 states that attended a conference in the Liberian capital, Monrovia, in May 1961: Benin, Burkina Faso, Cameroon, Central African Republic, Chad, Congo (Brazzaville), Côte d'Ivoire, Ethiopia, Gabon, Liberia, Libya, Madagascar, Mauritania, Niger, Nigeria, Senegal, Sierra Leone, Somalia, Togo, and Tunisia. One member of the Casablanca group, namely Libya, attended this meeting. Sudan accepted the invitation but changed its mind when it learned that Mauritania would be attending. The Monrovia and Brazzaville groups had similar views on Mauritania, which, they believed, had a right to independent statehood. They also supported the UN policy on Congo.

The Monrovia group agreed on several principles, which were later reissued as the "Lagos Charter of the Organisation of African and Malagasy States" after a meeting of the same countries (including Congo-Kinshasa) in Lagos, Nigeria, in January 1962. The five principles they endorsed later formed the basis of the OAU Charter:

1 absolute equality and sovereignty of African states
2 the right of each African state to exist and not to be annexed by another
3 voluntary union of one state with another
4 non-interference in the domestic affairs of African states
5 no state to harbor dissidents from another state

The above principles revolved around one institution: sovereignty. Other significant values, such as democracy and the rule of law, did not concern the protagonists.

Despite the differences among the three sub-regional groups, the OAU was established because they were united on other issues – as the OAU Charter and the organization's subsequent activities suggest.

The OAU Charter

The OAU Charter consisted of 33 Articles that defined its objectives, principles, and organs. The principal organs of the OAU were the Assembly of Heads of State and Government; the Council of Ministers; the General Secretariat; The Specialised Commissions; the Commission of Conciliation, Mediation and Arbitration; and the Liberation Committee. It was founded by 31 states in 1963, but had 53 members when it was dissolved in 2002.

The organization's purposes, which were stated in Article 2 [1], reflected the statist dimension of the pan-Africanist aspirations for liberation and integration. These included the promotion and solidarity of African states, the defense of state sovereignty, territorial integrity and independence, and the promotion of international cooperation having due regard for the UN Charter. However, the OAU Charter also touched on people-centered activities – such as the pledge to coordinate and intensify cooperation and efforts to achieve a better life for the peoples of Africa, and the promotion of international cooperation having due regard for the Universal Declaration of Human Rights (UDHR). Hardly any African leader paid attention to these people-centered activities. Indeed, despite the pledge to uphold the UDHR, most African states trampled on human rights. The OAU, and especially its Liberation Committee, pursued consistently its goal of eradicating colonialism. This goal was so crucial to the survival of the OAU that after the liberation of South Africa in 1994, the organization's days appeared numbered. It was fitting that its successor, the AU, was launched in South Africa.

The OAU was driven by seven statist principles that were enshrined in Article 3 of its Charter. These included the sovereign equality of all member states; non-interference in the internal affairs of member states; respect for the independence, sovereignty, and territorial integrity of each state; the peaceful settlement of disputes; unreserved condemnation of political assassination and subversive activities on the part of neighboring states; dedication to the total emancipation of all African territories; and affirmation of the policy of non-alignment. The first four of these principles correspond with those contained in the UN Charter and reflect the norms of international law. However, taken together, these seven principles reflected the power struggles and the fear that existed in Africa in the early 1960s. For this reason they acted like insurance policies or mutual preservation measures.

The protection of territorial integrity was revisited in 1964 when the Cairo OAU summit reaffirmed the principle of the inviolability of borders inherited from the colonial period. At the 1965 OAU Summit in Accra, Nkrumah and his supporters proposed a pan-African executive, but those who wanted to preserve their independence, sovereignty, and territorial integrity rejected it.

That the OAU devoted a considerable amount of its time to condemning racial discrimination in southern Africa reflected two things: the commitment to ending the continued humiliation of fellow Africans; and the concealed fear of South Africa. Much of the OAU's support for liberation struggles in southern Africa was funneled through its Liberation Committee, which was based in Dar es Salaam, Tanzania. The Liberation Committee's work was mainly diplomatic and the UN Security Council endorsed its goals when it met for the first time in Addis Ababa in 1972. However, many African states gave little or no support at all to the Liberation Committee, which, in turn, came to be closely identified with the foreign policy of Tanzania and other frontline states such as Angola, Botswana, Mozambique, Zambia, and Zimbabwe. As Gilbert Khadiagala has observed, the frontline states played an important role "in forging African and global consensus about the end of minority rule" in southern Africa.[27]

The OAU was keen to end colonialism, but it often had no answers to subsequent problems that could impede the realization of freedom. It had a dispute resolution mechanism that included negotiation, mediation, conciliation and arbitration, but this mechanism seldom functioned effectively. For example, the OAU admitted Angola to its membership in 1975 but it failed to find a solution to the tragedy that took place in the former Portuguese colony. Indeed, the Angolan civil war at one time paralyzed the OAU Assembly. It was eventually addressed through UN auspices in the 1990s. Among the controversial issues that embroiled the OAU in the 1980s was the admission of Western Sahara (The Saharoui Arab Democratic Republic) as a member in 1980. Subsequently, the admission of Western Sahara saw the organization torn between pro-Moroccans and pro-Polisario supporters – two summits in 1982 being aborted due to the massive boycott by Moroccan supporters and the withdrawal of Morocco from the organization in 1984. This issue, which accounted for Morocco's failure to join the AU, remains unresolved.

Regional Economic Communities and initiatives

Some of the weaknesses of the OAU were demonstrated at two levels: the Charter's failure to make clear the OAU's relationship with sub-regional organizations, formally known as Regional Economic

Communities (RECs); and the OAU's failure to pursue vigorously the economic goals and principles stipulated in its Charter. In one case, the weakness was apparently due to an oversight by those who formulated the OAU Charter. In the other case, the weakness was clearly due to an inability to fulfil the organization's mandate. These two weaknesses, in turn, demonstrated the organization's inability to take advantage of the complex relations among peace, globalization, security, and governance.

During its 39 years of operation the OAU co-existed with a number of RECs, including: the East African Community (EAC); the Economic Community of Western African States (ECOWAS); the Southern African Development Community (SADC), which was originally called the Southern African Development Coordination Committee; and the Intergovernmental Authority on Development (IGAD), which was originally known as the Intergovernmental Authority on Desertification and Development. These organizations had their own identities and interests derived from their respective sub-regions. One of these, the EAC, existed before the emergence of the OAU, but the others were established in the 1970s and 1980s. The UN Economic Commission for Africa (ECA) also existed before the OAU was created.

The OAU Charter failed to stipulate its relations with RECs. However, it settled for a protocol, which served as a diplomatic tool with which the OAU would formalize relations with RECs. RECs were not subsidiary organs of the OAU. Moreover, RECs could deal directly with the UN under Chapter VIII of the UN Charter – which theoretically meant that they could render the OAU an onlooker on major security initiatives on the continent. However, the OAU was in the process of formalizing relationships with seven RECs by the time it folded (OAU/AU relations with RECs are discussed in detail in Chapter 4).

The OAU Charter was quite clear about the organization's role in economic development. For example, the preamble of the Charter talks about the OAU's responsibility for economic development. Article 2 [2] requires member states to coordinate and harmonize their policies in "economic cooperation, including transport and communications." It also requires members to coordinate and harmonize their policies in "education and cultural cooperation" as well as in other areas like "health, sanitation, and nutritional cooperation." Given the fact that those who influenced the direction of the Charter after rejecting Nkrumah's ideas believed that African unity could be achieved only through economic cooperation, why did the OAU pay so little attention to economic issues? Failure to address economic and development issues effectively meant that the OAU was not equipped to address effectively the imperatives for peace and to utilize the processes of globalization.

It was partly due to the lack of expertise that the OAU appeared to cede the power for economic decision-making to the ECA, which, like the OAU, had its headquarters in Addis Ababa. In the initial period there appeared to be rivalry between the OAU and the ECA on major economic initiatives for Africa, but after some time the OAU appeared to follow the lead taken by the ECA. Nonetheless, the OAU participated in negotiations on major economic initiatives, including the discussions on the so-called new international economic order and the Lomé conventions. Another important economic initiative that the OAU took in the late 1970s and early 1980s was the Lagos Plan of Action (LPA), but it did not deliver the goods envisaged.

It is in the economic field that the OAU should have exploited the dynamic tension between globalization, security, and governance: but it did not. For this reason, it lacked the levers for peace building on the continent.

Conclusions

The OAU was a product of its time. The interests and identity of African states drove the organization's purposes, principles, concerns, and interpretations of its mission; but they also reflected the prevailing norms of global governance. The OAU's Charter was state-centric in tone, but this reflected the interpretation of the UN Charter at the time. Even the OAU's insistence on the inviolability of African state borders – which was driven by fear and concern for state security – reflected the message of UN General Assembly Resolution 1514 of December 1960, the Declaration on the Granting of Independence to Colonial Countries and Peoples. For example, paragraph 6 of the declaration stated: "Any attempt aimed at partial or total disruption of the national unity and the territorial integrity of a country is incompatible with the purposes and principles of the Charter of the United Nations."

With a view to discouraging political assassinations, the OAU exploited the ghost of Sylvanus Olympio in 1963 to canonize a policy that resulted in the protection of dictatorial leaders such as General Idi Amin of Uganda and General Sani Abacha of Nigeria – who were responsible for the insecurity and deaths of thousands of their citizens.

During the first two decades of the OAU, few countries in the world paid sufficient attention to good governance and respect for human rights. Indeed, in the 1960s, and owing to the existence of white minority regimes on the continent, African states appeared more interested in the promotion of self-determination – a part of human rights – than Western states were. Some of the weaknesses of the OAU in the post-Cold War era resulted from the fact that it was not designed to exploit effectively the complex relations among peace, globalization, security, and governance. Just as the OAU was a creature of its time, the successor organization – the AU – is a product of its time. Without the type of changes that took place after the Cold War it would not have been possible for African states to establish the AU.

Notes

1 Kwame Nkrumah, *Axioms* (London: Panaf Books) (1967): 19.
2 Nkrumah, *Axioms*: 9.
3 Hugh Trevor-Roper, "The Rise of Christian Europe," *Listener* (November 28, 1963).
4 Ibid.
5 Cited in Ezekiel Mphalele, *The African Image* (New York: Praeger) (1974): 68.
6 Ali A. Mazrui, *The Africans: A Triple Heritage* (London: BBC Publications) (1986): 23–38.
7 Ali A. Mazrui, *Towards a Pax Africana: A Study of Ideology and Ambition* (London: Weidenfeld and Nicolson) (1967): 46.
8 A. Adu Boahen, *African Perspectives on Colonialism* (Baltimore, MD: Johns Hopkins University Press) (1987): 95.
9 See Gideon Cyrus Mutiso, *Kenya: Politics, Policy and Society* (Nairobi: East African Literature Bureau) (1975): 3–45.
10 On the evolution of sovereignty, see Samuel M. Makinda, "The United Nations and State Sovereignty: Mechanism for Managing International Security," *Australian Journal of Political Science*, vol. 33, no. 1 (1998): 101–15; and Daniel Philpott, *Revolutions in Sovereignty: How Ideas Shaped Modern International Relations* (Princeton: Princeton University Press) (2001).
11 Jeffrey Herbst, "Responding to State Failure in Africa," *International Security*, vol. 21, no. 3 (1996–97): 120–44.
12 Robert H. Jackson, "Negative Sovereignty in Sub-Saharan Africa," *Review of International Studies*, vol. 12, no. 4 (1986): 247–64.
13 Preston King, *Toleration* (London: Allen & Unwin) (1976): 199–226.
14 UN press release, September 20, 1999.
15 See, for instance, Francis M. Deng, Sadikiel Kimaro, Terrence Lyons, Donald Rothchild, and I. William Zartman, *Sovereignty as Responsibility: Conflict Management in Africa* (Washington DC: The Brookings Institution) (1996). Moreover, the 2010 Kenyan Constitution states that sovereignty belongs to the people. See Special Issue of the *Kenya Gazette Supplement*, no. 55 (Nairobi: Government of Kenya), August 27, 2010: 13.
16 Colin Legum, "The Roots of Pan-Africanism" in Colin Legum (ed.) *Africa Handbook* (Harmondsworth: Penguin) (1969): 541.
17 Kwame Nkrumah, *Revolutionary Path* (London: Panaf Books) (1973): 206.
18 Kwame Nkrumah, *I Speak of Freedom* (London: Panaf Books) (1961): xii.
19 Nkrumah, *I Speak of Freedom*: 125.
20 Nkrumah, *Africa Must Unite* (London: Panaf Books) (1963): 203.

21 Zdenek Cervenka, *The Unfinished Quest for Unity: Africa and the OAU* (London: Africa Books) (1977): 1–11.
22 Cervenka, *The Unfinished Quest for Unity*: 1.
23 Nkrumah, *Neocolonialism: The Last Stage of Imperialism* (London: Panaf Books) (1965): 30.
24 Nkrumah, *Revolutionary Path*: 222.
25 Gilbert M. Khadiagala, *Allies in Diversity: The Frontline States in Southern African Security, 1975–1993* (Athens, OH: Ohio University Press) (1994): xi.

2 The African Union

Meeting the challenges of an ambitious and rapidly expanding agenda

The emergence of the African Union (AU) in July 2002 prompted a number of questions. What major factors were behind its creation? Does the organization have the capacity to meet the challenges of peace, security, and governance? Is the organization being driven by a statist agenda or an agenda that is geared towards satisfying the aspirations and needs of the people? We assume that it was new identity issues and interests that fueled the creation of the AU. In one sense, the AU could be regarded as a product of pre-Organization of African Unity (OAU) debates, but, in another sense, it could be seen as a response to the globalization and democratization processes that characterized post-Cold War changes in Africa and in the world as a whole. As early as 1961, Kwame Nkrumah had called for an organization similar in structure and ambitions to the AU, but the majority of other African leaders rejected it. However, as one analyst has suggested, the "tide" that necessitated the construction of the AU was "the end of the Cold War, globalization and the need for a fundamental change of the iniquitous international economic system."[1] Nkrumah had cautioned that a weak Africa was vulnerable to external pressures and manipulation, and could only "become one of the greatest forces for good in the world" if it was united.[2] Accordingly, the AU was envisioned as an organization that could render African unity more meaningful by creating, maintaining, and sustaining peace on the continent.

Speaking as if in reference to Nkrumah, the Saharoui Arab Democratic Republic president, Mohammed Abdelaziz, argued that "in this brave new world, there is no room for the weak."[3] Perhaps for this reason, African leaders sought to reconstruct their identities and interests by launching an organization with lofty objectives and ambitious structures which would require considerable skills, operational capacity, and international goodwill to succeed.[4]

At the establishment of the OAU in 1963, the shadow of apartheid South Africa and other minority white regimes was cast over debates among the delegates because the main interest that united African leaders was liberation. The liberation of South Africa in 1994 removed one of the pillars on which the OAU had been constructed. As the OAU was wound up, it was the newly liberated South Africa that hosted the summit that established its successor. If power struggles between Ghana and Nigeria had characterized the political debates prior to the creation of the OAU, rivalry among Africa's regional powers – especially Libya, Nigeria, and South Africa – surrounded the emergence of the AU.

To address in detail the questions raised at the start of this chapter, this analysis is divided into seven parts. The first looks at the legacies of the OAU, while the second examines the post-Cold War political climate that produced the momentum for change. The third part analyzes the objectives of the AU, while the fourth examines its principles. The fifth part discusses gender mainstreaming, the sixth examines the AU's organs, and the seventh looks at the AU's financial woes. The conclusion is that the AU is yet to realize many of the objectives stipulated in its Constitutive Act.

Legacies of the OAU

By the early 1990s globalization and the end of the Cold War had compelled African states to recognize the structural and normative weaknesses that had prevented the OAU from responding effectively to intrastate conflicts. At the same time, it was becoming evident that the West and the United Nations (UN) Security Council were not responding adequately to African problems,[5] particularly peace and security matters.[6] It was for these reasons that the OAU summit of 1990 issued the declaration on the "Political and Socio-Economic Situation in Africa and the Fundamental Changes Taking Place in the World." This declaration provided a framework in which African leaders pledged to work together towards the peaceful and rapid resolution of conflicts. Their pledge resulted in the Cairo Declaration of 1993 that established the OAU's Mechanism for Conflict Prevention, Management, and Resolution.

It was through this new mechanism that the OAU reacted to various conflicts, including those in Angola, Burundi, the Central African Republic (CAR), the Comoros, the Democratic Republic of Congo (DRC), Liberia, Guinea Bissau, Rwanda, Somalia, Sierra Leone, and on the Ethiopian-Eritrean border. Nevertheless, the persisting inadequacy and structural incapacity of the OAU, underpinned by the non-interference principle, led to a further realization that Africa needed a new organization that could take risks and responsibility in promoting integration, development, peace, and security. It was against this background that the OAU extraordinary summit in Sirte, Libya, agreed on the establishment of the AU in September 1999. The Constitutive Act of the African Union (CAAU) was signed at the OAU summit in Lomé, Togo, in July 2000.

The OAU bequeathed the AU many legacies, but given space constraints only a few of them are discussed here. Some of the organs, principles, and objectives of the AU are clearly different from those of the OAU, but others went through only cosmetic changes. Moreover, when the OAU was wound up, it had not achieved many of its objectives. Critics of the OAU had increasingly seen it as a "big men's club" or their "talking shop" – a forum where eloquent speeches were made and little else was accomplished. Amara Essy, the last OAU Secretary-General, regarded the Organization as "the most difficult" he had "ever seen."[7] Several OAU objectives, such as that of improving the living standards of the African people and creating intra-African cooperation, were not achieved.

If the liberation of the continent – which was concluded with South Africa's transition to democracy in 1994 – is taken as the OAU's most sterling achievement, the rest of its record is largely ineffectual since it failed to free Africa from poverty, disease, bad governance, violent conflict, and dependence on Western economic assistance. During the life of the OAU its member states were run, and run down, by dictators whose obsession with accumulating power resulted in wanton looting of state coffers and engagement in destructive habits and practices such as corruption and nepotism. The AU had the unenviable task of mopping up after nearly four decades of misguided and often self-interested political and economic policies.

The issue of disputed state boundaries was no longer a major problem, but this has cropped up again in the last decade to demand special attention. Related to boundaries is the institution of state sovereignty and its derivative: territorial integrity. In particular, the OAU used the principle of non-interference and non-intervention to turn a blind eye to horrendous and egregious acts of brutality that were taking place in almost all African states. The AU has tried to address this weakness through Articles 4 [h] and 4 [j], which permit the Union to intervene in member states "in respect of grave circumstances, namely war crimes, genocide and crimes against humanity." Article 4 [h] was subsequently amended to allow the AU to intervene where there is "a serious threat to legitimate order to restore peace and stability to the member state." Under Article 23 of the CAAU, the AU can also impose sanctions on member states that fail "to comply with the decisions and policies of the Union."

The OAU coddled some of the world's worst dictators – including Uganda's Idi Amin Dada, who served as OAU's chairperson from 1975–76 at the same time as his regime was butchering thousands of Ugandans. Other dictators who served terms as OAU chairmen included Ethiopia's Mengistu Haile Mariam, and Generals Mobutu Sese Seko of Zaire (now the DRC), Moussa Traore of Mali, Ibrahim Babangida of Nigeria, and Gaafar Numeiry of Sudan. As some dictators from the OAU era remain part of the AU Assembly, there is nothing in the CAAU that would preclude them from heading the AU. Although the AU has additional structures that require its members to govern well, observe sound economic policies, and respect human rights, some of the leaders who claim to have committed themselves to its objectives are autocrats. These include Robert Mugabe of Zimbabwe, Omar Hassan al-Bashir of Sudan, and Paul Biya of Cameroon – none of whom have demonstrated a willingness to observe good governance principles. While al-Bashir's bid to chair the AU in 2007 was rejected on these grounds, in January 2011 the AU Assembly picked President Teodoro Obiang Nguema Mbasogo of Equatorial Guinea to preside over its discussion on Africa's shared values – including those of good governance and respect for human rights. Equatorial Guinea has been ranked 45 out of 52, with a score of 38.4 out of 100, by the 2014 Ibrahim Index of African Governance. Moreover, it is the 12th most corrupt country in the world according to Transparency International.

The AU also inherited from the OAU several unresolved intra-state crises that have tested its credibility – the elusive peace and state reconstruction in Somalia and Burundi, the long-festering problems in the eastern DRC (despite the presence of one of the largest UN peacekeeping forces), and the continuing political crises in South Sudan, to name but a few. The AU has also been unable to resolve or provide leadership in solving the long-standing inter-state conflict between Ethiopia and Eritrea. In the first decade of its existence the AU had to address complex emergencies in Sudan's Darfur region, Guinea Bissau, Guinea, and the CAR; in addition to the Arab Spring that saw the fall of the dictatorial rules of Tunisia's Ben Ali, Libya's Muammar Gaddafi, and Egypt's Hosni Mubarak. Additionally, the AU had to deal with the secession of South Sudan and irredentist and secessionist impulses in Mali, Nigeria, Cameroon, and Somalia. Among the security issues that have consumed the attention of the AU are piracy off the coasts of the Horn of Africa and the Gulf of Guinea, transnational terrorism, and the proliferation of small arms and light weapons. Addressing these issues effectively requires appropriate political and diplomatic conditions.

The political climate for the African Union

Some of the factors that contributed to the emergence of the AU include the end of the Cold War, recognition of the power of the forces of globalization, the preeminence of neo-liberal economic ideology, increasing demands for respect for human rights and for transparency by civil society organizations (CSOs), the growing popularity of liberal democratic principles, and personal rivalries among some African political leaders.

The rivalry among political leaders appeared to revolve around three figures: Libya's Muammar Gaddafi, whose rediscovery of pan-Africanist ideals seems to have been influenced by the search for allies to break out of the US-led international isolation; Nigeria's Olusegun Obasanjo, partly owing to his country's political and economic clout in west Africa and an urge to spread Nigeria's influence across the continent; and South Africa's Thabo Mbeki, also due to his country's political and economic prowess, his reinvention of the "African renaissance," and his neo-liberal economic initiatives through the New Partnership for Africa's Development (NEPAD). The rivalry between Nigeria and South Africa, as displayed by their ambitions to create and then occupy new and permanent "African" seats in the UN Security Council, contributed to the formation of the AU and NEPAD.[8]

Gaddafi, an admirer of former Egyptian leader Gamal Abdel Nasser, had pursued various pan-Arabist projects during the Cold War, albeit without success. He took power in 1969 after overthrowing King Idris, who had attended the Casablanca group with Nkrumah and who had also called for an African political union in the early 1960s. In the 1970s and 1980s Gaddafi had also wanted to build a nuclear weapons capability. With the end of the Cold War, Gaddafi's room for maneuver on the nuclear issue had gone, and he was considering giving it up. Pursuing the pan-African project seemed an attractive option for advancing his regional power ambitions.

While Mbeki made the nexus between globalization, governance, peace, security, and development central to his pitch for continental leadership, Gaddafi's quest to unify Africa was partly influenced by his desire to forge closer ties with fellow African leaders after being subjected to a US-led campaign to isolate him following his implication in supporting international terrorism. For his part, Obasanjo was driven by his ambition to spread across Africa the idea of the four calabashes of security, stability, development, and cooperation.[9]

South Africa had also sought, from the late 1960s, to become a nuclear power, and had apparently developed a credible nuclear weapons program by the late 1980s. However, following the end of the Cold War, and with renewed pressure for liberation, the white minority government debated whether or not nuclear weapons would be passed on to the black regime. Accordingly, it dismantled the nuclear weapons program before signing the Non-Proliferation Treaty in July 1991. At the time Mbeki assumed the presidency in 1999, South Africa had given up its nuclear weapons ambitions.[10]

By waving the pan-African and African renaissance flags, Gaddafi and Mbeki respectively pursued the ideals that Nkrumah had enunciated. However, by pursuing NEPAD, Mbeki hoped to satisfy the concerns of those 1960s critics of Nkrumah who had sought African unity through economic cooperation. NEPAD, with its support for a peer review mechanism, was regarded as an appropriate governance tool for debt-ridden Africa. In this context, South Africa's initiatives were geared towards exploiting the complex relations among peace, globalization, security, and good governance for Africa's benefit.

It is in the context of the aforementioned developments that one can explain why the 43 African leaders attending the extraordinary OAU summit in Libya in September 1999 decided to establish the AU. Their decision was in conformity with the OAU Charter and the 1991 Abuja Treaty. From this meeting, the process moved fairly quickly. For example, the initial version of the Constitutive Act was adopted during the 2000 Lomé summit.[11] During the OAU's 5th extraordinary summit, also held at Sirte in March 2001 and attended by 40 African political leaders, the AU was born.

When the union was formally launched in Durban on July 8, 2002, some analysts described the meeting as "an array of personalities representing Africa's ruling elite, from the reprobates to the respected, from heroes to villains, and from the eccentric to the power-drunk demagogues."[12] Mbeki was the host, but it was Gaddafi who drew the most attention – while his critics vilified him for pursuing sinister motives, his supporters compared him to Nkrumah.

The Gaddafi speech that heralded Africa's freedom, the end of enslavement and colonialism, and African ownership of their own land and destiny, was termed "a militant rant, thick with rhetoric."[13] Gaddafi was labeled a dictator who had for more than 30 years denied his people free elections, a free media, and basic human rights; and hence the criticism was leveled that he lacked the credentials to promote the AU's new principles.

The rivalry between Mbeki and Gaddafi was not surprising given South Africa's status as a regional power. In this context, claims that – through the AU – Gaddafi sought "to establish a hegemony"[14] in

Africa, warranted closer examination. Some critics pitted Gaddafi's interest in the AU against NEPAD – Mbeki's brainchild. Some of Gaddafi's critics, favoring South Africa, argued that for the AU to succeed Gaddafi needed to "step back" and allow a leader "from a country grounded in the principles of democracy [to] pick up the mantle."[15]

Looking at the two leaders' projects superficially, one would conclude that Gaddafi's dream was to see a continental government, a single African military force, uniform trade and foreign policies, and one leader representing all the African states in dealing with the rest of the world. This was Nkrumah's dream. Nevertheless, Mbeki's mission was to create a multinational continent ruled multilaterally by like-minded African democrats who shared his goals of competitive markets, technological advancement, progressing economies, and industrious populations.[16]

However, in a profound sense both Mbeki and Gaddafi revealed certain leanings towards Nkrumah's project. Both had passionate feelings for Africa and grandiose plans for uplifting the continent from its deplorable state. The fact that it was Mbeki who hosted the summit that created the AU and became the first chairperson of the Union helped to combine, and go beyond, the visions of the Casablanca, Monrovia, and Brazzaville groups of the early 1960s. In about 40 years, South Africa had moved from casting a shadow over pan-African dreams to leading the most ambitious pan-African organization.

The United States also played an indirect role in the formation of the AU. US involvement can be traced back to November 1993 when the OAU established a conflict prevention, management, and resolution mechanism. Washington offered to assist it by providing the necessary infrastructure, and sharing with it standards and principles for the establishment and planning of peacekeeping operations. In late 1994 President Bill Clinton signed into law the African Conflict Resolution Act, which had provisions for US financial and technical support of the conflict resolution mechanism, and authorized funding to support the OAU's efforts at conflict resolution.[17]

However, this support was cut short due to the OAU's dalliance with Gaddafi. The fundamental reason for the US hostility to Libya was Gaddafi's use of terrorism and subversion, and his foreign military adventurism. Two cases show how the antagonism between the US and Libya worked to the detriment of the OAU. In October 1981 the US provided some funding for the OAU peacekeeping force in Chad after the Libyan forces that had been supporting Goukouni Oueddei pulled out. The Reagan administration was later accused of undermining the OAU effort in Chad by providing arms to Hissen Habre's forces – which

were fighting to oust Oueddei from power. It was with American support that Habre took government.

The second incident related to the bombing of the Pan-Am aircraft
over Lockerbie, Scotland, in December 1988. The US accused Libya of
involvement and subsequently campaigned to isolate it internationally.
As Libya became isolated, Gaddafi looked south to Africa for friend-
ship with non-Western leaning states and liberation movements – such
as South Africa's ANC. He also increased his participation in the OAU
and spearheaded efforts to transform it into a more viable and vibrant
pan-African organization. As Gaddafi developed closer ties with the
OAU, the US reacted by scaling back and eventually almost freezing
all its ties to the organization. It is notable that the OAU was the first
regional organization to defy sanctions against Gaddafi, and it was
through the diplomatic initiatives of former South African president,
Nelson Mandela, that the Lockerbie issue was resolved and sanctions
against Libya lifted. Thus, Gaddafi's decision in August 2003 to pay
compensation to the victims of the Lockerbie bombing after more than
a decade of denying his country's involvement was part of his strategy
to pursue pan-African ambitions without being undermined by the US
and the UK.

Nonetheless, the factors that gave birth to the AU go far beyond the
personal ambitions of Gaddafi and Mbeki. For example, the end of
the Cold War, the collapse of the Soviet Union, and the prevalence of
neo-liberal economic ideology helped to change domestic politics in
much of Africa. Western countries, which had courted African dictators
who had taken sides with them in the Cold War, increasingly distanced
themselves from these same leaders. Indeed, those Western states that
had turned a blind eye to human rights abuses in many African states
started to support the domestic forces that sought democratic reforms
in these countries. The initial success of democratic reforms and transitions in various African states had a double effect. First, the new and
pro-Western African leaders found the OAU outdated and sought to
replace it with an organization more attuned to democracy and transparency. Second, democratic reforms within states emboldened CSOs to
demand accountability on the part of the OAU. They wanted an organization that gave more respect to women's rights, human rights, and
sustainable development. Thus, the identities and interests of African
leaders were changing fast.

Another important factor in the emergence of the AU was the recognition of the significance of the forces of globalization. The intensity and breadth of interactions within the political, technological,
economic, social, and cultural domains that characterize globalization

had a major impact on the domestic policies of African states. The AU founders saw the union as a tool for the continent to face the "multifaceted challenges" posed by globalization. Hence, among the AU objectives (Article 3 [i]) is to "establish the necessary conditions which enable the continent to play its rightful role in the global economy and in international negotiations." Globalization also encourages imitation, and it was not surprising that African leaders sought to establish a continental body that mirrored some of the features of the European Union (EU). Besides adopting organs that are prototypes of EU structures, the AU also borrowed some of the UN organs and rules of procedure.

Objectives of the African Union

The AU's objectives, which are contained in Article 3 of the CAAU, articulate the agenda and underline the priorities of the union. Some objectives give priority to state interests ahead of people, while others promote the interests and aspirations of the people. To be pursued successfully, many of these objectives require a skilful exploitation of the interrelationships between peace, security, and governance.

Unlike its predecessor, which sought unity and liberation but was primarily state-centric in orientation, the AU makes the pledge to build "a united and strong Africa" and to establish partnerships between governments and business; in addition to achieving "greater unity and solidarity" among states and African peoples. The organ that has been given these responsibilities is the Economic, Social, and Cultural Council (ECOSOCC), which comprises the African CSOs. It was anticipated that the African people would gain more roles in influencing continental trends and policies through the election of members of the Pan-African Parliament (PAP), and through contributions to the work of the Peace and Security Council (PSC), the African Commission on Human and Peoples' Rights (ACHPR), and the African Peer Review Mechanism (APRM). However, many of these intentions are yet to be fully realized and it seems that African states and leaders are unwilling to cede power to the people through these organs. The priorities placed on the operationalization of the AU structures and organs can serve as a pointer. For instance, ECOSOCC, which adopted its statutes in 2004, has yet to play an active role in representing the voices of people in the AU decision-making process – as was originally envisioned. ECOSOCC appears to be one of the AU organs that has not met the objectives set out in the CAAU.

By May 2013, and as the AU celebrated the 50th anniversary of the founding of the OAU, it became clear that the Assembly gave higher priority to the interests of African leaders than to the promotion of norms and values such as political accountability. This was prominently highlighted by the rhetoric against the International Criminal Court (ICC) and other decisions that marred the golden jubilee anniversary celebrations. The CAAU pledges to defend the sovereignty, territorial integrity, and independence of member states, and there is nothing wrong with this. However, the defence of state sovereignty is stipulated in Article 3 [b], implying that it is a top priority for the AU; while the promotion of human rights and good governance is stated in Article 3 [h], suggesting that, in the minds of those who framed the CAAU, the state comes ahead of the people. The AU also proposes, through Article 3 [j], to accelerate Africa's economic, social, and cultural integration. The CAAU also refers to the promotion and defense of Africa's "common position on issues of interest to the continent and its people." Like its predecessor, the AU pledges to encourage international cooperation, taking into account the UN Charter and the Universal Declaration of Human Rights (UDHR). On paper, the above objectives are not markedly different from those of the OAU. Moreover, the way the AU approached the crises in the Darfur region of Sudan in 2003, Libya in 2011, and South Sudan in 2014 suggested that state interests had taken priority over the responsibility to protect suffering civilians.

However, the AU also pledges to "promote democratic principles and institutions, popular participation, and good governance." This is a major departure from the OAU, which did not take democratic governance seriously. Since its formation, the AU has assumed an increasing role in the observation and monitoring of elections. However, there have been criticisms about the results of some of the AU election reports.

The objective of promoting democracy and good governance was expected to assume extra significance once the PAP evolved into an organ with full legislative powers, with legislators elected by universal adult suffrage, and when the APRM became mandatory rather than voluntary – as it is at the moment. By 2014 the PAP had failed to transform itself from a body with only consultative and advisory powers and comprising legislators nominated by national parliaments to one with legislative and oversight powers – as had been initially planned to be achieved by 2009.

Another objective of the AU is to "promote and protect human and peoples' rights in accordance with the African Charter on Human and Peoples' Rights" and other human rights instruments. This is a major normative development in the AU's approach to governance. However, the continuing violation of human rights in many African countries – and in particular Sudan, Gambia, Zimbabwe, Egypt and

Equatorial Guinea – has raised introspective questions as to whether the AU has the capacity and the will to pursue this goal conclusively and consistently.

On research, the AU claims it aims to advance the development of Africa "by promoting research in all fields, in particular in science and technology." This objective is being met through the department headed by the Commissioner for Human Resources, Science, and Technology, and through relevant Specialized Technical Committees (STCs). The successful pursuit of this objective is crucial to Africa's sustainable development. Indeed, science, technology, and innovation are so important that Africa cannot effectively address many of its goals without them. However, apart from the Kwame Nkrumah Scientific Awards there is little evidence that the AU is investing adequately in research and knowledge.[18]

On the whole, the Commissioners and bodies charged with implementing the objectives of the AU could take advantage of the interrelationships between peace, security, and governance to realize the dream of Pan-Africanism. Whether they do so for the benefit of the people and societies – as opposed to the states – will depend on their understanding of Pan-Africanism, their perspectives on peace and security, the extent to which they permit non-state agents to participate in decision-making, and a fundamental understanding that globalization can be managed and controlled for the benefit of Africa and humanity.

Principles of the African Union

The AU's principles, as laid out in Article 4 of the CAAU, can be broadly categorized into four groups: traditional principles adopted from the OAU; peace and security; good governance and social justice; and socio-economic development.

The traditional principles adopted from the OAU – such as "sovereign equality and interdependence among member states," and "respect of borders existing on achievement of independence" – are based on the old-fashioned interpretation of state sovereignty. However, a radical departure is that while member states are forbidden to intervene in each other's internal affairs, the AU has a right to "intervene in a member state pursuant to a decision of the Assembly in respect of grave circumstances, namely war crimes, genocide and crimes against humanity." Following the 2003 amendment to Article 4 [h], the AU can also intervene in a member state upon the recommendation of the PSC if a member state requests it, or if the PSC believes there is "a serious threat to legitimate order." However, for reasons highlighted in Chapter 4, the

AU has faced serious challenges in implementing these principles in situations such as Darfur, Zimbabwe, the CAR, and South Sudan.

The governance and social justice principles were aimed at promoting the norms of gender equality, constitutionalism, the respect for the sanctity of human life, democracy, human rights, the rule of law, and good governance. While upholding these norms, the union also condemns and rejects impunity and political assassination, acts of terrorism, subversive activities, and unconstitutional changes of government. Through the APRM, established under NEPAD, African leaders were supposed to be monitored on their performance in regard to "policies, standards and practices that will lead to political stability, high economic growth, sustainable development and accelerated regional integration in the continent."[19] It was in reference to this principle that the African leaders, during the first AU Assembly summit, made a commitment to practice "the principles and core values" of democracy, and of political, economic, and corporate governance. These norms were also to be implemented through the Charter on Democracy, Elections and Governance, and the African Governance Architecture (AGA).

The peace and security principles of the AU relate to the "establishment of a common defence policy," "peaceful resolution of conflicts among member states," and the "prohibition of the use of force or threat to use force among member states." In forming the AU, African leaders acknowledged that "peace, security, and stability were prerequisites for Africa's development and integration agenda." The idea of relating the peace and security agenda to socio-economic development suggests that both peace and security were not conceived primarily in traditional and statist terms. However, it now appears that the AU does not have adequate means and commitment to implement this broad approach to peace and security. As will be shown later, in the implementation of the peace and security agenda, the AU has concentrated its resources and efforts mainly on conflict management rather than conflict prevention or post-conflict peace building and development.

The AU's socio-economic development principle is articulated in Article 4 [n] of the CAAU. However, the CAAU gives only scant attention to socio-economic matters, stating that "balanced economic development" will be sought through the "promotion of social justice." The AU's apparent lack of serious commitment to social issues is reflected in the fact that the department of social affairs is fully funded by international partners. The AU has also not been able to link social issues to bad governance – which could, in turn, be associated with rising youth unemployment, negative ethnicity, radicalization, political violence, and armed conflicts. Additionally, the AU's attention to social and economic issues has been hampered by the donor community's obsession with peace and security, and the lack of commitment to the implementation of social and economic-related policies.

Besides its complex architecture and ambitious goals, the AU differs from the OAU in the way it accords prominent roles in its affairs to both CSOs and gender matters. The PSC, for instance, has a provision that recognizes CSOs as key components of the AU peace and security architecture by encouraging them "to participate actively in the efforts aimed at promoting peace, security and stability in Africa." The PSC also encourages CSOs "to collaborate" with the Commission in the "effective functioning of the Early Warning System."[20] CSOs have also been given a role to play in the implementation of the AU agenda through ECOSOCC and the APRM. This is significant as the role of CSOs was crafted into the Constitutive Act to ensure that the AU does not degenerate into the "old boys' club" that the OAU was. Yet African CSOs' involvement in the AU has been undercut by their lack of resources, overdependence on foreign funding, and the lack of transparency in the management of their own affairs.

Gender mainstreaming

The AU has treated gender equality, gender balance, and gender mainstreaming more seriously than the OAU and most of its member states. Starting with the CAAU, the Preamble states that the formation of the AU was guided by "the need to build a partnership between governments and all segments of civil society, in particular women, youth, and the private sector in order to strengthen solidarity and cohesion among … (African) peoples." One of its principles (Article 4 [l]) is the "promotion of gender equality." Article 3 has also been amended to "(e)nsure the effective participation of women in decision-making, particularly in the political, economic and socio-cultural areas." However, the CAAU fails to highlight instruments such as the UN Convention on the Elimination of All Forms of Discrimination against Women in Article 3 [e]. Moreover, it has not established an STC to deal with gender issues.[21]

Nonetheless, gender equality and the importance of women in the promotion of the AU objectives are recognized in various statutes and practices. For instance, the Statute of the African Union Commission (AUC) (Article 18.6 [a]) states that the principle of gender equality will be upheld in the recruitment of staff, and that women will compose half of the ten commissioners (Articles 6 [3] and 13). The statute also assigns the portfolio of gender issues to the Office of the Chairperson of the Commission as these issues cut across all departments within the Commission (Article 12 [2]). Article 20 of the PSC protocol recognizes the role of women in promoting the AU peace and security agenda, and calls on women in non-governmental organizations (NGOs) to contribute to the functioning of the PSC.

Most notable, and of historical significance, was the election of Nkosazana Dlamini-Zuma – the former South African foreign minister – as the chairperson of the AUC in July 2012. Prior to her election women had also broken the proverbial glass ceiling in the Assembly when Liberia's Ellen Johnson-Sirleaf was elected president in 2006. Another woman joined the assembly when Joyce Banda served as Malawi's president between April 2012 and May 2014. However, more efforts need to be made to mainstream gender at all levels of the AU, including the Assembly. As Article 6 [1] of the CAAU states that those attending the Assembly sessions ought to be heads of state and government (or their accredited representatives), the Assembly can easily facilitate more female participation in this supreme organ by arranging every session to have a certain number of females participating.

By suggesting this we do not imply that more women in the Assembly would lead to qualitatively different types of decision. Gender mainstreaming should not be based on this claim. It is fundamentally about equality and representation. Our concern with the composition of the Assembly is that it defies logic for an organization which claims to be seriously concerned with gender mainstreaming to marginalize women from its own supreme decision-making organ.

Organs of the African Union

All 26 organs of the AU, displayed in Figure 2.1, were created to perform important governance tasks – but this section looks at only 10 of them that were established with a view to demonstrating how the Union handles the challenges of peace, security, and governance in a globalizing world.[22] The ten organs examined are: the Assembly; the Executive Council (EC); PAP; the African Court on Human and Peoples' Rights and the ACHPR; the PSC; the APRM; ECOSOCC; the Commission; and the STCs. Each organ is discussed in terms of how it meets the objectives and complies with the principles stipulated in the CAAU. An attempt is also made to see whether these organs have the potential to provide continent-wide leadership.

The Assembly

This is the supreme organ of the AU, which comprises heads of state and government or their representatives. Some of these were

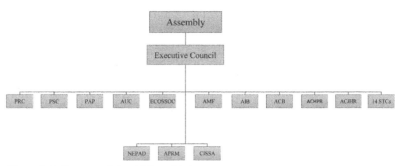

Figure 2.1 Organs of the African Union
Source: Authors

democratically elected, others were not – yet they all theoretically exercise the same level of power. In this respect the AU's Assembly is somewhat similar to the OAU's Assembly – despite the fact that the AU's peace, security, and governance agenda places a premium on public accountability. The Assembly's chairperson – elected by heads of state and government – serves a term of one year, which could be renewable under certain circumstances as was the case with Nigeria's President Olusegun Obasanjo, who served from July 2004 until January 2006. This organ meets in ordinary session twice a year (January and July) to make decisions that are implemented by other organs. However, it may also meet in extraordinary session if requested by a member state and if approved by at least two-thirds of the members. As of January 2014 the Assembly had sat in 22 ordinary sessions and 15 extraordinary sessions since the formation of the AU. The Assembly reaches its decision by consensus; where this is not possible it requires a two-thirds majority. However, on procedural matters it needs only a simple majority.

On the basis of the CAAU, the Assembly wields enormous power. It determines the AU's policies, admits new members, adopts the budget, appoints the chairperson of the Commission and his/her deputy as well as other commissioners, and decides on intervention in member states under Articles 4 [h] and 4 [j]. The Assembly can give "directives to the Executive Council on the management of conflicts, war and other emergency situations and the restoration of peace." This organ has the potential to become dictatorial since it is not accountable to, or balanced by, any other organ or authority.

While the CAAU invests the Assembly with enormous power, it provides no inbuilt checks on this power or any avenues for reviewing the appropriateness of its actions. The AU was established at a time when governance in Africa called for the participation of states and non-state agents in decision-making, but the CAAU provided no mechanisms for the people, CSOs, and the corporate sector to lobby the Assembly directly. Indeed, as of 2014 the Assembly did not meet the requirements for democracy, accountability, and popular participation. However, under Article 9 [2] of the CAAU, the "Assembly may delegate any of its powers and functions to any organ of the Union." Through this delegation, some of the Assembly's business has been handled by organs that have sought consultations with specialists and CSOs.

Since its inception the Assembly's record on African crises and conflicts has been a mixed bag. The first test case was the political crisis in Madagascar during the 2002 summit in which it needed to choose between Didier Ratsiraka, an incumbent who had refused to accept an election loss, and Marc Ravalomanana, the former mayor of Antananarivo, the capital city, who had claimed the election victory and demanded recognition. The AU chose neither and left Madagascar's seat empty for a year. The Assembly was forced to take similar action after Andry Rajoelina, a former disc jockey and mayor of Antananarivo, ousted Ravalomanana from power in March 2009. Since then, the Assembly has considered and made many decisions during each summit on addressing African governance problems and conflicts – including those in the CAR, Côte d'Ivoire, the DRC, Egypt, Guinea, Guinea Bissau, Kenya, Liberia, Libya, Mali, Mauritania, Niger, Sudan, South Sudan, Somalia, Togo, and Zimbabwe. At each meeting the Assembly receives implementation reports of the previous decisions from the Commission.

The Assembly's rules of procedure stipulate what forms the decisions may take: if it is issued as a regulation or directive, it will be binding on the member states and all measures will be taken to ensure it is implemented within 30 days. But if a decision is taken as a "recommendation, resolution or opinion," it will not be binding, since its intention is "to guide and harmonize the viewpoints of member states."[23] One of the grey areas in the Assembly's decision-making process relates to making decisions on intervention under Articles 4 [j] and 4 [h]. If the Assembly has to decide on intervention, it will need to do so in an extraordinary session, which requires approval "by a two-thirds majority of the member states" and 15 days' notice.[24] The meeting will take place only if at least 36 member states respond to the request for an extraordinary summit. It is notable, however, that the Assembly's rules of procedure go to extremes to define, in Rule 37, the process for imposing "Sanctions for Unconstitutional Changes of Government," but are silent on how decisions will be taken in response to "grave circumstances." The rules of procedure of all the other organs of the Union are also silent on this issue.

Despite the failure of Zimbabwe's internal governance system and the severe deterioration in the security, economic, and social situation, prior to, and following, the 2008 general elections, the Assembly did not take any meaningful action. Similar futile actions were witnessed in respect to the AU's involvement in the 2011 Libyan imbroglio as well as the 2011 and 2013 Egyptian crises. In the case of the former, the Assembly appeared confused as to whether to take action on behalf of one of its own member states or on behalf of segments of the Libyan population. In the case of Egypt, the Assembly has twice been forced to suspend its membership after the overthrow of Presidents Hosni Mubarak (January 2011) and Mohamed Morsi (June 2013). The AU decision was complicated by the fact that each of these countries contributes 25 percent of the AU's budget.

It is the Assembly that has to deal with the choice of excluding from the Union member states that flout the AU principles. It also has to develop compliance programs for such states, which they must implement within a specified period. According to Article 23(2) of the CAAU, member states that fail

> to comply with the decisions and policies of the union may be subjected to other sanctions, such as the denial of transport and communications links with other member states, and other measures of a political and economic nature to be determined by the Assembly.

Although the penalties for failure to comply with the objectives and principles of the AU are clearly stated, their implementation has lacked political will on the part of the leaders, and lacked the cooperation of all member states.

Only a few of the thousands of decisions made by the Assembly, EC, and other key organs of the AU are monitored, evaluated, and followed up. Every AU meeting results in decisions, resolutions, communiqués, declarations, and other policy-related outputs that are left without enforcement means and resources. The AU makes policy outputs without having the required inputs, particularly the resources needed to implement its decisions. Due to lack of monitoring of its decisions, more decisions are made in subsequent meetings without evaluation of, or reference to, previous ones. This has led to two things. The Commission is overwhelmed and ends up producing inadequate implementation reports to present to the EC and the Assembly. Second, the AU loses credibility in the eyes of the African people when it seems to do more talking than acting on its words. Among proposals made to rectify this problem are plans to impose a moratorium on decisions for a period of at least one year and to implement those ones made over previous years; reduce the number of meetings; ensure that meetings mostly focus on evaluation of implementation and outcomes of existing decisions rather than making additional ones; and to make only decisions that are informed by policy research and after securing resources to implement them.

The Executive Council

This body is comprised of the foreign ministers or any other minister designated by the member states. In composition it is similar to the OAU's Council of Ministers. Thus, the EC is filled with appointees of the Assembly and is accountable to the Assembly. It meets at least twice a year in ordinary session, but it can also meet more often at the request of a member state if this is approved by two-thirds of the members. As of January 2014, the Council had held 24 ordinary sessions and 15 extraordinary ones. Like the Assembly, the EC reaches its decisions by consensus; if this is not possible, it requires two-thirds of the members. On procedural matters it needs just a simple majority.

The EC has the mandate to make decisions on a wide range of issues, including foreign trade, science and technology, health, transport and communications, culture, environmental protection, humanitarian action, education, food, water resources, energy, and mineral resources. It is expected to delegate some of its powers and functions to the STCs. The EC has also the responsibility of monitoring the implementation of policies formulated by the Assembly. For example, the EC does not have the mandate to decide on intervention in member states, but once the Assembly has made such a decision the EC has responsibility for implementing it.

CSOs have opportunities to influence the agenda of the EC through the STCs, to which the Council delegates some of its responsibilities. Indeed, on security, science, and technology issues, CSOs and expert panels have played important roles. For example, *Freedom to Innovate: Biotechnology in Africa's Development*, the report of the High-Level African Panel on Modern Biotechnology[25] co-chaired by Professor Calestous Juma (Kenyan) of Harvard University and Dr Ismail Serageldin (Egyptian) of the Library of Alexandria, formed the main theme for the AU summit of January 2007.

On issues of governance and the promotion of peace and security, provisions have been made in various AU statutes for CSOs to make contributions.[26] Since the EC is the body that prepares the agenda for the summit and considers policy proposals before the Assembly decides on them, it can provide an avenue for non-state agents to have input in decision-making in the following way. A CSO can make a proposal for an issue of interest through its home government, which will then adopt it as its proposal and submit it to the Permanent Representative Committee (PRC) for possible consideration as a summit agenda item. The PRC will then consider and adopt the proposal, and recommend it as an agenda item for the EC meeting.

The Pan-African Parliament

The PAP, one of the AU's key organs, was inaugurated in Addis Ababa, Ethiopia, on March 18, 2004. Its objective is to serve as a deliberative continental body, providing a common platform for all the peoples of Africa and their grassroots organizations to get more involved in discussions and decision-making on the problems and challenges besetting the continent. Based in Midrand, South Africa, the PAP comprises five legislators nominated from each of the states that have ratified the CAAU. As of early 2014, it had 235 legislators from the 47 states that had ratified the Act. The legislators are expected to work only part-time in two sessions of 30 days each per year. The PAP has ten permanent committees: Co-operation, International Relations and Conflict Resolution; Justice and Human Rights; Rural Economy, Agriculture, Natural Resources and Environment; Monetary and Financial Affairs; Trade, Customs and Immigration Matters; Transport, Industry, Communications, Energy, Science and Technology; Health, Labour and Social Affairs; Education, Culture, Tourism, and Human Resources; Gender, Family, Youth, and People with Disability; and, Rules, Privileges, and Discipline.

Although it was supposed to transform itself into an institution with full legislative powers by 2010, by 2014 the PAP still had only a consultative and advisory role in relation to the other organs of the AU. Since its formation, the PAP has barely made any impact on substantive issues of significance to the continent – apart from sending missions to the CAR and Darfur, and to observe elections in member states. During this period, the Assembly, EC, and the PRC have cautioned the PAP to refrain from making its own rules, and to exercise financial discipline. Member states are also required to meet the expenses of their PAP delegates. Apart from financial scandals, the PAP has struggled to evolve into an organ with full legislative powers and to play the vital role of implementing "the objectives and principles enshrined in the Constitutive

Act ..., particularly, with regard to the protection of human rights, consolidation of democratic institutions, popularization, and promotion of good governance," as well as transparency, peace, security, and stability.[27] With limited powers, and lacking important legislative and supervisory powers to participate in important decision-making in the AU pertaining to the budget, the PAP cannot play the oversight role in the AU system. Its powers are limited to examining, discussing, or expressing opinions on any matter, such as respect for human rights, the consolidation of democracy, and the promotion of peace, stability, good governance, and the rule of law.

The annual budget of the PAP constitutes an integral part of the regular budget of the AU and is drawn in accordance with the financial rules of the AU and will continue to be approved by the Assembly until it starts to exercise legislative powers. This means that the PAP can only give opinions and make recommendations about its budget proposals submitted to the Assembly, and it is not able to prepare an independent work plan of its own according to its own priorities. In 2014 it had a budget of $14.3 million (up from $6.4 million in 2007).

Just as the current structure of the AU emulates the EU, the PAP shares a few characteristics with the European Parliament (EP). The PAP consists of equal numbers of parliamentarians, i.e., five legislators (at least one of whom must be a woman) drawn from each member state representing their national parliaments. That means the PAP members are elected or designated by the respective national parliaments or any other deliberative organs of the member state, from among their legislators. During the nomination of representatives to the PAP, the national parliaments are supposed to pay due regard to the diversity of political opinions among their national legislators. EP members were elected in a similar manner until 1979. The fact that 20 percent of the PAP members (as of 2014) were women was significant. This contrasted sharply with the fact that there were only six female foreign ministers in the very important EC, which processes all matters and makes recommendations to the Assembly.

However, the composition of the PAP poses some difficulties and dilemmas. One of these is the acceptance of the principle of representation by equal numbers of legislators from each member state irrespective of their population. Nigeria has complained that while it has a population of over 170 million, it is represented by the same number of legislators in the PAP as Cape Verde, which has a population of 500,000. It appears that ensuring fair and balanced representation that takes into account the member states' respective population sizes should be one of the issues the PAP needs to address.

The PAP also faces the practical problem of ensuring representation of various political opinions in the continental legislative body. Presently, there are no common rules of procedure that are being applied by the national parliaments in the appointment of their legislators to the PAP. Indeed, in the majority of countries there is no clear ideological alignment of political forces, but rather an alignment on ethnic and religious lines. During the first and subsequent sessions, the members had to be repeatedly reminded that they were serving in the PAP in their personal capacities and not as national delegates. Since it appears that PAP members have usually pursued personal agendas, promoted their national interests, and entered into regional groupings and alliances, it follows that their decision-making has not been based on any common political platform. If PAP members could unite along certain commonly defined political programs transcending the prevailing diversity among the African political cultures, there would be some hope of their promoting pan-African ideals and tackling continent-wide problems. However, serious concerns have been raised about PAP members' behavior – particularly on financial matters – leaving many to wonder whether the PAP should have oversight over other organs.

The protocol is also silent on how the PAP relates to other AU organs, particularly those with the responsibilities of promoting good governance, the rule of law, human rights, and peace and security. However, protocols – such as those establishing the PSC and the ACHPR – recognize the role of the PAP in promoting peace and human rights respectively.

Since its launch the PAP has faced a number of challenges that seem to form part of a common trend with regard to the establishment and operationalization of AU structures. The PAP, like other AU organs, was established despite the continent's weak capacity and despite the considerable financial implications of such a move both at national and continental levels. For instance, the protocol provides that allowances shall be paid to PAP members to meet expenses in the discharge of their duties – but is silent as regards the sources of finance for such allowances. In the initial period it seemed that PAP parliamentarians from some countries were not aware that their own governments were expected to cover the full cost of their attendance, including allowance and transport, presumably in accordance with their own national practice as far as the determination of the amount of allowance was concerned. However, this arrangement has not worked well since rich countries, like Libya under Gaddafi, could pay a $600 daily allowance; while poorer ones, like Guinea, could pay only $150. Consequently, legislators from poorer countries have found it difficult to attend PAP meetings.

Despite its institutional growth challenges, the PAP could contribute immensely to the promotion of peace, security, and good governance in Africa if its members used their national parliaments to ensure that relevant AU instruments were signed, ratified, and implemented in their respective countries. The problems that afflict the PAP are similar to those that affect other AU organs, including the legal and human rights instruments.

The African Commission on Human and Peoples' Rights and the African Court on Human and Peoples' Rights

The idea of an African Court can be traced back to 1961 when a meeting of African jurists in Lagos, Nigeria, suggested such a body. However, it was not until 1981 that the OAU summit in Nairobi, Kenya, adopted the African Charter on Human and Peoples' Rights. It also established the African Commission on Human and Peoples' Rights (ACHPR) with limited advisory powers for interpreting and promoting the Charter, ensuring compliance with its objectives, and examining state party's reports. One of the major weaknesses of the Charter and the Commission is that they lack enforceable remedies and mechanisms. They do not have levers through which they may encourage or ensure state compliance with the Commission's decisions. The ineffectiveness of the Commission was displayed in January 2006 when the AU Assembly adopted and authorized, "in accordance with Article 59" of the Charter, "the publication of the 19th Activity Report of the African Commission on Human and Peoples' Rights (ACHPR) and its annexes, *except for those containing the Resolutions on Eritrea, Ethiopia, the Sudan, Uganda, and Zimbabwe.*"[28]

However, the weakness of the ACHPR had become glaringly apparent in the 1990s, giving impetus to existing claims by human rights scholars and activists that the protection of human rights in Africa needed stronger mechanisms. This led the OAU summit in Ouagadougou, Burkina Faso, to adopt the Protocol to the African Charter on Human and Peoples' Rights on the establishment of the African Court on Human and Peoples' Rights in June 1998. The protocol came into force on January 25, 2005, after its 15th ratification in the Comoros.

The Court, which is based in Arusha, Tanzania, has 11 judges who are chosen by the EC and endorsed by the Assembly. The judges serve for periods of six years, renewable once. The Court has both judicatory and advisory powers, and met for the first time on May 2, 2006. Its powers include the interpretation and implementation of the Charter, the protocol, and other instruments concerning human rights. Although the power *rationae personae* (who is entitled to submit cases to the Court) is mainly conferred upon the AUC, state parties, and Regional Economic Communities (RECs), optional powers are also extended to individuals and NGOs with observer status in the AUC. No appeals will be allowed, but under certain circumstances the Court may interpret or review cases on which it has ruled. The African Court on Human and Peoples' Rights and the Court of Justice of the African Union were merged into the African Court of Justice and Human Rights (ACJHR) through the Protocol on the Statute of the African Court of Justice and Human Rights (which was signed on July 1, 2008). The ACJHR Protocol has yet to come into force since only five countries have ratified it.

As of April 2014, only 27 of the 54 AU member states had ratified the protocol that established the African Court on Human and Peoples' Rights. The Court's first major judgment on the merits of a case was delivered in June 2013, when it found that Tanzania had violated a citizen's right in relation to participation in politics. The second was a ruling against Burkina Faso in March 2014, which related to a former journalist who was murdered in 1998. The Court has faced several challenges since its formation. Among these is a lack of resources. In 2014, for example, it had a budget of $8.3 million. While member states fund its entire operating budget – which covers salaries, maintenance, and related costs – donors fund its activities ($1.7 million).

The ACHPR, which was established on November 2, 1987, and headquartered in Banjul, Gambia, has the mandate to promote and protect human and peoples' rights in Africa. Moreover, Article 19 of the PSC protocol recognizes the ACHPR as one of the organs required to promote peace and security. However, the contributions and impact of the Commission on the promotion of peace in Africa are minimal. The 2007 High Level Panel of Audit of the AU – chaired by Adebayo Adedeji (Nigeria) (hereafter the Adedeji panel) – found that the Commission was facing multiple problems, including member states' refusal to "grant the ACHPR authorization to undertake missions in their countries even though all Member States have ratified the Charter."[29] The panel also pointed out that "the bulk of Member States do not submit their mandatory reports," and that some of them refuse "to comply with the recommendations of the ACHPR."[30]

The panel found that although the Commission was understaffed, it spent only 4 percent of its budget on its core mandate. The Commission also relies heavily on donor funds – to the extent that it would not be able to operate without them. For instance, in 2014 the Commission's program budget of $1.6 million was fully funded by donor organizations even though member states are fully funding its operating budget of $4.1 million. The Commission's strategic plans have also been drawn up by foreign human rights groups, some of which have deployed technical advisors. This apparent "meddling" in its affairs by "outsiders" has worked against the Commission, and member states have criticized donor funding for promoting external interests. In December 2013 the Commission was called upon by the PSC to play a major role in South Sudan, and to form a team to investigate the atrocities being carried out there. But instead this role was taken over by an AUC of Inquiry headed by former president, Olusegun Obasanjo.[31]

The Peace and Security Council

This is the main AU body charged with the responsibility of promoting peace, security, and stability. Conceived as a tool for promoting collective security in Africa, the PSC is composed of 15 members elected on the basis of equal rights – ten for two-year terms, and five for three-year terms – and equitably distributed among the continent's five regions. Among the criteria for PSC membership is a country's "contribution to the promotion and maintenance of peace and security in Africa," and "respect for constitutional governance ... (and) rule of law and human rights." The protocol that established the PSC was ratified in December 2003 and the first meeting of the PSC at ministerial level took place in March 2004. The AU Assembly formally launched the PSC two months later.

The PSC's other functions include anticipating conflicts and undertaking preventive diplomacy; and making peace through the use of good offices, mediation, conciliation, and enquiry. The PSC may also undertake Peace Support Operations (PSOs) and intervention, pursuant to Article 4 [j] of the CAAU; engage in peace building and post-conflict reconstruction; and undertake humanitarian action and disaster management. It has the power to institute sanctions whenever an unconstitutional change of government takes place in a member state in contravention of the Algiers Decision and the Lomé Declaration. The PSC also has the mandate to promote and implement the Common African Defence and Security Policy; the Convention on the Prevention and Combating of Terrorism; and international conventions and treaties on arms control and disarmament. It may also take appropriate measures to defend the national independence and sovereignty of a member state that is threatened by acts of aggression, such as mercenaries.

Article 8 of the PSC protocol provides for three types of meetings: closed, open, and informal consultations. Although the number of meetings it holds is impressive, the Council's business has often been characterized by poor time management and confusion. For instance, the PSC combines consultations, decisions, procedural debate, and deliberations in a single meeting; and turns briefing sessions into formal meetings without proper preparation. The outcomes of PSC deliberations are released in two forms: communiqués and press statements. Implementing and enforcing compliance of its decisions is a challenge even though they are binding on the member states.

Over the past ten years the PSC has developed a mode of work that includes chamber deliberations, retreats in exotic locations, and field (fact-finding and assessment) visits (or missions) to conflict zones or post-conflict recovery areas. Although the PSC has a comprehensive mandate that enables it to deal with complex peace and security issues, it has mainly been reacting to conflicts. It has paid inadequate attention to other security issues such as the use of child soldiers, the role of mercenaries, the abuse of women, and the illegal exploitation of natural resources in armed conflicts. In addition, the PSC has not paid adequate attention to domestic and transnational terrorism, rebels and militant groups, the proliferation of small and light weapons, violations of international humanitarian and human rights laws, and piracy.

The membership criteria, laid out in Article 5 of the PSC protocol, are designed to ensure inclusiveness and equitable participation. These include: upholding the AU principles, promoting its peace, security, and governance agenda; capacity and commitment to promote and maintain peace and security; past experiences in resolving regional and international conflicts, peacemaking and peace building; the willingness and ability to assume the responsibilities of regional and continental peacemaker; and the ability and willingness to make financial contributions to peace activities and to honor its financial obligations to the Union. However, these membership criteria are not followed. For instance, most of the countries that have served in the past, or are currently serving, do not meet the requirement of having adequate and appropriate staffing of their embassies. The election of the members has also been left to the regions to determine, using their own criteria. For instance, the west Africa region has decided to have a "permanent member" contrary to the letter and spirit of the protocol. Some members in the past did not even have military attachés in Addis Ababa to participate in meetings on military-related matters before the PSC or Military Staff Committee (MSC).

Most of the permanent representatives in the PSC lack the skills, knowledge, and resources to address critical issues brought before them. Additionally, too many meetings overburden the PSC. Although it was supposed to meet at least twice a month, the PSC has – since its inauguration – been meeting more than five times a month due to increased demands on it to address a growing number of disputes in Africa. The PSC secretariat lacks staff with competence in legal matters and in conflict analysis, conflict resolution, and peace building. Besides being serviced by a skeletal secretarial staff that is insufficiently trained, PSC meetings are in most cases poorly conducted and deliberated. It usually makes decisions without inputs from experts and without the type of well-researched information that is needed in such complex matters. Between 2003 and 2010 the PSC held more than 250 meetings and briefings that mostly resulted in decisions on issues such as the deployment of peacekeepers – even though the AU did not have the capacity, capability, and will to deploy them. The PSC is also grossly underfunded for the activities that it is expected to undertake. For example, in 2014 the Assembly allocated it only $759,253 for its operations.

Although regions are expected to practice the principle of rotation, Nigeria has become a de facto permanent member of the PSC by being allowed (since 2004) to continuously occupy the three-year membership seat. The justification for this violation of the PSC protocol is that, being a powerhouse, the region is best served by allowing its regional anchor to serve on this major decision-making body. This then leads to justification by other major regional powerhouses, such as South Africa, to make the same claim. If this were allowed it would eventually work to the detriment of the PSC.

The PSC protocol calls for the establishment of the Continental Early Warning System (CEWS), the Panel of the Wise (PoW), the African Standby Force (ASF), the MSC, and the Peace Fund to act as instruments for promoting its peace and security agenda. These structures and related issues are discussed in more detail in Chapter 4.

While the PSC has given a regional power – Nigeria – an opportunity to act like the first among equals, the AU has a leveling structure in the form of the peer review system, which treats all states as equals.

African Peer Review Mechanism

The APRM was established on March 9, 2003, as an instrument for monitoring participating AU member states in four thematic areas: democracy and political governance; economic governance and management; corporate governance; and socio-economic development. The original idea was that for African leaders to win foreign financial assistance and investment, they had to first put their own houses in order. The APRM was the tool to be used to assess their good governance performance. The Peer Review Mechanism is constituted as follows:[32]

- the Committee of Participating Heads of State and Government (APR forum), which is the highest decision-making authority in the APRM
- the Panel of Eminent Persons (APR panel), which oversees the review process
- the APRM Secretariat, which serves as the secretarial, technical, coordinating, and administrative body, and
- the Country Review Mission Team that conducts the review progress and produces APRM Reports on countries.

By January 2014, 31 countries[33] had joined the APRM, but only 14 had been peer reviewed.[34] Although it is the best AU instrument conceived to promote peace and good governance, the APRM's early warnings have been generally neglected. For instance, the APRM accurately predicted the outbreaks of post-election violence in Kenya in 2007–08 and of xenophobic violence in South Africa in 2008. As is pointed out later, receding support in this process has cost Africa one of its most effective tools for conflict prevention and good governance promotion.

The Economic, Social, and Cultural Council

ECOSOCC, which was launched in Addis Ababa on March 29, 2005, aims to give African CSOs a role in AU policy formulation and decision-making. Composed of professional groups, NGOs, social groups, community-based organizations, workers, religious and cultural groups, and consisting of 150 members, ECOSOCC is an advisory organ of the AU. Its main objectives are: to promote dialog and partnership between African governments and their people, and among the African people themselves; and to participate in the programs and activities of the AU, including promoting the overall principles and objectives of the Union. During the inauguration of ECOSOCC, the AUC chairperson, Alpha Konare, claimed this organ was created to serve as a tool "against authoritarian regimes, hostile external efforts and the negative waves of globalization."[35]

ECOSOCC was expected to provide a solid foundation for democracy, and to promote respect for the rule of law and human rights, democratic transformation, and good governance. It had an interim mandate from March 2005 to March 2007, during which time it was to ensure that its sub-regional and national structures were in place and that CSOs had started influencing policy changes within the AU by engaging its sectoral clusters.[36] This goal was not attained. The inclusion of ECOSOCC in the AU system is of great historical significance in the sense that it recognized the role of African CSOs in the continent's development. It is also a reaffirmation of the 1990 Arusha Charter on Popular Participation that recognized the importance of CSOs in governance and development. ECOSOCC represents a radical departure from the OAU days when civil society was viewed with hostility. The 2001 OAU summit in Lusaka stressed the importance of involving CSOs in Africa's integration process, as well as in the formulation and implementation of the AU program through ECOSOCC.[37]

When fully operational, ECOSOCC will not only enable African people to contribute to the programs and decisions of the AU, but also to assume ownership of these programs and play a role in their implementation. This engagement will also be extended to other AU organs such as the PSC, the PAP, the African Court on Human and Peoples' Rights, and specialized committees. Nevertheless, ECOSOCC faces a number of critical challenges that could hinder its effectiveness. First, most African CSOs and community-based organizations are not able to fully meet the conditions for eligibility. This is due to the fact that most of them are heavily dependent on foreign funds, which makes them ineligible. Second, like the other AU organs, it has insufficient funds. In 2014 the Assembly allocated it only $993,710 for its operations. Third, many African governments are still uneasy with CSOs and would like to keep them at a distance. Most governments criticize CSOs for relying on foreign donors, although the governments are also dependent on the same sources of funding. Fourth, most African CSOs have weak institutional capacity and most of them would fail the "good governance, transparency, and accountability" test.

The African Union Commission

The AU appears to have centralized power within the Commission – the administrative structure that effectively runs the organization inbetween summits. The Commission is the secretariat of the Union and its executive organ. There are major differences between the AUC and the former OAU secretariat in that one individual does not, theoretically, dominate the Commission. As displayed in Figure 2.2, the chairperson of the Commission – currently Nkosazana Dlamini-Zuma – is assisted by a deputy and eight commissioners who represent different sub-regions of the continent. The commissioners, half of whom are women, were supposed to be selected on the basis of their competence, experience, and leadership. Although a decision was taken during the January 2007 summit in Addis Ababa to expand the number of commissioners to 11, this decision was not implemented due to the proposal to transform the Commission into an authority.

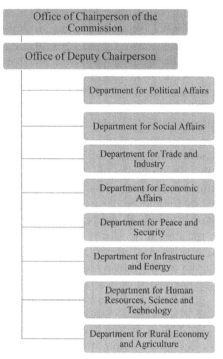

Figure 2.2 Current structure of the African Union Commission
Source: Authors

The last OAU Secretary-General and interim chairperson of the AUC, Amara Essy, expressed serious concern that the commissioners would be elected – which would make them political appointees answerable to the Assembly rather than being responsible to the Commission chairperson.[38] He argued that this would undermine the performance of the new organization since it would be bogged down in a struggle similar to the one the OAU experienced between "the secretary-general and his assistants, because they were all elected" and had political support that encouraged them to "do what they wanted."

The Commission faces serious problems within itself and in its relations with other structures in the Union. There is an overwhelming concern within the Union that the Commission is doing everything and wants to run the entire AU system. In particular, the Commission has had acrimonious and checkered relations with the PRC, characterized by tensions and mistrust. The hostilities are mutual and evident whenever the two organs meet to review documents or plan events. On the one hand, the PRC believes it has the responsibility to monitor and check the Commission's excesses; while on the other, the latter body feels that PRC members are pursuing hidden agendas that include personal or national interests.

Since the Commission has been providing the secretarial support for the PSC, PSC members often appear like invitees of the Commission. The Commission sets the PSC timetable, proposes its agenda, prepares its draft reports, and drafts the PSC communiqués – which are usually provided for consideration and adoption only minutes before the meeting. The PSC has also shown little commitment to the technical matters of drafting and analysis. Ideally, countries on the PSC should have full-time ambassadors serving in the Council for the duration of their terms, instead of the present arrangement under which they concurrently serve the AU, the UN, Ethiopia, and other countries in the region.

As a result of the weaknesses of the PSC members, the Commission has assumed the lead role in implementing the AU's peace and security agenda – including the management of funds donated for its implementation. There have also been cases where the Commission has taken decisions that should have been taken by the PSC. For instance, during the 50th PSC session members felt that they were being presented with a fait accompli to send an AU military force to eastern DRC to disarm groups operating in the region with impunity. While the Commission argued that PSC member states ought to have acted quickly in view of the deteriorating security situation, the latter felt that such an important operation that required the use of force should have a clear mandate and that any decisions taken in pursuit of this should have followed consultation with their respective governments. On another occasion the Commission did not seek an endorsement of the PSC before asking South Africa to send extra troops to the AU Mission for the Support of Elections in the Comoros in April 2006.

The above is an indication of serious flaws in the organizational structure. Ideally, the Commission is supposed to be the administrative arm of the Union and not a decision-making body. It should only implement decisions made by other bodies. By acting as the custodian of AU documents – as well as the maker and interpreter of rules, procedures, and regulations – it has acquired considerable power. Bodies such as the PSC are further held at the Commission's mercy, since the latter controls the purse strings.

Within the Commission there is also concern about how one department is the darling of the donors, while others go virtually unnoticed and their work unheralded. For instance, the department of political affairs – which deals with issues related to political stability, human rights, and humanitarian assistance – is generally ignored even when it comes to responding to complex emergencies such as those in Darfur, the CAR, Mali, and South Sudan. Indeed the PSC protocol mostly ignores this important department, despite the fact that its work is relevant to the PSC's functions.

The Adedeji panel found the relationship between the chairperson, the deputy, and the eight commissioners to be "dysfunctional with overlapping portfolios, unclear authority and responsibility lines and expectations, due to inadequate comprehension on their part."[39] The commissioners have been operating independently –unanswerable to the chairperson, the chief executive officer – on the basis that they were elected by an Assembly which gave them complete authority to manage their departments in the way they saw best. The panel found that the dysfunctionality of the AUC could be attributed to the "lack of operational clarity as to the lines of authority," the lack of international exposure and previous experience of working for an international organization, and the fact that the commissioners never go through induction training that would prepare them for serving a multicultural and complex organization.

The panel also found that the AUC lacks a professional and collegiate culture, operates in "an unhealthy organisational culture," and is composed of unwieldy and illogical portfolios.[40] It pointed out that the AUC head did not exercise full authority as the chief executive and accounting officer, and did not follow the statutes and rules of procedure. The panel claimed that the AUC had been headed by people with no "known vision of and commitment to pan-Africanism and continental integration."[41] Adedeji and his team further claimed that the AUC had "inadequate in-house leadership and weak management systems" that "have resulted in poor supervision in the commission, within and between departments, and low morale among staff. Few commissioners and directors can claim to have had a respectful and productive relationship."[42]

According to the Adedeji panel, the AUC had also failed to "articulate and accept a chain of command," and to clarify authorization levels – that is, the exercise of power and its delegation. It claimed the AUC also had "ineffective accountability mechanisms" which were "central to the disempowerment of and demoralisation among staff." The panel warned that unless these undesirable practices were checked, the departments would "continue to work in silos, producing gaps, overlaps and a fragmented institution."[43]

Although the panel had warned that failure to fundamentally reform the AUC "would be detrimental and costly" to the "quest for political and economic integration", no action was taken until January 2013 when the EC made decision EX.CL/Dec.754(XXII). This conferred upon the chairperson the power to take "necessary actions aimed at enhancing the operational efficiency of the Commission." The chairperson was specifically asked "to take the necessary measures to modernize and strengthen the Commission in line with international best practices, and performance standards, to achieve a high level of Excellence, Accountability, Transparency, Integrity, Professionalism, Gender Equity and Respect for Diversity."

Specialized Technical Committees

STCs are provided for in Article 15 of the CAAU, partly to prepare projects and programs of the Union and submit them to the EC. They also have responsibility for ensuring the supervision, follow-up, and evaluation of the implementation of decisions taken by the organs of the Union. The STCs are also expected to ensure the coordination and harmonization of projects and programs of the Union, and to submit them to the EC – either on its own initiative or at the request of the EC. The STCs may also carry out any other function assigned to them for the purpose of ensuring the implementation of the provisions of the CAAU.

Article 14 of the CAAU provides for the following STCs: the Committee on Rural Economy and Agricultural Matters; the Committee on Monetary and Financial Affairs; the Committee on Trade, Customs and Immigration Matters; the Committee on Industry, Science and Technology, Energy, Natural Resources and Environment; the Committee on Transport, Communications and Tourism; the Committee on Health, Labour and Social Affairs; and the Committee on Education, Culture and Human Resources. Although Article 14 does not identify an STC on peace and security matters, the AU Assembly, in February 2009, decided (Assembly/AU/Dec.227(XII)) to restructure STCs on the following thematic areas:

- Agriculture, Rural Development, Water and Environment
- Finance, Monetary Affairs, Economic Planning and Integration
- Trade and Industry and Minerals
- Transport, Transcontinental and Interregional Infrastructure, Energy and Tourism
- Gender and Women Empowerment
- Justice and Legal Affairs
- Social Development, Labour and Employment
- Public Service, Local Government, Urban Development and Decentralisation

- Health, Population and Drug Control
- Migration, Refugees and Internally Displaced Persons (IDPs)
- Youth, Culture and Sports
- Education, Science and Technology
- Communication, Information Communications Technology (ICT)
- Defence, Safety and Security.

The STC on Defence, Safety, and Security (STCDSS) – which is composed of the African ministers of Defence, Safety, and Security – has met on a number of occasions to consider the Gambari report on the African Standby Force.[44]

STCs are structures that were borrowed from the EU system, but without adequate consideration of how they are funded or how they fit into the AUC portfolio and member states' ministries. Some governments have been allowed to send between three and six ministers to attend a committee meeting. There have also been regular meetings of ministers on issues that are identified in the CAAU. For instance, ministers in charge of border issues have been meeting every two years to discuss matters related to delimitation, demarcation, and management of African boundaries. Since 2007 these ministers have passed three declarations that have been endorsed by the Assembly and EC meetings.

Aside from the STCDSS, the AU has yet to make the STCs a reality and is still grappling with defining their terms of reference and the modalities for their functions. It is also facing the challenge of aligning these bodies to the Union's structures and programs, the RECs, and national level ministerial structures. For instance, some countries have at least five ministers with portfolios that fall under the auspices of the Committee on Industry, Science and Technology, Energy, Natural Resources, and Environment. Furthermore, there are no budgetary allocations for the STCs. Consequently, the Committee on Health, Labour, and Social Affairs relies on money from donors who include the Bill and Melinda Gates Foundation, the World Bank, UNICEF, and the Global Fund.

AU financial woes

Although African leaders adopted one of the most ambitious agendas and institutional structures when they created the AU, they did not assign or secure the financial resources needed to implement them. Without adequate resources the AU has struggled not only to establish the key structures, but also to run the existing ones and to implement the Union's agenda. As a result the AU has depended on funding from international partners (see Table 2.1, Table 2.2 and Table 2.3). Since Decision AHG/Dec.1(XXXVII) of the OAU Assembly was taken at the Lusaka summit of 2001, several studies have been carried out to explore "alternative sources of funding" for the AU. Since then numerous other Assembly and EC decisions have been taken on the same issue.[45] One of the latest efforts to find sustainable and reliable sources of funding for the AU's ambitious and growing peace, security, governance, integration, and development agendas was the appointment in July 2011 of another panel of eminent persons – this time headed by former Nigerian president, Olusegun Obasanjo.

The Obasanjo panel[46] completed its work in December 2013 and acknowledged that "the current system of statutory contributions, which has been in place since the OAU days is no longer adequate to meet the growing financing needs of the union due to greater operational requirements and increased scope of activities." The AU derives its funding from two sources: the assessed contributions of its members, and donations from external partners. The organization has been struggling financially as a result of member states defaulting on their payments, making late payments, or withholding contributions – for different reasons. Donors, meanwhile, only fund projects that they have identified and whose implementation they control. This last form of funding is also unsustainable since the "partners" can attach strings that make it difficult for the AU to spend the money.

In the process, the absorptive capacity of the AU has become very low due to "unspent" money being returned or carried forward from year to year. The AU also depends on six of its members to pay 85 percent of the budget.[47] Three of these six are in North Africa, where political turmoil has resulted in the withholding, or delayed disbursement, of their payments. The delinquency rate (non-payment of dues) has hovered between 35 percent and 60 percent over the last ten years. Although the arrears owed by members fell from $72.4 million in 2011 to $43.8 million in 2012, this still represents a staggering amount when one bears in mind that members' contributions pay for an AU operating budget of just $126 million.

The Obasanjo panel received a number of proposals for funding the AU, and after evaluating them it decided to recommend:

- private sector funding
- a levy on insurance premiums at 1 percent
- a levy on international (US$2.50) and continental (US$1) travel, and a tourism and hospitality tax of US$1
- a levy of 0.2 percent on goods imported from outside the continent.

Table 2.1 AU budget ($), 2014

Organ	Member states			Partners		
	Operational	Program	Total	Operational	Program	Total
AUC	91,508,707	5,520,089	97,028,796		125,881,823	125,881,823
PAP	10,891,648		10,891,648		3,400,476	3,400,476
AfCHPR (the Court)	4,076,044		4,076,044		1,569,423	1,569,423
ACHPR (the Commission)	6,938,014		6,938,014		1,681,571	1,681,571
ECOSOCC	993,710		993,710			-
NEPAD	4,410,000		4,410,000	6,304,442	29,687,801	35,992,243
AUCIL	371,024	44,100	415,124		203,892	203,892
Advisory Board on Corruption	492,436		492,436		1,015,421	1,015,421
Peace and Security Council		759,253	759,253			-
ACERWC		45,873	45,873		353,696	353,696
Sub-total	119,681,583	6,369,315	126,050,898	6,304,442	163,794,103	170,098,545

Additional Sources	Member states			Partners		
	Operational	Program	Total	Operational	Program	Total
General Fund	8,916,329		8,916,329			-
Acquisition of Properties Fund	2,105,986		2,105,986			-
Government of China	876,619		876,619			-
Sub-total	7,148,933	-	7,148,933	-		-
Grand Total	131,580,516	6,369,315	137,949,831	6,304,442	163,794,103	170,098,545

Source: AU Directorate of Programming, Budget, Finance and Accounting

Table 2.2 Sources of funding for overall AU budget, 2004–14 ($ millions, percentages)

Sources	2004(%)	2005(%)	2006(%)	2007(%)	2008(%)	2009(%)	2010(%)	2011(%)	2012(%)	2013(%)	2014(%)
Member states	40.4	60.2	69.4	87.8	107.6	106.9	116.8	122.6	122.4	122.9	137.9
	(94)	(40)	(51)	(71)	(77)	(65)	(47)	(48)	(45)	(44)	(45)
Partners	2.6	89	66.6	36.3	32.4	57.4	133.7	134.2	151.7	155.4	170.1
	(6)	(60)	(49)	(29)	(23)	(35)	(53)	(52)	(55)	(56)	(55)
Total	**43**	**149.2**	**136**	**124.1**	**140**	**164.3**	**250.5**	**256.8**	**274.1**	**278.2**	**308**

Source: AU Directorate of Programming, Budget, Finance and Accounting

Table 2.3 Sources of funding AU programs, 2007–14 (million $, percentages)

Sources	2007(%)	2008(%)	2009(%)	2010(%)	2011(%)	2012(%)	2013(%)	2014(%)
Member states	13.7	14.7	11.3	11.2	10.2	7.6	5.4	6.4
	(27)	(31)	(16)	(8)	(7.1)	(4.8)	(3.3)	(3.8)
Partners	36.3	32.4	57.4	133.7	134.2	151.7	155.4	163.8
	(73)	(69)	(84)	(92)	(92.9)	(95.2)	(96.7)	(96.2)
Total	**49.7**	**47.1**	**68.7**	**144.9**	**144.4**	**159.3**	**160.7**	**170.2**
	(100)	**(100)**	**(100)**	**(100)**	**(100)**	**(100)**	**(100)**	**(100)**

Source: AU Directorate of Programming, Budget, Finance and Accounting

The Obasanjo panel calculated that if the levies were to be imposed on imports (0.2 percent), insurance premiums (0.2 percent), air travel (US$5), and tourism (US$1 per tourist) an extra US$1.45 billion per year would be generated. In the event the panel adopted the option of levying US$10 on tickets for international flights into and out of the African continent; and a US$2 hospitality levy per stay in a hotel, the total revenue that will be generated from these taxes will be $763 million annually for the AU.

However, several member states – particularly those whose economies heavily rely on tourism – opposed the panel's recommendations as inequitable.

In view of its failure to directly connect to the African people, or to make itself relevant to their everyday lives, it will not be easy for the AU to attract direct funding from the people. Africans are likely to protest against any attempt to raise taxes to support the AU bureaucracy and activities. This means that the AU will continue to depend on foreign support to implement its agendas.

Conclusion

It is apparent that power struggles, alongside donor interests, have played key roles in establishing and shaping the AU organs, structures, and mechanisms. Those who control political power and financial resources appear to be driving institution-building from back to front; instead of first identifying Africa's needs and priorities – and then designing strategies for addressing them – the structures were set up and their missions identified only afterwards. Many of the structures and mechanisms are operational, but some of them are not functioning as they were expected to. Even ECOSOCC has yet to live up to the expectation of it as the forum through which CSOs influence Africa's peace, security, governance, and development agenda.

Thus, the AU is an over-ambitious organization that was modeled on the EU, a body which itself took more than four decades to evolve to its present state. Although the mantra of the AU in 2002 was "new organization, new ideals, new objectives, new leaders, and a new era for Africa," the jury is still out as to whether it has lived up to these expectations. In the final analysis it will be political will, money, and the adoption of a new mindset (or lack thereof) that will ultimately determine whether the AU succeeds or remains as just another African experiment.

The success of the AU will depend on several factors. The first is the extent to which its members are willing to pool their sovereignty in the interest of the continent. It is only with a single voice that Africa can address issues of common concern – such as threats to peace, debt, unfair international trade terms, ecological problems, the HIV/AIDS pandemic, and, most recently, the Ebola virus. The second factor is that the integration process needs to be directed by an astute, inspiring, consistent, and focused political leadership – one that is fully committed to Africa's transformation and unification.

Third, the AU needs unwavering, universal goodwill, and the support of the African people. The Union will continue to be challenged for its lack of democracy, accountability, and transparency, so long as some of its members continue to score low marks on the Ibrahim governance index. So far it is governments that have driven the AU – but the Union will have to broaden its ownership to include the African people, who need to be consulted regularly.

Fourth, the AU needs to ensure that it has adequate funding for capacity building, and to support its activities. Among the things that the OAU bequeathed the AU have been defaulting membership payments and inadequately trained staff. When the OAU was folded, all but four members owed a total of $53 million. While the OAU had an annual operating budget of $30 million, the AU budget is conservatively estimated at $500 million. It is still unclear where the AU will get this kind of money from to run its 26 or more organs. Many proposals have been put forth. These have ranged from taxing air travel to imposing a special tax on all citizens of the member states. Whatever methods are adopted, the AU faces a major challenge in raising funds from its members because their individual prospects for economic growth vary so widely. To put this into perspective, 35 of the 42 poorest countries in the world are in Africa; but at the same time six of the ten fastest growing economies are in Africa. That said, these fast-growing economies are starting from a low base and are still relatively poor.

As a result of Africa's weak financial base, the AU has come to rely heavily on donors to implement its programs and projects. This, in turn, has exposed the organization to the donors' agenda, which, in some cases, has been different from Africa's. The donors' support of AU activities – including the peace operations in Darfur, Somalia, and Mali – has been mostly laudable, but has also caused some concerns about making the Union dependent upon external support.

Last, but not least, the AU needs to proceed at speed to adopt and implement common continental policies. The AU's "Agenda 2063," which will be discussed in the concluding chapter, provides a framework for long-term strategic planning. However, good policies and planning per se amount to nothing unless there are competent people to carry them out. In the final analysis the mantra of the AU as a new organization, with new ideals, objectives, and leaders, will be determined by a strong political will, the availability of resources, and a new mindset.

Notes

1 See Pusch Commey, "African Union – What Next?" *New African*, vol. 1, no. 410 (September 2002).
2 Kwame Nkrumah, *I Speak of Freedom* (London: Panaf Books) (1961): xii.
3 Cited in Commey, "African Union – What Next?"
4 See Wafula Okumu, "The African Union and the Challenges of Integration in Africa" in Charles Okigbo and Festus Eribo (eds) *Development and Communication in Africa* (Lanham, MD: Rowman & Littlefield) (2004): 187–204.
5 Ironically, the UN drastically reduced the deployment of its Blue Helmets in the late 1990s while the demand for peacekeepers in Africa was growing. Out of the 75,000 UN peacekeepers deployed in 1993, about 40,000 were deployed in seven concurrent missions in Africa. This contrasts with 1999 when there were 12,000 Blue Helmets, out of which 1,600 were deployed to three concurrent missions in Africa. See Eric G. Berman and Katie E. Sams, "Keeping the Peace in Africa," *Disarmament*, vol. 3 (2000): 22.
6 After the Somali debacle and the Sierra Leone humiliation, the UN limited its participation in peace support operation (PSO) to situations where all the parties have signed ceasefires and peace accords and are willing to cooperate in disarmament, demobilization and reintegration, and post-conflict reconstruction. Consequently, the UN has laid down minimum criteria that must be met to allow it to deploy its peacekeepers.
7 Amani Daima, "The Biggest Show in Africa: The Launching of the African Union," *Perspective* (Smyrna, Georgia), July 11, 2002.
8 Nigeria was at first lukewarm towards NEPAD, since it appeared to pose a threat to the Conference on Security, Stability, Development, and Cooperation in Africa (CSSDCA) – which was regarded as President Obasanjo's idea.
9 See Olusegun Obasanjo, *Hope for Africa – Selected Speeches* (Abeokuta, Nigeria: ALF Publications) (1993).
10 Obasanjo, *Hope for Africa – Selected Speeches*.
11 Although the CAAU abrogated the OAU Charter, it integrated the other existing legal instruments such as the 1991 Abuja Treaty setting up the African Economic Community, and the Cairo Declaration on a mechanism for conflict prevention, management, and settlement.
12 Ranjeni Munusamy and Mondli Makhanya, "Gaddafi parades on Mbeki's reign," *Sunday Times*, July 14, 2002). Available at: www.sundaytimes.co.za/specialreports/africanunion/ (no longer accessible).
13 See Munusamy and Makhanya, "Gaddafi parades on Mbeki's reign"; and Mondli Makhanya, "Ordinary Folk Need to Rein in the Dictators," *Sunday Times* (July 21, 2002). One African newspaper called Gaddafi "a self-styled, self-aggrandizing showman whose paramount obsession is to conquer and rule Africa by pickpocketing emotional votes and support from nations that … are considered less significant in the continent." See *Accra Mail* (July 24, 2002).
14 E. Ablorh-Odjidja, "Ghadaffi Strutting His Stuff," *Accra Mail* (July 24, 2002).

15 Ablorh-Odjidja, "Ghadaffi Strutting His Stuff."
16 It was Mbeki, as AU chairperson, who put this issue to rest when he informed the Group of Eight (G8) – through Canadian prime minister, Jean Chretien – that NEPAD was a program of the AU. See *Business Day*, November 18, 2002.
17 For analysis of AU-US relations, see Wafula Okumu, "AU-US Relations" in David Levinson and Karen Christensen (eds) *Global Perspectives on the United States Volume III: Issues and Ideas Shaping International Relations* (Great Barrington, MA: Berkshire Publishing) (2007): 293–6.
18 The Kwame Nkrumah awards ceremonies are symbolic events that are not taken seriously at national level.
19 "Declaration on the Implementation of the New Partnership for Africa's Development (NEPAD) (ASS/AU/Decl. 1 (I)) made by the Assembly of Heads of State and Government." See: www.au2002.gov.za/docs/summit_council/ (last accessed March 27, 2015).
20 See Articles 20 and 12 of the Protocol Relating to the Establishment of the Peace and Security Council.
21 However, such a committee can be established under Article 14 [2] by the Assembly, which can also restructure one of the committees to assume more responsibilities over gender issues.
22 Although the Permanent Representative Committee (PRC) is one of the organs that has been established and is functioning, it is deliberately left out of this overview of the AU organs since it is essentially an extension of the Assembly and the EC.
23 See Rules 33 and 34 of Rules of Procedure of the AU Assembly. The decision-making procedures for both the Assembly and the EC are similar except that the former makes its decisions on the recommendation of the latter, which in turn makes its decisions on the recommendations of the PRC (ambassadors). Notably, the decisions of the PRC are only recommendations until such time as they are adopted by the EC. See Rule 26 of the PRC Rules of Procedure.
24 See Rules 11 and 12 of AU Assembly Rules of Procedure, Assembly/AU/2 (I). The procedure and requirements for holding an extraordinary session of the EC are the same.
25 *Freedom to Innovate: Biotechnology and Africa's Development.* Draft Report of the High-Level African Panel on Modern Biotechnology of the African Union and the New Partnership for Africa's Development (14 July 14, 2006).
26 For instance, Article 20 of the Protocol Relating to the Establishment of the PSC calls on civil society to play a role in promoting peace and maintaining security in Africa. CSOs are also assigned key roles in NEPAD's APRM.
27 Speech of the Chairperson of the AUC, Alpha Konare, on the opening day of the PAP on March 18, 2004, in Addis Ababa.
28 AU Executive Council Decision on the 19th Activity Report of the African Commission on Human and Peoples' Rights. Doc. Ex.Cl/236 (VIII). Available at: http://www.au.int/en/content/khartoum-16-%E2%80%93-21-january-2006-council-ministers-organization-african-unity-meeting-its-eig-0 (last accessed on 10 March 2014). (emphasis added).
29 AU Audit Report (hereafter referred to as Adedeji panel), 2007. Available at: www.pambazuka.org/actionalerts/images/uploads/AUDIT_REPORT.doc (last accessed March 10, 2015): 84.

30 Adedeji panel: 84.
31 Other members of the Commission include Professor Mahmood Mamdani, Ms Bineta Diop, Professor Pacifique Manirakiza and Lady Justice Sophia Akuffo. The Commission is supported by an AUC technical team rather than the ACHPR.
32 See: www.nepad.org/economicandcorporategovernance/african-peer-review-mechanism/about (last accessed March 27, 2015).
33 Algeria, Angola, Benin, Burkina Faso, Cameroon, Congo, Djibouti, Egypt, Ethiopia, Gabon, Ghana, Kenya, Lesotho, Liberia, Malawi, Mali, Mauritania, Mauritius, Mozambique, Nigeria, Rwanda, Sao Tome & Principe, Senegal, Sierra Leone, South Africa, South Sudan, Sudan, Tanzania, Togo, Uganda, and Zambia.
34 Algeria, Benin, Burkina Faso, Ethiopia, Ghana, Lesotho, Kenya, Mali, Mauritius, Mozambique, Nigeria, South Africa, Rwanda, and Uganda.
35 See Irungu Houghton, "Reflections on African Union, NEPAD and African CSO engagement with an eye on Continental Citizenship, Public Accountability and Governance", 12 December 2005. <www.sarpn.org/.../AU_Nepad_Houghton_Dec2005.pdf> Accessed on 7 May 2015.
36 These clusters are peace and security, political affairs, infrastructure and energy, human resources, science and technology, rural economy and agriculture, economic affairs, women and gender-related issues, and crosscutting issues such as NEPAD.
37 See the Durban Declaration in Tribute to the Organisation of African Unity and on the Launching of the African Union of 10 July 2002 (Ass/Au/Decl. 2 (I)). Available at: http://au.int/en/content/durban-8-july-2002-assembly-heads-state-and-government-first-ordinary-session (last accessed 28 April 2014).
38 See Ofeibea Quist-Arcton, "AU's Interim Boss Essy Struggles to Shed OAU Legacy," available at: www.allAfrica.com, July 23, 2002. Available also at: http://allafrica.com/stories/200207240003.html (last accessed 25 April 2015).
39 AU Audit Report (hereafter referred to as Adedeji panel), 2007. Available at: www.pambazuka.org/actionalerts/images/uploads/AUDIT_REPORT.doc (last accessed March 10, 2015) 44.
40 Adedeji panel: 45.
41 Adedeji panel: 46.
42 Adedeji panel: 47.
43 Adedeji panel: 47–8.
44 Another STC that has come up covers the domain of public service, decentralization, and urban development.
45 Decision EX.CL/DEC.285 (IX) in June 2006; Declaration (Assembly/AU/Decl.2 (IX) of July 2007; Decision EX.CL/Dec.643 (XVII) of January 2011; and Decision Assembly/AU/Dec.364 (XVII) of July 2011.
46 The Obasanjo panel was appointed in July 2011 and was composed of former OAU Secretary-Generals Edem Kodjo and Salim Ahmed Salim (who withdrew for personal reasons), former prime minister of Mozambique Luisa Diogo, and the then AU Commissioner for Economic Affairs, Maxwell Mkwezalamba.
47 In 2011, the contributions from the "Big Five" (Algeria, Egypt, Libya, Nigeria, and South Africa) were reduced to 13.271 percent, which is 66.36 percent of the total budget. Under the new arrangements, Angola has been added to make it six main contributors.

3   The challenge of promoting governance, democracy, and the rule of law

One of the main factors behind the formation of the African Union (AU) was the determination of its founders to promote and protect human rights, enhance democratic structures, and encourage good governance. They considered these issues, as well as others such as constitutionalism and respect for the rule of law, to be crucial for the pursuit of peace, security, and development. The Constitutive Act of the African Union (CAAU) adopted these ideals as some of its objectives and principles, in addition to popular participation, gender equality, and social justice.

The African Charter on Democracy, Elections, and Governance (hereafter the Charter on Democracy) was adopted by the AU Assembly on January 30, 2007, and entered into force on February 15, 2012. By May 2014, 23 out of 54 AU member states had ratified it. The main objectives and principles of the Charter are to elaborate the elements of democracy and governance in the Constitutive Act. The Charter on Democracy also seeks to eradicate corruption, embed a culture of peace, and establish an enabling environment for democratic consolidation – including the institutionalization of opposition political parties. It aims also to promote the separation of powers and checks and balances, representative government through free and fair elections, and civilian control of the security sector (Article 3).

In addition, the AU Assembly adopted the African Governance Architecture (AGA) at its 16th ordinary session in January 2011. On paper, the AGA is the overall political and institutional framework for the promotion of good governance. It seeks to achieve its aims by enhancing interactions and synergies between the decision-making AU organs and structures. Based on three pillars – norms, an institutional framework, and interactions – the AGA also intends to encourage the generation of shared governance values and a vision for the continent.

Achieving these objectives would require collaboration among various agents: the AU, Regional Economic Communities (RECs), African states, civil society organizations (CSOs), and the donor community. A crucial element in this process is the recognition that the African people need to be consulted and to participate in the pursuit of the AU's objectives and principles. Theoretically, this represents a normative jump from the state-centrism of the Organization of African Unity (OAU) to apparently people-centered processes and activities. If successful, it could represent a move away from the culture of impunity to one of responsible sovereignty.

Governance, democracy, and the rule of law require appropriate mechanisms at the local, state, and continental levels. Indeed, the AU objective of promoting "democratic principles and institutions, popular participation and good governance" (Article 3 [g]) cannot be achieved across the continent unless there is cooperation between the local, national, and continent-wide governance structures. Ideally, this means not only the existence of democratic mechanisms at the three levels, but also the absence of corruption and a commitment by those who manage these mechanisms to permit CSOs and the people to participate in decision-making. Such a situation is a long way off for a number of reasons: the differing political and legal systems in Africa; the lack of knowledge of the AU's activities among people at the local level; and the fact that some African states are still ruled by leaders who do not accept that they are accountable to the people they rule. The rest of this chapter is divided into three parts. The first discusses briefly some of the terms, concepts, and shared norms referred to in the AGA. The second examines the nature of corruption, and efforts by the AU and New Partnership for Africa's Development (NEPAD) to address it. The third analyzes political leadership and examines options for overcoming the constraints that African leaders face.

Conceptual issues

What do we understand by the terms governance, democracy, and the rule of law? The simple answer is that the meanings of these concepts are historically contingent and, therefore, vary from one period to another; and from one geographical location to another. Even in the same era and within the same geographical location their definitions can be hotly contested.

Governance

As stated in the Introduction, governance occurs at various levels of social activity – from the village, to the state, to the global system. The

Commission on Global Governance has claimed that governance is "a continuing process through which conflicting and diverse interests may be accommodated and co-operative action may be taken."[1] From this perspective, governance would describe the structures, rules, and institutions which African people have established for managing their political, cultural, economic, and social affairs. Governance has also been used to refer to formal and informal sets of arrangements. For example, Goran Hyden has defined governance as "the conscious management of regime structures with a view to enhancing the legitimacy of the public realm."[2] Governance sometimes implies that the management of mega-policy issues such as the environment, security, and development cannot be left to governments alone. Therefore, village associations, women's organizations, ethnic networks, and other non-governmental organizations (NGOs) may be involved in decision-making processes.[3]

This means that the legitimacy of government decisions is judged, in part, by the level of consultation that policy makers have had with civil society. It is for this reason that governance has been used to refer to sub-national, national, and transnational networks. A system of governance can be crucial for the utilization of globalization processes and the management of security because it involves institution building, the generation of new norms, and the management of societal change. This is why the Charter on Democracy seeks the creation of an enabling environment for sustainable development, stability, peace, and security through political, economic, and social governance.

There are also various types of governance: bad governance, cooperative governance, corporate governance, global governance, and good governance, among others. Since the 1980s the World Bank and the International Monetary Fund (IMF) have used the term "good governance" to refer to a particular type of political and economic order underpinned by a neo-liberal ideology.[4] Although the IMF and the World Bank had in the 1990s incorporated a requirement for "good governance" as part of their structural adjustment packages, they had only narrowly defined it "in terms of governmental efficiency and the absence of corruption."[5] It was not until 1999 that the Bank and the IMF broadened the definition to include governmental transparency and accountability, increased popular participation in the policy making process, and the building of democratic structures.[6] Hence, for the World Bank and the IMF, "good governance" is associated with the spread of liberal democracy, leaner bureaucracies, accountability, transparency in government, and free markets.

However, the World Bank and the IMF's version of "good governance" has also had undesirable features that have caused considerable pain to the African people and diminished the internal legitimacy of African governments. Their model of good governance has raised serious ethical questions. For example, is it morally acceptable for African policy makers to give export crops priority over food crops? Is it ethical for poor African states to spend large portions of their income on debt repayment while their own people are starving? Why should the new generations of Africans meet the cost of debts attributable to borrowers and lenders from earlier periods? There are no simple answers to these questions but democracy empowers the African people to raise them.

Democracy

Although definitions of democracy have varied widely, it has generally been described as a political system whose "main features are free competition among political parties, periodic elections, and respect for the fundamental freedoms of thought, expression, and assembly."[7] This is why the Charter on Democracy (Article 3) identifies the following among its principles: regular, transparent, free, and fair elections; representative government; respect for human rights; separation of powers; popular participation; and constitutional transfers of political power. It goes further and links democracy to human security, sustainable development, and peace. The Charter also associates democracy with human rights by seeking the commitment of African states to promote democracy alongside the rule of law and human rights (Article 4 [1]). In Article 27 it also recognizes "freedom of expression, in particular freedom of the press," as an essential ingredient of good governance.

As one of us has posited, democracy is "a way of government firmly rooted in the belief that people in any society should be free to determine their own political, economic, social, and cultural systems."[8] Larry Diamond also describes democracy as "a civilian, constitutional, multiparty regime, with competitive elections."[9] A survey of the literature reveals that the different definitions of democracy revolve around several themes: consent, popular participation, and accountability.

Consent simply refers to the unforced agreement of the electors on the procedures governing the distribution of political power and decision-making within their society. This does not mean unanimity on specific issues, but it does imply recognition that all human beings are equal. Consent also conveys the view that citizens are sovereign in their own political community. This latter position has been accepted only by some African leaders; others believe that sovereignty resides in them and that they can do as they like within their own states.

Popular participation, particularly through "universal suffrage," is recognized by the Charter on Democracy (Article 4 [2]) as "the inalienable right of the people." It is used in this chapter to refer to conditions in which the majority of the African people have relatively equal opportunities to express their views about the policies and decisions that govern them. It implies equal access to elections – including the one-person, one-vote formula – as well as equality before the law, which connotes an opportunity to redress grievances and resolve conflicts peacefully. Popular participation also implies the freedom to organize political parties and civic organizations, and equal access to the mass media. Chapter 7 of the Charter on Democracy defines the conditions under which democratic elections should be conducted, with particular reference to the AU Declaration on the Principles Governing Democratic Elections in Africa.

Accountability in this context means the existence of mechanisms in which those who exercise power – namely the African leaders – have to justify their actions to the electorate. It entails continuing efforts by political leaders to seek the approval of those they rule. Accountability is only possible if the citizens of African states understand their rights, responsibilities, and opportunities. Some African states which consider themselves democratic appear to fall short of meeting the requirements for consent – i.e. popular participation and accountability. This could also explain why such states are dogged by violence and rampant violations of human rights. The Charter on Democracy seeks to stem this practice by calling on African states to "commit themselves to democracy, the principle of the rule of law and human rights." It further calls on African states to "ensure that citizens enjoy fundamental freedoms and human rights taking into account their universality, interdependence and indivisibility."

Efforts by the AU to promote democracy need to be understood in a context in which this form of rule has eluded Africa. African states briefly enjoyed democracy following independence in the 1950s and 1960s, but before it could take root dictatorship set in and lasted until the early 1990s. In such situations it is one thing to have a multi-party system and regular elections, but quite another to consolidate democracy.

Democratic consolidation refers to a situation in which a transition from an authoritarian phase is completed. The introduction of democratic ideals and practices in societies that have lived under oppressive regimes for many years is a daunting challenge. As some critics have argued, the transition from authoritarian rule is one in which there is an "interval between one political regime and another ... delimited, on one side, by the launching of the process of dissolution of an authoritarian regime and, on the other, by the installation of some form of democracy."[10] In other words, a transition takes place when wholescale change has occurred in a political system and "not just in the individuals holding positions of political power." This change has to take place also "in the assumptions and methods of the political system, in how the system legislates, formulates, and implements policies, and in the ways in which individuals gain access to power."[11]

Such a transition can be influenced by a number of factors – such as the length of time the authoritarian regime was in power, the methods it employed to exercise power, and the level of knowledge people have about their rights and responsibilities. In a country like the Democratic Republic of Congo (DRC), where Mobutu's dictatorship lasted more than three decades, democratic consolidation is likely to be a slow process. According to Juan Linz and Alfred Stepan, a society has consolidated its democracy when there is broad consensus among its members that democratic practice is the only acceptable type of rule, or as they put it: "the only game in town."[12]

Democracy is consolidated when democratic norms and institutions are strengthened and the new regime "does not have the perverse elements undermining [democracy's] basic characteristics."[13] Adam Przeworski contends that for democratic structures to last they must be fair by giving "all the relevant political forces a chance to win from time to time," and make "even losing under democracy more attractive than losing under non-democratic alternatives."[14] In the current international climate democratic consolidation in Africa is likely to be undermined by corruption, external interference, and the so-called "War on Terror" – which has tempted some governments to disregard the rule of law.

The rule of law

The rule of law is predicated on a number of factors, including the assumption that the law must "be universally heeded, that is, obeyed and complied with."[15] According to Ishmail Mohammed, the rule of law implies five assumptions. First, the law is sovereign over all authorities, including the government. Second, the law must be clear and certain in its content, and accessible and predictable to those subject to it. Third, the law must be general and universal in its application. Fourth, the judiciary must be independent and accessible to every aggrieved person, whatever his/her status. Finally, the law must have procedural and ethical content.[16] Based on the above understanding, it could be argued that the rule of law in Africa is achievable where there is a clear separation of powers between the judiciary and the executive, and the judiciary is insulated "from political pressure to decide particular cases in certain ways."[17]

The former Chief Justice of Tanzania, Francis Nyalali, has said: "[I]ndependence of the judiciary, impartiality of adjudication, fairness of trial, and integrity of the adjudicator are so universally accepted that one may reasonably conclude that these principles are inherent to any justice system in a democracy."[18] Nyalali further observed:

> [T]here is no doubt that these same principles are part of the African dream, resulting from the liberation struggle against colonial and racial oppression ... They are inherent to the statehood which came into being when our respective countries became politically independent.[19]

The consolidation of the rule of law in Africa is dependent upon political leaders and other powerful individuals or groups desisting from attempting to subvert justice for their own private interests. Article 10 of the Charter on Democracy identifies constitutionalism as a way of universalizing democratic principles. Additionally, the principles of "the right to equality before the law and equal protection by the law" are regarded "as a fundamental pre-condition for a just and democratic society" (Article 10 [3]). Being cognizant of the fact that principles need to be reflected in societal norms and values, and implemented through concrete structures, Chapter 5 of the Charter on Democracy calls on African states to "develop the necessary legislative and policy frameworks to establish and strengthen a culture of democracy and peace."

Military coups and unconstitutional changes of government have significantly decreased since the adoption of the 2000 Lomé Declaration on Unconstitutional Changes of Government, and the adoption of a principle in the Constitutive Act that condemns and rejects this practice. However, the 2005 military and constitutional coups in Mauritania and Togo respectively, pointed to the need to strengthen the existing mechanisms. It is in meeting this need, and in recognition of the negative impact of security apparatuses on the consolidation of democracy and the rule of law, that the Charter on Democracy, in Article 14, seeks to "strengthen and institutionalise constitutional civilian control over the armed and security forces." To give teeth to the AU's mechanism, Chapter 8 of the Charter prescribes various measures that are to be taken in cases of unconstitutional changes of government. Table 3.1 shows a drastic reduction in the number of successful and attempted coups since the adoption of the Lomé Declaration of July 2000 and the adoption of the Charter on Democracy.

Table 3.1 Coups in Africa, 1960–2014

	1960–79	1980–99	2000–14
Successful military coups	46	34	16
Attempted military coups	47	46	23
Total	93	80	39

Source: Habiba Ben Barka and Mthuli Ncube, "Political Fragility in Africa: Are Military Coups d'Etat a Never-Ending Phenomenon?" *AfDB Chief Economist Complex*, September 2012. Available at: www.afdb.org/fileadmin/uploads/afdb/Documents/ Publications/Economic%20Brief%20-%20Political%20Fragility%20in%20Africa%20 Are%20Military%20Coups%20d%E2%80%99Etat%20a%20Never%20Ending%20 Phenomenon.pdf (last accessed March 18, 2015)

Although the above concepts and issues are enshrined in the CAAU, they require well-established structures, strategic and transformative leadership, as well as the political will to entrench them as African norms that can, in turn, lead to the emancipation and empowerment of the African people. The extent to which the AU implements its principles will depend on the existence of an enabling environment that is free of corruption.

Preventing and combating corruption[20]

Africa's chances of turning globalization into a force "with a human face," pursuing peace and security, and achieving social, economic, and political development, are closely linked to good governance. However, good governance cannot co-exist with rampant corruption, as shown in Table 3.2. Corruption has taken advantage of the globalization of markets and is increasingly involving a wide range of activities. Some of these include drugs and arms smuggling; money laundering; the forging of passports, some of which been used by terrorists; and plundering Africa's resources, including minerals, oil, forestry products, and wildlife. These criminal activities have denied African economies the fuel they need to propel themselves forward. There are, indeed, correlations between corruption and poverty, and between corruption and insecurity, as the situations in Liberia and Sierra Leone demonstrated in the 1990s. In order to make progress on development, the AU and its member states need to tackle corruption by exploiting the complex relations among peace, globalization, security, and governance.

According to John Githongo, a former senior anti-corruption official in Kenya, "corruption – in particular grand corruption and looting of the kind that has tangible economic implications – is at the epicenter of

Table 3.2 Corruption ranking of African countries, 2006–2012

	2006	2007	2008	2009	2010	2011	2012
	Country rank/163	*Country rank/179*	*Country rank/180*	*Country rank/180*	*Country rank/178*	*Country rank/182*	*Country rank/174*
Algeria	84	99	92	111	105	112	105
Angola	142	147	158	162	168	168	157
Benin	121	118	96	106	110	100	94
Botswana	37	38	36	37	33	32	30
Burkina Faso	79	105	80	79	98	100	83
Burundi	130	131	158	168	170	172	165
Cameroon	138	138	141	146	146	134	144
Cape Verde	–	49	47	46	45	41	39
CAR	130	162	151	158	154	154	144
Chad	156	172	173	175	171	168	165
Comoros	–	123	134	143	154	143	133
Congo	142	150	158	162	154	154	144
Congo DR	156	168	171	162	146	168	160
Côte d'Ivoire	151	150	–	154	164	154	130
Djibouti	–	105	102	111	91	100	94
Egypt	70	105	115	111	98	112	118
Equatorial Guinea	151	168	171	168	168	172	163
Eritrea	93	111	126	126	123	134	150
Ethiopia	130	138	126	120	116	120	113
Gabon	90	84	96	106	110	100	102
Gambia	121	143	158	106	91	75	105
Ghana	70	69	67	69	62	69	64
Guinea	160	168	173	168	164	164	154
Guinea Bissau	–	147	158	162	154	154	150
Kenya	142	150	147	146	154	154	139
Lesotho	79	84	92	89	78	75	64
Liberia	–	150	138	97	87	91	75
Libya	105	131	126	130	146	168	160
Madagascar	84	94	85	99	123	100	118
Malawi	105	118	115	89	85	100	88
Mali	99	118	96	111	116	118	105
Mauritania	84	123	115	130	143	143	123
Mauritius	42	53	41	42	39	46	43
Morocco	79	72	80	89	85	80	88
Mozambique	99	111	126	130	116	116	123
Namibia	55	57	61	56	56	56	58
Niger	138	123	115	106	123	120	113
Nigeria	142	147	121	130	134	57	139
Rwanda	121	111	102	89	66	134	50
São Tomé & Príncipe	–	118	121	123	123	123	123
Senegal	70	71	85	99	105	112	94

Table 3.2 (cont.)

	2006	2007	2008	2009	2010	2011	2012
	Country rank/163	Country rank/179	Country rank/180	Country rank/180	Country rank/178	Country rank/182	Country rank/174
Seychelles	63	57	55	54	49	50	51
Sierra Leone	142	150	158	146	134	134	123
Somalia	–	179	180	180	178	182	174
South Africa	51	43	54	55	54	64	69
Sudan	156	172	173	176	172	177	173
South Sudan	–	–	–	–	–	–	–
Swaziland	121	84	72	79	91	95	88
Tanzania	93	94	102	126	116	100	102
Togo	130	143	121	111	134	143	128
Tunisia	51	61	62	65	59	73	75
Uganda	105	111	126	130	127	143	130
Zambia	111	123	115	99	101	91	88
Zimbabwe	130	150	166	146	134	154	163

Source: Transparency International. Available at: www.transparency.org/ (last accessed March 18, 2015)

the failure by many African countries to achieve economic objectives so finely articulated in their development plans."[21] In a report presented in September 2002, the AU estimated that corruption costs African economies in excess of $148 billion a year. The direct and indirect costs of corruption represent 25 percent of Africa's gross domestic product (GDP), and often increase the cost of goods by as much as 20 percent.[22]

These figures hardly tell the whole story, namely the fact that a huge number of Africans have been denied opportunities for emancipation and empowerment. In a nutshell, corruption has retarded development and thereby enhanced the potential for insecurity by weakening state institutions, diverting public resources into private hands – undermining indigenous entrepreneurship, scaring away foreign investors, and closing off avenues for human emancipation.

It was against this background that the AU Assembly adopted in July 2003 the Convention on Preventing and Combating Corruption (hereafter the Anti-Corruption Convention), which aims at establishing effective measures and actions that prevent, detect, punish, and eradicate corruption and related offenses. This Convention entered into force on August 5, 2006, and had been ratified by 35 countries as of January 2014. This Convention was supposed to be complemented by the NEPAD Action Plan, which calls for setting up a coordinated mechanism to combat corruption. However, this top-down approach to fighting corruption appears to have been aimed at hoodwinking donors and has borne few results, as Transparency International reports indicate. Moreover, this approach does not appear to take into account the possibility that, in some cases, the state may have become "a vehicle for organized criminal activity."[23] The remaining part of this section looks at how corruption in Africa needs to be understood, explains the nature of the AU and NEPAD measures for addressing the problem, and offers options for tackling this vice more effectively.

Understanding corruption in Africa

Corruption is prevalent in Africa as a result of many factors, including personal greed; the internalization of bad habits; the misperception that politics is the road to prosperity; weak government structures; ethnic ties and considerations; and the poor remuneration of civil servants. These factors have generated corruption from the local governance authorities, through to the state and RECs, and as far as the OAU/AU.

The plundering of the Congolese, Liberian, and Sierra Leonean economies by Mobutu Sese Seko, Charles Taylor, and Foday Sankoh, respectively, was largely the result of personal greed. However, these leaders – who used the state for criminal activities – exploited an atmosphere in which the populace thought it was acceptable to steal from the state. Thus, the people had internalized bad habits.

By the internalization of bad habits we mean the existence of a culture of corruption, which cannot be eliminated by the mere removal of a president, the sacking of a corrupt minister, or the jailing of a corrupt judge/magistrate. Corrupt practices have shaped the identities and interests of individuals and social groups to the extent that some of them cannot tell the difference between right and wrong. People acquire bad habits through schools, football clubs, social groups, and the recruitment to political party and government offices. This form of corruption is produced by, and helps to generate, vices such as nepotism, cronyism, patronage, and tribalism. It also helps to buttress other criminal activities such as drugs and arms smuggling, and the plundering of national economies. It is these activities that continue to undermine good governance, democracy, and the rule of law. These vices are likely to make it difficult for some states to benefit from the complex relations among peace, globalization, security, and governance.

In addition, and since independence, aspiring politicians and civil servants have regarded the African state as a "cash cow." African politicians and civil servants have reversed Karl Marx's thesis that it is the economic base that determines political power. In Africa, political office – or a senior civil service position – has served as the road to prosperity for those who occupy them. The desire to exploit the state for personal gain has led to corruption in recruitment processes, the awarding of tenders, and the management of parastatal organizations. According to Jeremy Pope, the founding executive director of Transparency International, most corrupt governments have "a hopelessly corrupt political elite – a political class across the spectrum that simply sees politics as a way of becoming wealthy."[24] Pope warns that it will be difficult to combat corruption in Africa "as long as politics is seen as the path to wealth." Bayart *et al.* have observed that while countries in other parts of the world have been tainted with corruption, "in Africa, the interaction between the practice of power, war, economic accumulation and illicit activities ... forms a particular political trajectory."[25]

The exploitation of the state for private gain has left state structures weak. According to William Kalema, a member of the Commission for Africa – a body instigated by the then British prime minister, Tony Blair – one of the reasons why corruption is widespread in Africa is the steady erosion of governance structures to the point that they are too weak to function properly.[26] This is why Aminatta Forna claimed:

> Corruption is not, as is often hinted, some sort of cultural weakness – even if it has, sadly, become the norm. Africa's problem is that the structures designed to provide checks and balances on the leadership are often neither sufficiently strong nor independent.[27]

Fighting corruption in Africa cannot be the responsibility of Africans alone. Multinational corporations, international organizations, Western countries, and increasingly China, have to play a part. As of this writing, China was not interested in joining this drive. The West has frequently expressed concern about the adverse effects of corruption and demanded that Africans adhere to certain standards of behavior, but Germany and Japan have not ratified the United Nations (UN) Convention Against Corruption. However, all the African countries except Chad, Equatorial Guinea, Eritrea, South Sudan, Sudan, and Somalia have ratified the Convention.[28] Disturbingly, the West has sometimes turned a blind eye to "the criminalization of the state in Africa."[29] For example, Western banks and businesses have assisted corrupt African leaders in stealing from their governments. In July 2013 the French government auctioned luxury cars belonging to Teodorin Obiang, son of Equatorial Guinea's president, Teodor Obiang, after he had been found guilty in 2011 of embezzling public funds.[30] At the same time, it was revealed that the young Obiang had purchased, with the assistance of the banks, a luxury home worth $30 million in Malibu, California, and collected art worth $24 million. In October 2013 Malawian president, Joyce Banda, was forced to sack a number of civil servants implicated in a $100 million scandal involving the looting of government coffers. In January 2014 the government put on mass trial 100 civil servants, politicians, and business people; while foreign donors suspended $150 million of aid – 40 percent of which supported the national budget.

Another case involved officials in the West conniving with African leaders who had illegally permitted Western chemical industries to dump toxic waste on the continent. Moreover, Western companies have not only continued to bribe African public officials, they also continue to deduct such bribes from their tax returns. In addition, offshore tax havens such as British Jersey are used as conduits for bribery payments made in Africa. Despite the Organization for Economic Cooperation and Development's (OECD') promise in 2004 to close these channels, the companies registered on these offshore islands have continued to pay bribes with impunity. This partly explains Aminatta Forna's argument that "Africa doesn't have the monopoly on corruption."[31]

AU and NEPAD anti-corruption measures

The AU and NEPAD have issued blueprints for fighting corruption – the Anti-Corruption Convention and the NEPAD Action Plan. However, both documents appear to be predicated on the assumption that African leaders, many of whom still benefit from corruption, will spearhead the fight.

The AU's Anti-Corruption Convention has the following objectives:

- promoting and strengthening the development of mechanisms to prevent, detect, punish, and eradicate corruption and related offenses in the public and private sectors
- promoting, facilitating, and regulating cooperation among states of effective measures and actions to eradicate corruption and related offenses
- coordinating and harmonizing policies and legislation among African states that will eradicate corruption
- promoting socio-economic development by removing obstacles to the enjoyment of economic, social, and cultural rights, as well as civil and political rights; and
- establishing the necessary conditions to foster transparency and accountability in the management of public affairs.

The NEPAD Action Plan makes a similar commitment "to combat and eradicate corruption,"[32] and calls for specific actions. In the short term it seeks measures to facilitate financial sector assessments, international assistance for training in anti-money laundering measures, and placing the recovery of stolen assets at the highest level of the global agenda.

In the medium term, the NEPAD Plan calls on African states to adopt relevant international conventions, standards, and best practices; permit international legal assistance in anti-money laundering matters based on accepted international legal standards; establish laws regulating the duties and responsibilities of participants in financial institutions; strengthen laws relating to anti-corruption measures and prosecutorial capacities; adopt national laws that provide for the criminalization of money laundering and the financing of terrorism; and improve cooperation within and outside Africa to help recover funds illegally acquired through corruption and criminal activity that are subsequently deposited in foreign countries. In the long term, the NEPAD Plan calls on African states to develop and strengthen judiciaries to enhance their independence and international credibility; strengthen arrangements for access to courts and investigative authorities, especially in developed countries; and establish strong and reliable regulatory and intelligence authorities.

NEPAD was established to promote good governance in return for aid, investment, and debt relief. This initiative appears to have been influenced by the desire for a rethinking of the African state's responsibility towards its citizens. It is a poverty reduction initiative that reflects the belief that African states can make progress in development only if internal governance is based upon solid foundations, and external trade and investment climates are transformed.

NEPAD's commitment to good governance is reflected in the African Peer Review Mechanism (APRM), an instrument for fostering political, economic, and corporate good governance, improving the efficiency and effectiveness of governments in delivering goods and services to their citizens, and creating confidence in target countries to attract support and investment.[33] As was stated in Chapter 2, the APRM was designed to track the progress and performance of member states in their quest for democracy, human rights, and good governance. It draws its strength from the provision that allows the peer review report to be released publicly, giving members of the public a chance to suggest areas that need correction. Among the indicators on which countries are assessed are their ratification and implementation of international codes – including the AU anti-corruption code – and the enactment and enforcement of effective anti-corruption and anti-money laundering laws. Of the 31 countries which agreed to undergo the first "peer review" (at the time of writing), 20 had ratified the AU's Anti-Corruption Convention and 29 had ratified the UN Convention Against Corruption. Yet most of these

Table 3.3 APRM members that are parties to AU and UN anti-corruption conventions (out of 177 countries)

AU members acceded to APRM	AU member peer reviewed	Ratified AU Convention of Preventing Corruption	State Party to UN Convention Against Corruption	Transparency International ranking (2013)
Algeria	x	x	x	94
Angola		-	x	153
Benin	x	x	x	94
Burkina Faso	x	-	x	83
Cameroon		-	x	144
Congo		x	x	154
Djibouti		-	x	94
Egypt		-	x	114
Ethiopia	x	x	x	111
Gabon		-	x	106
Ghana	x	x	x	63
Kenya	x	x	x	136
Lesotho	x	x	x	55
Liberia		x	x	83
Malawi		x	x	91
Mali	x	x	x	127
Mauritania		-	x	119
Mauritius	x	-	x	52
Mozambique	x	x	x	119
Nigeria	x	x	x	144
Rwanda	x	x	x	49
São Tomé & Príncipe		-	x	72
Senegal		x	x	77
Sierra Leone		x	x	119
South Africa	x	x	x	72
South Sudan		-	-	173
Sudan		-	-	174
Tanzania		x	x	111
Togo		x	x	123
Uganda	x	x	x	140
Zambia		x	x	83

Sources: AU Legal Office, United Nations Office on Drugs and Crime, NEPAD Secretariat and Transparency International

countries also performed poorly on Transparency International's list of the "most corrupt countries" in the world, as indicated in Table 3.3.

The APRM has a number of shortcomings. Although it is African leaders who are supposed to review each other's performances, this function is actually carried out by technical experts who are themselves governed by an independent panel of seven eminent persons and the African Peer Review secretariat. The heads of state and government receive the report prepared by the experts, and make recommendations. This is the end of the process; they have no mandate to punish wayward member states. Furthermore, participation in the peer review process is voluntary. So far, 31 countries have acceded to the program and fewer than half have completed the review. Even after undergoing the review process there are no indications that the recommendations dealing with corruption and other governance-related matters will be taken seriously by the country under review. If fully implemented, the APRM has the potential to be one of the best tools for anticipating and preventing conflicts – but only if its work is taken seriously. To put this into some kind of context, the post-election and xenophobic violence that broke out in Kenya and South Africa in 2008 could have been prevented had the respective governments heeded the APRM warnings.

Possible ways of tackling corruption

Although the AU Anti-Corruption Convention was signed in July 2003, and entered into force in August 2006, it was not until 2009 that the AU Advisory Board on Corruption was formed under Article 22 [1] of the Convention. The 11-member Board has the primary functions of:[34]

- promoting and encouraging adoption and application of anti-corruption measures on the continent
- collecting and documenting information on the nature and scope of corruption and related offenses in Africa
- developing methodologies for analyzing the nature and extent of corruption in Africa, disseminating information, and sensitizing the public on the negative effects of corruption and related offenses
- advising governments on how to deal with the scourge of corruption and related offenses in their domestic jurisdictions
- collecting information and analyzing the conduct and behavior of multinational corporations operating in Africa, and disseminating such information to national authorities designated under Article 18 [1] of the Convention
- developing and promoting the adoption of harmonized codes of conduct for public officials; and
- building partnerships with the African Commission on Human and People's Rights (ACHPR), African CSOs, and governmental,

intergovernmental, and non-governmental organizations, to facilitate dialog in the fight against corruption and related offenses.

However, these goals are only attractive on paper since the Board will not be able to meet them because it is currently staffed by only an executive secretary, one professional officer and nine support staff; has a budget allocation of only $1.5 million (2014); and relies on donor funding for all its activities.

The top-down approach to tackling corruption proposed by the AU and NEPAD has not been tried in any other part of the world. Given the nature of corruption in Africa, this approach is unlikely to succeed. Moreover, the lukewarm reception to the Anti-Corruption Convention is a clear indication that African leaders, many of them products of corrupt practices, are not ready to dismantle the patron-client political systems that promote corruption.

Corruption is in people's minds because it has been internalized since childhood. Therefore, it is in people's minds that anti-corruption measures should start. Just as the consolidation of democracy calls for the promotion of certain values over a period of time, the elimination of corruption requires the dissemination of particular values and norms over a protracted period.

This is not to imply that corruption might not be addressed in other ways. Indeed, some African leaders have taken commendable actions that demonstrate a seriousness about containing corruption. For example, in May 2005 South African president, Thabo Mbeki, fired his deputy, Jacob Zuma, after he was implicated in shady and corrupt deals.[35] In Nigeria, the second most corrupt country according to the 2005 Transparency International list, President Olusegun Obasanjo fired a number of high-ranking officials, including the minister for education and the chief of police, after they were implicated in corruption.

However, as the Nigerian case shows, efforts against corruption cannot be won by firing a few high-ranking officials. Strong leadership must be complemented by a substantial clean-up of the civil service, the dismantling of institutionalized corruption networks, encouragement of a high level of public awareness, citizen participation in the fight against corruption, and the creation of watchdog groups. Furthermore, as Ray Matikinye points out, "studies indicate that governments lacking a strong framework of good governance, the rule of law and adequate banking regulations while clinging on to unsound investment decisions, provide fertile grounds for corruption to thrive."[36]

In order for the AU/NEPAD anti-corruption measures to be successful, they must be based on a bottom-up strategy. This would entail strengthening national legislation, tightening procedures and audit systems, improving public service performance, developing a culture of outrage, positively encouraging public service integrity, and strengthening governance structures.[37] Good governance, based on effective mechanisms of public financial management and structures of political accountability, would contain corruption by dismantling patron-client networks.

The AU and NEPAD can only play the complementary role of promoting the continental norms of accountability, transparency, and good governance. They could also play a role in erecting an anti-corruption architecture composed of CSOs, national anti-corruption bodies, RECs, international anti-corruption bodies, and international financial houses.

The above anti-corruption strategy would work best if driven by public ownership and a committed political leadership. In other words, the ultimate responsibility for combating and eradicating corruption lies on the shoulders of the people. People need to be educated about their rights and responsibilities. They need to be made aware of how corruption closes off avenues for their emancipation and empowerment. It is when the people begin to reject corrupt politicians and leaders that the battle to contain corruption can start in earnest.

Strategic leadership

The success of the AU, and particularly its capacity to exploit the relations among peace, globalization, security, and governance, will depend on Africa's strategic leadership. It is plausible to argue that every state has leadership. Some states have good and forward-looking leaderships, while others have poor and backward-looking ones. Strategic or transformative leadership is a prerequisite for the realization of the AU's objectives and principles. The term "strategic leadership," in this context, means the ability to provide clear vision, inspiration, and effective strategies for mobilizing human, financial, scientific, and social resources. This talent requires creative and imaginative thinking, innovation, and entrepreneurship. Africa's strategic leaders should clearly understand the needs and aspirations of the people, and value their people's input in governance.

In the context of the AU, strategic leadership is crucial for the achievement of greater unity and solidarity between African states and peoples. It is necessary for the establishment and consolidation of democracy.

Such leadership is also vital for the attainment of sustainable development, the promotion of science and technology, the consolidation of peace and security, and the containment of corruption. This leadership has to be underpinned by at least three ethical principles which are listed in the AU Constitutive Act: human welfare, security, and socio-economic justice. These principles have the potential to facilitate human emancipation and empowerment.

Since independence in the 1950s and 1960s, African states have had many types and styles of leadership. Ali Mazrui has identified at least four historical leadership "traditions" in Africa: the elder tradition, like that of Jomo Kenyatta, 1963–78; the warrior tradition, like that of Idi Amin, 1971–79; the sage tradition, like that of Julius Nyerere, 1961–85; and the monarchical tendency.[38] The monarchical tendency, charisma, and the personality cult among some African leaders may have been attractive during the struggle for liberation but in subsequent years such styles hindered the development of democratic rule and strong governmental structures, and established a fertile ground for authoritarianism.

One of those leaders who had a weakness for the personality cult was Kwame Nkrumah. Mazrui, who admires Nkrumah's organizational skills, criticizes him for his dictatorial policies. Mazrui claims that "while Nkrumah strove to be Africa's Lenin, he also sought to become Ghana's Czar." He goes on: "Nkrumah's tragedy was a tragedy of excess, rather than of contradiction. He tried to be too much of a revolutionary monarch."[39]

Some of the aforementioned leadership traditions and styles would be regarded as subversive of the AGA, and the values, norms, rules, and principles on which it is based. Even during the Cold War these traditions and styles of leadership had mixed results. For example, Idi Amin's warrior tradition and intimidating style drove intellectuals out of Uganda, expelled Ugandans of Indian extraction, impoverished the country, and destroyed institutions of learning. His leadership was a classic case of dictatorship, which led to internal anarchy. Indeed, Amin's eight-year rule is one reason why Uganda fell behind its neighbors in developmental terms. Julius Nyerere's political experiment with socialism, however, attracted the world's leading leftist intellectuals to Tanzania, but as a result of the West's hostility to his policies Tanzania's economic development stagnated. If Africa is to create conditions that might achieve human welfare, security, and socio-economic justice, the continent will have to recast the old-fashioned leadership traditions and styles. It will also need to keep out of power the likes of Charles Taylor and Mobutu Sese Seko, who led their countries to ruin through dictatorship and misguided or self-serving goals, policies, and strategies.

The AU and many African states are crying out for strategic and transformative leadership that might help their governments and CSOs work out the most appropriate ways of utilizing the relationships among peace, globalization, security, and governance. Strategic leadership should help to identify the resources on which policies should focus, secure markets for Africa's goods, construct structures that empower the people, and initiate productive linkages between internal agents, regional actors, and the global community.

Leadership is also about providing a role model. Libya, Nigeria, and South Africa have in the past vied to be role models for Africa. As of this writing, none of them had the credentials to serve in such a capacity. Libya is in turmoil after the ousting and assassination of Gaddafi in 2011. Even during Gaddafi's time it did not have a decent track record on democracy. While Gaddafi may be credited with spearheading the creation of the AU, the Union espoused principles and norms that went far beyond what Libya itself achieved in terms of human rights and democracy. Moreover, Libya's clandestine nuclear activity, at a time when it was a member of the Non-Proliferation Treaty (NPT), disqualified it as a role model.

Since the transition to democratic rule in 1999, Nigeria has made many efforts to display its democratic credentials. It has also played a key role in Peace Support Operations (PSOs) in West Africa over more than a decade. However, Nigeria has not been a democracy long enough to demonstrate that democratic rule has taken hold. Moreover, attempts by its former president, Olusegun Obasanjo, and his supporters, to manipulate the constitution to enable him to run for a third term in 2007, coupled with the deep divide between the northern and the southern parts of the country and the failure of the central government to decisively address a growing Muslim militancy in the country, shows that Nigeria lacks the capacity to lead the continent in promoting values such as democracy and good governance.

Would South Africa serve as a good role model? Since the transition to democratic rule in 1994 South Africa has assumed a prominent position in African politics. Like Libya, South Africa gave up its nuclear ambitions and is a strong supporter of nuclear disarmament. However, unlike Libya, South Africa is a democracy with a multi-party system. One feature that illustrates the limitations of South Africa's democratic practices, however, is its societal tendency towards one-party rule. While the state is constitutionally multi-party, its society appears to prefer one-party dominance. This is why only two parties have ruled South Africa since 1948. Under the apartheid system the National Party dominated the political scene (1948–94). Since then the African National

Congress (ANC) has dominated politics, and there are no signs of a serious challenge. South Africa's ability to lead Africa has been tested on a number of fronts. The first relates to how it treats Africans who migrate to, or visit, the country. Most African visitors for business or other legal reasons have faced stringent immigration measures. In one case a group of Nigerian officials was not allowed to enter the country for not having yellow fever certificates. Nigeria reciprocated by imposing similar restrictions on South African visitors. The South African debacle in the Central African Republic (CAR) and its confused approach to the crises in Côte d'Ivoire and Libya also cost it respect as a potential continental leader. The latest South African initiative to take over leadership of the African Union Commission (AUC) has not gone down well among most other African countries, particularly the small states that had assumed over the years that a "gentleman's agreement" existed in which the "big states" left leadership of the AUC to them. President Zuma's former wife, Nkosazana Dlamini-Zuma, was elected as AUC chairperson in 2012, but her victory came at a high price. Internationally, however, South Africa has fared extremely well – it is a member of the BRICS (Brazil Russia India China South Africa) group and of the Group of Twenty (G20), and an "associate member" of the Group of Eight (G8).

Nevertheless, there is still a question mark over South Africa as a role model. Its prominence in global debates over such issues as UN reform, climate change, and the global financial crisis, is due to wealth. It appears to be a leader largely because it has one of the largest economies on the continent. At a time when the AU is promoting human rights, the rule of law, and the idea that all people and states are equal irrespective of their wealth, should leadership be accorded to South Africa merely on account of its wealth? It is quite obvious that South Africa's quest for continental leadership is driven by two goals – the prestige of serving as a permanent member of the UN Security Council, and its economic interest in securing markets for its rapidly expanding industrial sector.

The idea of role models should not be limited to states. Individuals such as the late former South African president, Nelson Mandela, can also serve as role models for Africa's future leaders. Africa need not wait for the emergence of leaders like Mandela; it can make them. After all, contrary to the old-fashioned perception that leaders are born rather than made, it has been shown that leaders of all kinds are made.[40] For this reason, African policy makers need to give top priority to the training, development, and nurturing of strategic leaders at all levels of society. Most critically, such leadership must have a strong grounding in Pan-Africanism. Contemporary Africa lacks leaders with credentials that are equal to those of Kwame Nkrumah or Julius Nyerere. Only Mandela had the vision and leadership skills to match these great Pan-Africanist leaders. His successor as president of South Africa, Thabo Mbeki, demonstrated leadership potential by playing instrumental roles in the formations of NEPAD and the AU. By proclaiming an "African renaissance," Mbeki created a fertile environment for ideas such as "African solutions for African problems" to germinate. NEPAD came to symbolize this new mindset of Africans taking ownership of their own destinies by practicing good governance, respecting the rule of law, and maintaining a culture of human rights. Mbeki's ideas were well-received by other influential African leaders such as Nigerian president, Obasanjo, and Libyan leader, Muammar Gaddafi. Together with Algeria's president, Abdelaziz Boutfleka, Senegalese president, Abdoulaye Wade, and Egyptian president, Hosni Mubarak, these leaders carried the flame of pan-Africanism in 1999 that led to the formation of the AU within two years. Ironically, Mbeki and Obasanjo stepped down in disgrace after trying to prolong their rules by vying for third terms; Bouteflika successfully changed the Algerian constitution to rule for an unlimited term; and Gaddafi and Mubarak were ousted from power by popular uprisings after having ruled their countries with an iron fist for decades. Africa is in dire need of leadership with a vision and a mission to change the lives of its people.

The AU has a responsibility to provide this leadership, or at least contribute to its creation. Over the past decade the AU has been something of a retirement club for former leaders who need to be kept busy so that they do not continue to meddle in the affairs of their countries. By January 2014 such former leaders were serving, or had served, the AU in different capacities as members of panels to review or find alternative sources of financing for its activities. Others were requested to find peaceful solutions to crises in Kenya, Sudan, and Egypt, as members of the Panel of the Wise (PoW), and as special envoys and representatives to the DRC, Somalia, and Mali. Although some of these individuals have performed commendably, others – such as former Guinean strongman General Sekouba Kounate – have been given highly questionable roles within the AU. General Kounate was appointed in December 2010 as the AU's High Representative for the Operationalization of the African Standby Force, a position that did not previously exist in the AU staff structure. In another case the international community objected strongly to the AU's appointment of a former president who had previously carried out two coups in his own country, one of them accompanied by the massacre of thousands of people. Others, such as the late Ahmed Ben Bella and Kenneth Kaunda, were made members of the PoW at a time when they were probably too old to be effective in performing the high-profile positions to which they were appointed.

The AU's organs should be used to train continental leaders and not to reward former or current government officials for service elsewhere. Where possible, policy makers should seek to identify young people who have the potential to be effective leaders, and give them the opportunity they need to develop leadership skills. It is through such measures that the AU, and the states that comprise it, can exploit the complex relations among peace, globalization, security, and governance for the benefit of their people. Indeed, initiatives such as NEPAD are predicated on the assumption that Africa will have strategic leaders.

Conclusions

The AGA was designed largely to enhance the coordination of actions among AU organs with a view to strengthening their capacity and optimizing their impact. Its purpose is also to share and implement a set of norms and values, especially good governance, democracy, and respect for human rights and the rule of law. Without these norms and values, the Union would not be different from the OAU. By coming up with these values and principles, Africa's leaders signaled that they were willing to reconstruct their identities or transform themselves from dictators to democrats.

However, implementing these principles requires an environment that is free of corruption at various levels: local, national, and continental. Rampant corruption is likely to undermine the AU's ability to pursue its norms, principles, and objectives effectively. Unfortunately, the top-down approach the AU and NEPAD have taken towards tackling corruption is unlikely to eliminate the problem. The anti-corruption task requires cooperation between the AU, African states, international organizations, multinational corporations, CSOs, and the people of Africa.

Moreover, fighting corruption requires strategic and transformative leadership. Without such leadership, African states and the AU might not be able to pursue their principles and objectives, or contain corruption. As one observer has argued, the AU ought to recognize that the "crises bedevilling Africa are a result of lack of leadership of high personal integrity, weak governing institutions and uninstitutionalised democracy or outright dictatorship."[41] African states and the AU need leaders who are ready to work with the business sector and CSOs to enhance good governance. The organs of the Union also play crucial roles in the pursuit of the AU's objectives and the implementation of its principles. These organs also require strategic and transformative leadership. For this reason, the future of the AU depends on its capacity to train strategic leaders who will capitalize on the interrelationship between peace, security, and governance.

Notes

1 *Our Global Neighbourhood*, Report of the Commission on Global Governance (Oxford: Oxford University Press) (1995): 2.
2 Cited in S. H. Eriksen, "Shared River and Lake Basins in Africa: Challenges for Cooperation," *Ecopolicy*, no. 10 (Nairobi: African Centre for Technology Studies) (1998): 8.
3 For interesting case studies of governance, see Thomas G. Weiss and Leon Gordenker (eds) *NGOs, the UN and Global Governance* (Boulder, CO: Lynne Rienner) (1996).
4 For a good analysis of the work of the IMF, see, for instance, James R. Vreeland, *The International Monetary Fund: Politics of Conditional Lending* (London: Routledge) (2007).
5 Joel Barkan, "Protracted Transitions Among Africa's New Democracies," *Democratization*, vol. 7, no. 3 (2000): 242.
6 Ibid.: 242.
7 Samuel M. Makinda, "Democracy and Multi-Party Politics in Africa," *Journal of Modern African Studies*, vol. 34, no. 4 (1996): 556.
8 Ibid.: 557.
9 Larry Diamond, *Promoting Democracy in the 1990s: Actors and Instruments, Issues and Imperatives*. Report to the Carnegie Commission on Preventing Deadly Conflict (New York) (1995): 9.
10 Guillermo O'Donnell and Phillipe C. Schmitter, *Transitions from Authoritarian Rule, Volume 3: Tentative Conclusions about Uncertain Democracies* (Baltimore: Johns Hopkins University Press) (1986): 6.
11 Mary Ellen Fischer, "Introduction" in Mary Ellen Fischer (ed.) *Establishing Democracies* (Boulder, CO: Westview Press) (1996): 5.
12 Juan Linz and Alfred Stepan, "Toward Consolidated Democracies," *Journal of Democracy*, vol. 7, no. 2 (1996): 14–33.
13 J. Samuel Valenzuela, "Democratic Consolidation in Post-Transitional Settings: Notion, Process, and Facilitating Conditions" in Scott Mainwaring, Guillermo O'Donnell and J. Samuel Valenzuela (eds) *Issues in Democratic Consolidation: The New South American Democracies in Comparative Perspective* (Notre Dame, IN: University of Notre Press) (1992): 57–104.
14 Adam Przeworski, *Democracy and the Market* (Cambridge: Cambridge University Press) (1991): 26.
15 James Gibson and Amanda Gouws, "Support for the Rule of Law in the Emerging South African Democracy," *International Social Science Journal*, no. 152 (1997): 174.
16 Ishmail Mohammed, "Preventive Detention and the Rule of Law," *South African Law Journal*, no. 106 (1989): 547–9.
17 Jennifer A. Widner, *Building the Rule of Law: Francis Nyalali and the Road to Judicial Independence in Africa* (New York: W. W. Norton & Co.) (2001): 28.

18 Ibid.: 29.
19 Ibid: 29–30.
20 An earlier version of this section appeared as Wafula Okumu, "The Role of AU/NEPAD in Preventing and Combating Corruption in Africa – A Critical Analysis," *At Issue Ezine*, no. 4 (2005): 6–10. Available at: www.africafiles. org/atissueezine.asp?issue=issue2#art2 (last accessed March 17, 2015).
21 See John Githongo, "Corruption is the Bane of African Countries," *East African Standard* (April 15, 2005).
22 See BBC News, September 18, 2002; and the *Economist*, September 19, 2002.
23 Jean-Francois Bayart, Stephen Ellis and Beatrice Hibou, *The Criminalization of the State in Africa* (Oxford: James Currey) (1999): xii–xviii.
24 Cited in Virginia Gidley-Kitchen, "Corruption Getting Worse in Africa?" BBC News, February 11, 2005.
25 Bayart *et al.*, *The Criminalization of the State in Africa*: xvi.
26 Gidley-Kitchen, "Corruption Getting Worse in Africa?"
27 Aminatta Forna, "The West must own up to its part in African corruption," *The Independent*, March 9, 2005.
28 The following African countries have ratified it: Algeria, Benin, Djibouti, Egypt, Kenya, Libya, Madagascar, Mauritius, Namibia, Nigeria, Sierra Leone, South Africa, Tanzania, Togo, and Uganda.
29 Bayart *et al.*, *The Criminalization of the State in Africa*: xiv.
30 See Tom Murphy, "Study: West Facilitates African Corruption," *The Christian Science Monitor*, July 15, 2013. Available at: www. csmonitor.com/World/Africa/Africa-Monitor/2013/0715/Study-West-facilitates-African-corruption (last accessed March 17, 2015).
31 Aminatta Forna, "The West must own up to its part in African corruption," *The Independent*, March 9, 2005.
32 A Summary of NEPAD Action Plans, paragraph 8. See www.uneca.org/sites/default/files/publications/nepadactionplanssummary.pdf (last accessed March 30, 2015).
33 See W. L. Nkuhlu, "The New Partnership for Africa's Development – The Journey So Far," NEPAD Secretariat, June 2005. Available at: www.africarecruit.com/downloads/NEPAD-JOURNEYSOFAR.pdf (last accessed March 30, 2015).
34 See www.auanticorruption.org/auac/en (last accessed March 17, 2015).
35 In an ironic turn of events, the dismissal of Zuma contributed to Mbeki losing the presidency in September 2008. Later, in April 2009, Zuma assumed the presidency, but his administration has faced a series of major scandals, including one in which he was accused of misappropriating public funds to reconstruct his private home in Nkandla.
36 Ray Matikinye, "Corruption Gnaws Away at Body Politic," *Zimbabwe Independent*, April 15, 2005.
37 See Willy Mamah, "NEPAD, Good Governance and the Rule of Law," a paper presented at the Nigerian Civil Society Conference on the New Partnership for Africa's Development, held at the Airport Hotels, Ikeja, Lagos (April 2002).
38 Ali A. Mazrui, "Political Leadership in Africa: Seven Styles and Four Traditions" in Hans d'Orville (ed.) *Leadership for Africa: In Honour of Olusegun Obasanjo on the Occasion of His 60th Birthday* (New York: African Leadership Foundation) (1995): 161–4.

39 Ali A. Mazrui, "Nkrumah: The Leninist Czar," *Transition* (Kampala), vol. 6, no. 26 (1966): 9–17.
40 See, for example, C. Otto Scharmer, *Theory U: Leading from the Future as It Emerges* (San Francisco: Berrett-Koehler Publishers) (2009); Samuel M. Makinda, "Africa's Leadership Malaise and the Crisis of Governance" in Kobena T. Hanson, George Kararach and Timothy M. Shaw (eds) *Rethinking Development Challenges for Public Policy: Insights from Contemporary Africa* (London: Macmillan) (2012): 54–82; and Wisdom J. Tettey, "Africa's Leadership Deficit: Exploring Pathways to Good Governance and Transformative Politics" in Kobena T. Hanson, George Kararach and Timothy M. Shaw (eds) *Rethinking Development Challenges for Public Policy: Insights from Contemporary Africa* (London: Macmillan) (2012): 18–53.
41 See Tee Ngugi, "Dream on, Nkosazana, in the Waking World Africans are Living out a Nightmare," *The East African*, March 1, 2014. Available at: www.theeastafrican.co.ke/OpEd/comment/Africans-are-living-out-a-nightmare-/-/434750/2226688/-/item/1/-/lrtjyd/-/index.html (last accessed March 18, 2015).

4   The challenge of maintaining security and building peace

Given the continuing al-Shabaab terrorist attacks in Kenya and Somalia, the ease with which Boko Haram have wreaked havoc in Nigeria, and the evaporation of law and order in both the Central African Republic (CAR) and South Sudan, it is plausible to draw the conclusion that security and peace have been, and remain, some of the scarcest commodities in Africa. The creation of the African Union (AU) raised hopes that African governments and civil society organizations (CSOs) would have opportunities to address insecurity issues more promptly and effectively. However, the problems we have cited above, in addition to those in Sudan's Darfur region, Guinea, Mali, the eastern Democratic Republic of Congo (DRC), Libya, and Somalia, have led to at least two contradictory reactions. On the one hand they triggered a growing disillusionment about the AU's capacity to build and sustain peace; on the other, they have provided the AU with an opportunity to put into practice the principles, norms, and strategies that underpin its Peace and Security Architecture.

Since the 1980s, Africa has experienced more wars, conflicts, and crises than any other continent. Most of these have taken place within, rather than between, states. Owing to the fragility of African state boundaries, some intra-state conflicts have spilled over the borders and exerted pressure on neighboring countries. For example, Rwanda's conflict severely affected Burundi, the DRC, Tanzania, and Uganda. Similarly, Somalia's conflict continues to affect Djibouti, Ethiopia, and Kenya, while the Libyan conflict has contaminated the Sahel region, particularly Mali, Niger, and Mauritania. African states have also witnessed different levels of insecurity in the form of piracy, radical militancy, and terrorism – both local and transnational.

Insecurity has stemmed from various factors, including bad governance, ethnic rivalry, struggles over natural resources, human rights abuses, failure to respect the rule of law, nepotism, poverty, and the lack of access to affordable health, shelter, and education. For the AU to address Africa's security issues and violent conflicts promptly, effectively, and on a sustained basis, it needs to erect a framework that pays adequate attention to the impacts of globalization and governance on security.

Some of the wars, conflicts, and other sources of insecurity which emerged in the 1980s and 1990s have continued into the twenty-first century. For example, the civil war in southern Sudan, which started in 1983, was not resolved until early 2005. Prior to the conclusion of this war another conflict erupted in the Darfur region in 2003. Although South Sudan gained its independence in July 2011, its people are yet to benefit from the fruits of self-rule and have been engulfed in a brutal civil war since December 2013. The civil war in Somalia, which started in the late 1980s and intensified following the overthrow of former dictator Siad Barre in 1991, had not been resolved by late 2014. Indeed Somalia, which has had no effective governance structures at the national level since the early 1990s, has been subject to an African peacekeeping force drawn from Burundi, Djibouti, Kenya, Sierra Leone, and Uganda since 2007.

Moreover, the civil war in eastern DRC, which started in the mid-1990s, continued into 2014, notwithstanding the fact that the country has held two presidential elections in 2006 and 2012. In 2014 the largest United Nations (UN) peacekeeping operation, which has been operating in the DRC since 1999, was given a robust mandate to directly engage rebel groups acting as peace spoilers.[1] In Algeria, the civil war that erupted in 1992, when the military intervened in politics and nullified the general elections, has continued into the twenty-first century. These wars, conflicts, and crises have outlasted the Organization of African Unity (OAU).

The AU was established partly for the purpose of finding solutions to these, and similar, problems. Article 3 [f] of the Constitutive Act of the African Union (CAAU) states that one of the Union's aims is to "promote peace, security and stability." In addition, Article 4 [e] states that one of the AU's principles is the "Peaceful resolution of conflicts among member states." Moreover, the CAAU, under Article 4 [h], gives the Union the right "to intervene in a member state … in respect of grave circumstances, namely war crimes, genocide and crimes against humanity." Thus, the AU has a mandate to help resolve inter-state and intra-state conflicts, deal with terrorist threats, and engage in peace building activities. In order to implement its peace and security agenda, the AU has adopted very elaborate structures, as shown in Figure 4.1.

This chapter explores the AU's capacity to implement the peace and security agenda, particularly preventing, managing, and resolving

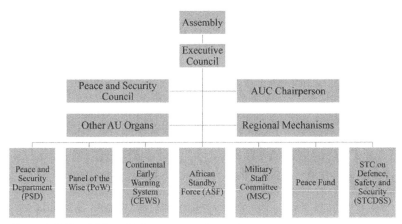

Figure 4.1 The African Union peace and security organs
Source: Authors

conflicts, and engaging in peace building processes. It also examines the roles of Regional Economic Communities (RECs) in facilitating conflict resolution. Accordingly, the rest of this chapter is divided into four seven sections. The first explains briefly the security concepts used broadly by the AU and its member states. The second examines the nature of war, conflict, and terrorism. The third looks at the AU's mechanisms for peace and security known as the African Peace and Security Architecture (APSA). The fourth discusses APSA's guiding principles while the fifth examines the roles of member states. The sixth section explores the roles of RECs while the seventh analyzes the contributions of civil society.

Conceptual issues

How do the AU and its member states view security? How do their definitions of security relate to identity and the concept of African solutions to African problems? How is peace building understood in Africa?

As the meanings of peace and security were explored in the Introduction, this section will not further elaborate these. The Introduction made it clear that all security, not just human security, ought to be concerned with the needs, aspirations, and dignity of the people. States have the primary responsibility of affording security to their people. However, some states continue to neglect and even violate human rights and democratic processes in the pursuit of state security.

This is why it is necessary to define security as the protection of the people – as well as the preservation of their norms, rules, interests, institutions, values, aspirations, and resources – in the face of military and non-military threats. This definition, which is underpinned by good governance, suggests that security and identity are inseparable. In other words, it is identity and interests that determine perceptions of security.

The OAU/AU definition of security has evolved over many years and has reflected certain identity issues. Following independence, African states and the OAU pursued security through traditional frameworks. Their perspective on security was state-centric because they often explained it in terms of state survival, territorial integrity, self-help, and protection of the ruling elites. While the security challenges of most states were internal, many African governments organized their security forces as if they were preparing to address threats that emanated from outside. Indeed, the OAU and its member states were traditionalists because they often prescribed the use of military force even if the threats in question were not ones that had military solutions. For example, many states routinely used military force to harass and intimidate legitimate opposition political groups. Thus, ordinary governance issues were militarized. In this traditional approach to security there was no room for CSOs or the consideration of gender issues.

The OAU started to redefine security shortly after the Cold War ended. Its broadened definition encompasses non-military issues, but is not sufficiently sensitive to gender questions. Moreover, it does not provide sufficient room for CSOs. For example, at a summit in Kampala in 1991, the OAU, in reference to the Conference on Security, Stability, Development and Cooperation, suggested that:

> The security of a nation must be constructed in terms of the security of the individual citizen to live in peace with access to basic necessities of life while fully participating in the affairs of his/her society in freedom and enjoying all fundamental human rights.[2]

The AU's draft Common African Defence and Security Policy (CADSP) adopted this view of security. CADSP claims that security includes human rights, the right to participate fully in the process of governance, the right to development, education and health, and the right to protection against poverty, marginalization, and natural disasters. This broad understanding of security provides room for the AU to utilize the dynamic relations among peace, security, globalization, and governance.

In addition, various African scholars have adopted new security frameworks and applied them to African problems. These have ranged from critical security perspectives[3] to human security and feminist frameworks.[4] Indeed, a group of seven non-governmental organizations (NGOs) in Africa established an African human security initiative through which it sought to influence policy on other initiatives – including NEPAD and the CADSP.[5]

Apart from providing a broader definition of security, the OAU and AU have championed the concept of applying "African solutions to African security problems," which underlines the identity dimension of security considerations. This concept, which has been part of African political thought since the 1950s, is derived from self-determination and self-government. Self-determination, in turn, is about the realization of African agency. These concepts were endorsed by many African thinkers, especially those who participated in the early phase of the liberation struggle such as Frantz Fanon, Kwame Nkrumah, Julius Nyerere, Sekou Toure, Kenneth Kaunda, Edward Mondlane, Ndabaningi Sithole, Nelson Mandela, and Tom Mboya. Seeking "African solutions to African problems" amounts to a proclamation of self-pacification. This is part of what Ali Mazrui described in the 1960s as a *Pax Africana*.[6] However, as we point out later, given Africa's multiple political, economic, social, ideological, and financial problems, self-pacification was honored in breach rather than in observance.

Another security concept that the AU has alluded to relates to the universality and indivisibility of security. For example, at the launch of the Peace and Security Council (PSC) in Addis Ababa in May 2004, the chairperson of the African Union Commission (AUC), Alpha Oumar Konare, underlined the view that security was universal, global, and indivisible. He said: "An Africa at peace cannot stand without a world at peace. Our security policy must be focused on the notion of collective and general security."[7] Thus, genuine security knows no racial, religious, ideological or national boundaries. It is meaningful only when it is enjoyed by all. This concept of collective security, like that of self-pacification, is not new. Nkrumah expressed it more than 50 years earlier, when he argued that peace, security, and freedom were universal and indivisible.[8] However, the universality and indivisibility that Nkrumah had in mind was a two-way street, while the indivisibility and universality to which the AU refers appears to be one-way only. Nkrumah believed that while Africa welcomed outside efforts to end colonialism in southern Africa, it also had a responsibility and the capacity to help other parts of the world enjoy peace, security, and freedom. The AU, nevertheless, expects the Group of Eight (G8) states and other Western countries to fund its programs and activities.[9] In this sense, the concept of the universality and indivisibility of security appears to undermine the idea of self-pacification.

Overall, it has been difficult to maintain security in Africa, partly because of the poorly constructed platforms upon which peace can be built. As in the case of security, it is leadership, identity, and interests that underpin peace building activities and processes in Africa. The term "peace building" is used here to encompass various activities that are designed to create the capacity to sustain democratic processes, the respect for human rights and the rule of law, poverty alleviation, and the provision of basic services such as health and education. In *An Agenda for Peace*, former UN Secretary-General, Boutros Boutros-Ghali, himself an African, employed the term "peace building" to refer to capacity building, societal transformation, and reconciliation among the parties in dispute.[10] In this chapter the term is used to encompass long-term transformative processes that facilitate the movement towards durable peace, while at the same addressing the root causes of conflict and war. Thus, there is considerable overlap between peace building and development (see Chapter 6). There is also an overlap between peace building and human security. These overlaps highlight the interconnections between peace, globalization, security, and governance. These interconnections should become clearer as the nature of war, conflict, and insecurity is explored.

The nature of war, conflict, and terrorism

In the past few decades Africa has been associated with hunger, famine, HIV/AIDS, Ebola, unending warfare, ethnic tension, political upheaval, social breakdown, economic deprivation, and, most recently, terrorism. It is these issues that underpin the insecurity that the AU needs to address.

As stated above, the AU's approach to peace and security is predicated on the idea of finding "African solutions to African problems," which dates back many decades. The OAU, which sought to promote this approach, put in place a conflict resolution mechanism that involved mediation, conciliation, and arbitration. Thus, African leaders in the 1960s, as now, were concerned with Africa's capacity for self-pacification. However, as a result of inadequate resources, a lack of institutional mechanisms, bad governance, power struggles, and the lack of political will, maintenance of security in Africa was largely underwritten – and has continued to be shaped – by external forces. The former colonial masters – especially France and the UK – and other global powers including the US, the Soviet Union, and China, played prominent roles in shaping the direction of African wars and conflicts. When external agents resolve African problems, the solutions often reflect not just the interests but also the identities of these external agents. Therefore it was not surprising that during the Cold War African security problems were frequently interpreted in terms of the US-Soviet competition. This applied to most wars and conflicts, irrespective of the nature of the local identity issues and interests behind them. In other words, the global East-West competition often dictated the way that African conflicts were resolved, regardless of whether they stemmed from territorial claims, the marginalization of local ethnic groups, or ideological differences. For example, the Shaba uprisings in the DRC (formerly Zaire) in 1977 and 1978 were not understood in terms of the bad governance of President Mobutu Sese Seko or the interests and identity of the people of Shaba province itself. Instead they were addressed in terms of how the US and the Soviet Union and their respective allies gained or lost influence.

A notable feature of the Cold War era is that good governance was not a major issue for African political leaders and their foreign backers. Human rights were abused, multi-party systems were outlawed, and the citizens of various African states were denied opportunities to participate in decision-making. In this sense, Western countries, like their communist counterparts and African dictators, were complicit in exacerbating insecurity in Africa. It was this situation that prompted former US president, Jimmy Carter, in May 1977, to ridicule his predecessors:

> Being confident about our own future, we are free of that inordinate fear of communism which once led us to embrace any dictator who joined us in our fear. For too many years we have been willing to adopt the flawed principles and tactics of our adversaries, sometimes abandoning our values for theirs. We fought fire with fire, never thinking that fire is better fought with water.[11]

This gave hope to those who believed that the United States might pursue a human-rights-based foreign policy. However, by the end of his term Carter had gone back to his predecessors' tactics of fighting fire with fire.

During this period there was no talk of failed states in Africa. A poorly performing state could play the East-West card and obtain the support it needed, even if this support meant obtaining arms to suppress legitimate political opposition groups. In one sense, African state failure is a construction of the post-Cold War climate. It was only after the Cold War had ended, and once the external powers saw no need to prop up unpopular and dictatorial African regimes, that the "orphaned" African states were seen to be failing to perform as required.

In the period following the end of the Cold War, especially in the early 1990s, African leaders discovered that they no longer had leverage in Western capitals. This meant that Western leaders could now afford to either ignore Africa altogether, or at least handle its problems at arm's length. During this period the West and the international organizations – especially the World Bank and the International Monetary Fund (IMF) – imposed certain political and economic conditions that African states would have to meet before they could obtain aid. Some of these conditions, dubbed structural adjustment programs, were so misguided and unfair to the poor that they resulted in enormous suffering, instability, and insecurity. This was when state collapse set in.

In the immediate post-Cold War era the UN also played a greater role in the resolution of Africa's wars than it had done before – amid claims that African crises were not accorded the same priority as those in Europe. It was at this time that the UN Security Council decided to implement Resolution 435 that led to Namibia's independence in 1989. This resolution, which authorized the UN to assume legal responsibility for Namibia's transition to independence, had been adopted by the Security Council in September 1978. However, there had been no political will to implement it until the Cold War was over.[12] Since Namibia, the UN has been involved in several other peacekeeping operations in Africa, including Angola, Burundi, the DRC, along the Ethiopian-Eritrean border, Côte d'Ivoire, Liberia, Rwanda, Sierra Leone, Somalia, Sudan, South Sudan, and Western Sahara. Some of these activities were undertaken as humanitarian interventions only, which had the effect of saving many lives but provided only Band-Aid type solutions to chronic security problems. For instance, US$1.3 billion and US$900 million was spent annually on the African Union-United Nations Hybrid Operation in Darfur (UNAMID) and the United Nations Mission in the Republic of South Sudan (UNMISS), respectively. But might it have been wiser to invest that money in development projects that enhanced human security?

The majority of Africa's wars have been intra-state. The immediate post-Cold War period was characterized by internal and external demands for good governance. Globalization, and particularly the revolution in communications technology, had reached a point where African governments could not conceal their misguided policies and other weaknesses. Indeed, the speed of external reaction to some of these wars was partly a result of what has been described as the "CNN effect" – another symptom of globalization.

In the early part of the twenty-first century the African security agenda was shaped largely, but not exclusively, by the so-called War on Terror. Africa's concerns with terrorism go back several decades, but since the 1990s terrorism has morphed through various phases.[13] A decade prior to the US government making counter-terrorism a cornerstone of its national security policy, the OAU had started debating ways of containing terrorism and "extremism." For example, in July 1992 the OAU summit in Dakar, Senegal, adopted a Declaration Against Extremism which was designed to enhance cooperation among African states to deal with "manifestations of extremism." It should be noted that Algeria, where civil war broke out after the general elections were abandoned, was one of the main drivers behind this initiative.

Later, in 1999, the OAU summit in Algiers adopted the Convention on the Prevention and Combating of Terrorism (hereafter the Algiers Convention). Support for the Algiers Convention also partly stemmed from the fact that al-Qaida agents had carried out simultaneous terrorist attacks against American diplomatic missions in Nairobi (Kenya) and Dar es Salaam (Tanzania) in August 1998. By committing itself to fighting terrorism in the 1990s, the OAU took a major step in enhancing security in some countries. But the genesis of this initiative was the Algerian government's move in early 1992 to undermine security by nullifying the general elections. The authorities feared that had the general election gone ahead, it would have been won by the Islamist group, Front Islamique du Salut, or Islamic Salvation Front. Having been denied the chance to take power through the democratic process, the Islamic Salvation Front resorted to violence, alongside other insurgent groups such as Groupement Islamique Armé or Armed Islamic Group. In response the government used brutal measures to suppress the Islamic Salvation Front.

Since the terrorist attacks in New York and Washington DC in September 2001, and the subsequent adoption of UN Security Council Resolution 1373, African states have been required to implement counter-terrorism measures that go far beyond what the local situation would demand. Some African states, such as Algeria and Egypt, have faced problems with terrorism for many years – but these can be explained in terms of local governance structures and policies. However, these countries' counter-terrorism strategies have subsequently been incorporated into the global War on Terror.

Unfortunately, African states, as well as external powers, have used the War on Terror to try to distort the nature of security problems. For example, Ethiopia's invasion of Somalia in December 2006, which had little to do with transnational terrorism, was justified in terms

of the global War on Terror. Somalia's problems predate the formation of the al-Qaida network and are unlikely to be resolved through
a strategy aimed at al-Qaida. One effect of distorting African security
problems through the prism of the global War on Terror is that the
counter-measures end up undermining security rather than enhancing
it. It was anticipated that the African Centre on the Study and Research
on Terrorism (ACSRT), established in Algiers in 2004 by the AU, would
serve as a vital tool for coordinating counter-terrorism measures in
Africa. However, there is little to show for its efforts.[14]

While we might be critical of those African states that have blindly
endorsed the global War on Terror logic, we do not play down the seriousness of terrorist threats in some African countries. It is important
to note that terrorism in Africa is evolving and requires greater efforts
to understand its local context. The In Amenas (Algeria) hostage crisis
of January 2013, the al-Shabaab attack on the Westgate shopping mall
in Nairobi in September 2013, and Boko Haram's kidnapping of more
than 200 schoolgirls in Chibok (Nigeria) in April 2014, are indicators
of how terrorism in Africa is changing. It is not enough to claim that
al-Shabaab and Boko Haram are affiliated with al-Qaida. It is important to raise questions about their local bases, their recruitment tactics,
and their claims to pursue Islamic goals. For example, al-Shabaab is
said to be a Somali organization, but in Kenya it has recruited operatives from the poverty-stricken populations of various ethnic groups. It
is said to be a fundamentalist Islamic group, yet some of its operatives
are not Muslims. Indeed al-Shabaab is a good example of how terrorism
in Africa is metamorphosing.

In addition to terrorism, Africa has witnessed extensive violence and
warfare in several countries since the creation of the AU. Although violent conflicts in Africa are not new, they have drawn special attention
due to the fact that they are both intense and extensive in scope, highly
destructive, and produce large numbers of both civilian casualties and
refugees. For instance, the war in southern Sudan claimed more than
two million lives. In the Rwandan genocide of 1994 an estimated one
million people perished in just three months. Violence in Africa has
taken various forms ranging from genocide, as in Rwanda and Darfur
between 2003 and 2007, to interpersonal violence. Quite apart from
their extremism in terms of brutality, armed conflicts in Africa have also
been characterized by warlordism, the targeting of vulnerable groups –
such as children, women, and refugees – the use of children as soldiers,
state sponsorship of violence, and war economies.[15]

In a 2007 study based on 23 countries that had experienced violent
conflicts between 1990 and 2005, the IANSA, Oxfam and Saferworld

organizations collectively estimated the cost at $284 billion. This represented "an average annual loss of 15 per cent of GDP" and "an average of $18bn per year lost by Africa."[16] When the Darfur crisis captured international attention in 2003, it was the AU that was called upon to lead negotiations between the Sudanese government and the rebel groups – the Justice and Equality Movement and the Sudan Liberation Movement. The AU's efforts culminated in the signing of a Humanitarian Ceasefire Agreement in April 2004 and the deployment of 60 ceasefire monitors and 300 soldiers to protect it. This protective force had grown to more than 7,000 by September 2006. After many delays and several rounds of negotiation, the Darfur Peace Agreement was signed in Abuja, Nigeria, in May 2006.

The situation in Darfur continues to be an acid test for the AU as a regional force for peace, and for its ability to respond to horrific crimes against humanity. This conflict, as with many others in Africa, has destroyed homes, damaged the environment, disrupted social, educational and health services, destroyed the economic and physical infrastructures, interrupted government operations, and displaced large groups of people from their homes and farms and thus rendering them dependent on humanitarian assistance.[17] Moreover, the International Commission of Inquiry on Darfur reported in January 2005 that war crimes and crimes against humanity had been committed by the government-backed militia group known as "Janjaweed." In addition, the Chief Prosecutor of the International Criminal Court (ICC) has indicted the Sudanese president, Omar Hassan Al-Bashir, on ten counts of war crimes, crimes against humanity, and genocide.

African Peace and Security Architecture

The AU structures and mechanisms for peace and security, commonly known as the African Peace and Security Architecture (APSA), are anchored on a number of legal instruments and revolve around the PSC, which was formally launched in May 2004. The PSC Protocol only mentions the term "architecture" once in Article 16, where it identifies "Regional Mechanisms" as "part of the overall security architecture of the Union, which has the primary responsibility for promoting peace, security and stability in Africa." However, the acronym APSA has become a very popular one in analyzing the work of the AU in the promotion of peace and security. APSA has evolved over the years and it has acquired a new meaning from its original conceptualization.

The peace and security architecture, as shown in Figure 4.2, has three main components: the structures, the legal instruments, and the guiding

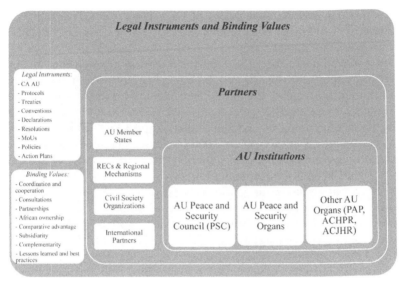

Figure 4.2 The African Union Peace and Security Architecture
Source: Authors

principles. This section explains each of these components, which aim at implementing the peace and security agenda.

APSA structures and arrangements

Article 3 [f] of the CAAU states that the promotion of peace, security, and stability on the continent is one of the AU objectives, but it does not establish the structure for achieving it. Using Article 5 [2] of the CAAU, the Assembly adopted the protocol that created the PSC and formulated the CADSP. The functions, powers, and structures of the PSC were discussed briefly in Chapter 2, but we would like to discuss them here in detail. These mechanisms include the Continental Early Warning System (CEWS), the Panel of the Wise (PoW), the African Standby Force (ASF), the Military Staff Committee (MSC), and a few other arrangements highlighted in Figure 4.1. Given space constraints, we shall examine only a few of these mechanisms.

The Continental Early Warning System CEWS

The CEWS was designed to anticipate and make recommendations for measures to prevent conflicts. When fully operational, the CEWS will consist of an observation and monitoring center (situation room) directly linked to observation and monitoring units of Regional Mechanisms (RMs). This system will collaborate with "the UN, its agencies, relevant international organizations, research centres, academic institutions, and NGOs" in collecting information to be fed into "an early warning module based on clearly defined and accepted political, economic, social, military and humanitarian indicators."[18]

The CEWS is supposed to collect and analyze developments on the continent and recommend to the African Union Commission (AUC) chairperson "the best course of action." Once the information reaches him or her, the chairperson is supposed to "timeously ... advise the Peace and Security Council on potential conflicts and threats to peace and security in Africa and recommend the best course of action."

Although the CEWS claims to be coordinating and collaborating with regional early warning systems, this is only partially the case because it is only the Intergovernmental Authority on Development (IGAD) that has one. Moreover, the IGAD system is specific to pastoralist conflicts in limited areas of the Horn of Africa. The AU situation room is mainly equipped with TV monitors tuned to CNN, BBC, and Aljazeera, and a conference table. This is one area that would benefit from extra training for staff in information collection and analysis. The main activity of the CEWS is the production and circulation of the *Africa News Brief* and *Daily News Highlights* that are essentially feeds from major news outlets on the internet. There is no evidence indicating that decision-makers have used the CEWS's raw and unanalyzed data to formulate policy and intervention actions.

The CEWS is not being developed from bottom up, but rather from the top down. The negative attitude the AU has towards CSOs and African thinktanks has prevented collaboration with these key actors in information collection and analysis – as required by the PSC Protocol. The most evolved regional Early Warning Systems (EWSs) are the ECOWAS Early Warning and Response Network (ECOWARN) and the Conflict Early Warning and Response Mechanism (CEWARN) that were also set up by the same consultants and partners who established the CEWS. In other RM, the establishments of the EWSs are still in the embryonic stages of developing policy frameworks, concepts and approaches to early warning. Data collection and reporting for early warning are yet to be effective in Communauté des États Sahelo-Sahariens (CEN-SAD), East African Community (EAC) and Common Market for Eastern and Southern Africa (COMESA). One of the Wikileaks cables revealed how, in 2005 during the Ethiopian political crisis, the then AUC chairperson, Konare, relied on the ambassadors of the US, the UK, and the European Union (EU) for information, and how he pleaded with them to assist the AU to build its capability to collect data on conflict situations in Africa.

The CEWS is not being set up to reflect African realities and needs. It is a "fire alarm prototype [that has been] under construction" for the past ten years, and which has experimented with various software modules that are supposed to facilitate the collection, sharing, and distribution of information within the AU and with the RECs. So far the CEWS has failed to monitor potential, actual and post-conflict situations in Africa. The CEWS's development, operations and personnel are fully funded by the US, the UK, and Germany. The AU has relied heavily on foreign consultants to develop its methodology, and its data collection and analysis tools. These foreign consultants have ended up reconceptualizing this conflict prevention tool, a situation that has led to the development of an inappropriate information technology system that cannot focus on the root causes of conflicts – i.e. poor governance, state mismanagement, human rights abuses, poor investment in youth opportunities, etc. The failure to anticipate the political, economic, and security implications of the Ebola epidemic in early 2014 is partly a result of inappropriate CEWS tools.

The CEWS is faced with a major challenge of harmonizing approaches to information collection. While it collects its information from open sources, IGAD collects from the field and the Southern African Development Community (SADC) prefers to gather its information using traditional intelligence methods. There are also questions about the quality and timeliness of the CEWS information, particularly with regard to how it is processed and prepared for use. There is no evidence showing that the CEWS has effectively prevented any conflict, or contributed to a mediation and preventive diplomacy effort. By 2014 the CEWS had still not attained the desired and expected levels of strategic and operational capacity necessary for the anticipation and prevention of conflicts, the enhancement of security, or the ability to build peace.

But while the member states are suspicious of sharing information with the CEWS for fear that this might fall in the hands of their enemies – and thereby compromise their own sovereignty – the AUC chairperson has mainly been consuming the confidential intelligence briefs of the Intelligence and Security Committee and the Committee of Intelligence and Security Services of Africa (CISSA), neither of which have any working relations with the CEWS. So the AU leadership receives briefs from three sources that operate mostly in contradiction to one another as a result of their differing data collection and analysis methods. This causes confusion and inertia in the decision-making process.

The Panel of the Wise PoW

Article 11 of the PSC Protocol establishes the PoW "to support the efforts of the Peace and Security Council and those of the Chairperson of the Commission" in preventing conflicts. The PoW is "composed of five highly respected African personalities from various segments of society who have made outstanding contribution to the cause of peace, security and development on the continent."[19] The PoW is supposed to advise the PSC and the AUC chairperson on how to promote and maintain "peace, security and stability in Africa," and to undertake, at the request of the PSC, the AUC chairperson, or on its own initiative, "such action deemed appropriate to support the efforts" of the PSC and those of the AUC chairperson to prevent conflicts, and "to pronounce itself on issues relating to the promotion and maintenance of peace, security and stability."

Only the Economic Community of Western African States (ECOWAS) has established a Council of the Wise, and it has used it to intervene in a number of conflicts in Liberia, Sierra Leone, Niger, Guinea, Guinea Bissau, and Togo. ECOWAS has also established a permanent Mediation Facilitation Division to support the Council of the Wise; and a Forum of Former Presidents to complement its work. CEN-SAD has a Permanent High Level Mediator for Peace and Security that has been deployed to mediate peace in Chad, Mali, Niger, and the Central African Republic (CAR). COMESA plans to establish the "Committee of Elders as part of its preventive diplomacy strategy." IGAD has also expressed interest in establishing a Mediation Support Unit. IGAD's past roles in mediating peace in Somalia and Sudan, and currently in South Sudan, have heightened the urgency of establishing such a unit. While the Economic Community of Central African States (ECCAS) wants to establish a "Committee of Ambassadors", the EAC has plans to establish the Council of Eminent Persons as part of its Conflict Prevention, Management, and Resolution Protocol. Although SADC has not shown interest in establishing its PoW, it has a forum of former heads of state that has been called upon to mediate in the Tanzania-Malawi border dispute.

Despite the above intentions and actions to establish regional mediation units there is no institutional linkage between the PoW and the PSC, and between the PoW and the ECOWAS Council of the Wise. Besides going on "confidence-building missions" to a number of countries, the PoW has issued statements on the crises in Guinea, Guinea Bissau, Zimbabwe, Madagascar, Somalia, and Sudan (Darfur), and has held meetings on thematic issues such as "Election Related Conflicts,"

"Non-Impunity, Justice and National Reconciliation," and "Women and Children in Armed Conflicts in Africa."

The PoW has faced enormous challenges to its role of preventing conflicts, for the following reasons: (1) its conflict prevention role is not clearly conceptualized or properly defined – the PoW's role has yet to be clarified in terms of intervening to prevent, manage, or resolve conflicts; (2) a lack of financing from member states – the PoW is fully donor funded; (3) it has a support staff of just two people, who are coordinated by a non-AU staffer seconded by the South African-based ACCORD; (4) members of the panel have other commitments and are often unavailable when needed to undertake peace missions – the AU Assembly tried in 2010 to overcome this challenge by approving the establishment of a "friends of the Panel group,"[20] but this has not improved its performance as a conflict prevention or management instrument; (5) the PoW is located in the Conflict Management Division – which has not had a substantive leader for several years – instead of in the office of the chairperson or of the PSC secretariat.

Although the panel is composed of people who have previously held respectable positions, they have generally been ineffective. This could be the result of them having other commitments, the AU's neglect of the Panel, or a lack of support from the AU – all of which could be interpreted as a lack of appreciation for its work. It is impossible for these elders to perform the following broad-ranging tasks that are assigned to them, without the necessary support staff:

- advise the PSC and the AUC chairperson on "all matter pertaining … to the promotion and maintenance of peace, security and stability in Africa"
- "facilitate the establishment of channels of communication" between the PSC and the AUC chairperson and parties engaged in a dispute "in order to prevent such dispute from escalating into conflict"
- "carry out fact-finding missions" to prevent conflicts from "either breaking out or seriously escalating"
- "conduct shuttle diplomacy between parties to a conflict in cases where parties are not ready to engage in formal talks"
- "encourage parties … to engage in political dialogue, adopt confidence-building measures, and carry out reconciliation processes"
- "assist and advise mediation teams engaged in formal negotiations"
- assist and advise "parties on how to resolve disputes related to the implementation of peace agreements," and
- "develop and recommend ideas and proposals that can contribute to promoting peace, security and stability in the continent."[21]

The African Standby Force

The operationalization of the ASF has been guided by three roadmaps:

* Roadmap I – covering the period June 2006 to March 2008, was adopted in March 2005. This period saw the establishment of planning elements and mechanisms in all the regions, and the production of core ASF documents on Doctrine, Logistics, Standard Operating Procedures, Training and Evaluation, and Command and Control, Communications and Information System.
* Roadmap II – covering the period April 2008 to December 2010, was supposed to complete outstanding issues from Roadmap I, evaluate progress in operationalization of the ASF, and consolidate the progress it had made.
* Roadmap III – covering the period December 2010 to December 2015, is supposed to be building on the work and lessons learned from Roadmaps I and II, and to address issues related to enhancement of the ASF's structures and capabilities, political decision-making, and mission planning processes, operational concepts, logistics and legal and financial frameworks. It was during this phase, by 2012, that the Rapid Deployment Capability (RDC) of the ASF was to be tested, evaluated, and operationalized.

A Panel of Experts, headed by Ibrahim Gambari (Nigeria), appointed in 2013 to conduct a comprehensive assessment of the ASF, found it "unlikely that FOC [full operational capability] will be achieved by the end of 2015." The Gambari panel also found that although "the AUC and RECs/RMs were all very aware of the goal" – which was to have FOC by 2015 – they were not aware "what FOC actually entailed."[22]

The panel also noted that the establishment of the ASF has faced a number of challenges. The first is that the dissipate mandating processes in the UN Charter, the CAAU, the RECs/RMs legal instruments, and national constitutions of troop-contributing countries, makes it impossible for the ASF "to respond urgently and robustly to mass atrocity crimes." The second is that there is a lack of clarity of "the specific roles and obligations of the AU and RECs/RMs when cooperating in ASF operations." There is no "legal and procedural basis for the transfer of authority from a REC/RM to an AU mission, or vice-versa." Currently, there is no instrument or guideline on how the AU and RECs/RM can mandate, plan, deploy, manage, support, and liquidate ASF operations.

The third challenge for the ASF is that there are no procedures or internal guidelines on how relevant divisions and departments within the AUC should cooperate and coordinate within the AUC "in support of the mandating, planning, management, support and liquidation of ASF operations." The fourth is that despite the characterization of ASF as multi-dimensional, its development is a military affair, as civilian and police representatives have been excluded from the annual meetings of the African Chiefs of Defence Staff and of the Specialized Technical Committee on Defence, Safety, and Security (STCDSS) meetings held so far. There is also an imbalance in the way the ASF military, civilian, and police capacities are being developed.

The fifth ASF challenge is that it has been conceived, designed, supported, and staffed at all levels by external partners. The sixth is that there is no "functional strategic headquarter capability at the AUC that can plan, manage, support and liquidate ASF operations." The seventh is that there is a lack of "strategic leadership and guidance from the AUC," as well as poor information sharing and inconsistent "coordination of policies, programmes and planning for the establishment and deployment of the ASF." The eighth is that there are no generic tables, mechanisms, procedures, and guidelines for verifying the pledged equipment for military, police, and civilian components.

The ninth ASF challenge is that the AUC and some RECs/RMs, compared to the UN and the EU, have very little and limited integrated mission support experience, which is fraught with corrupt procurement and hiring practices.[23] The panel also found that "the AUC lacks the mechanisms, systems and processes needed to bring together support functions such as human resources, finance, supply, procurement, engineering and communications, in order to support AU operations." The tenth challenge is that the AU and the RECs/RM have been unable to establish and maintain continental and regional logistical depots. In addition, there is lack of strategic lift capability unless it is offered by major powers such as the US, Russia, Germany, and France.

Other structures and arrangements

The fourth mechanism is the MSC, whose role is to advise and assist the PSC on all questions relating to military and security matters, including those concerning military intervention to stem humanitarian crises. The implementation of the AU peace and security agenda will be carried out by the above mechanisms within a governance structure that comprises the Pan-African Parliament (PAP); the African Commission on Human and People's Rights (ACHPR); RMs for conflict prevention, management, and resolution; international organizations (particularly the UN); and CSOs. While this governance structure is dominated by state representatives, it was designed to provide room for non-state agents. When fully operational, it will be driven by the complex relations between peace, globalization, security, and governance.

There are other APSA structures and arrangements that have been established through various instruments. These include the African Peace Academy (APA), the ACSRT, and the African Union Commission on International Law (AUCIL), which are stipulated in Article 9 of the African Union Non-Aggression and Common Defence Pact. This Pact, adopted in Abuja, Nigeria, on January 31, 2005, and entered into force on December 18, 2009, has the overall objective of dealing "with threats to peace, security and stability in the continent and to ensure the well being of the African peoples." The PSC is responsible for the implementation of the Pact with the assistance of the APA, the ACSRT, and the AUCIL.

Under Article 12 of the African Union Non-Aggression and Common Defence Pact, the APA is "to serve as a framework for the promotion of peace and stability in Africa, and as a centre of excellence for research and development of an African peace doctrine," while the AUCIL is "to study all legal matters related to the promotion of peace and security in Africa, including the demarcation and delineation of African borders." The ACSRT, which is located in Algiers and has been in existence since 2004, is to "assist Member States develop the expertise and strategies for the prevention and combating of terrorism."

Article 7 of its Statute that came into force after its adoption by the Assembly in January 2009, states that the AUCIL "shall contribute to the objectives and principles of the Union as enshrined in Articles 3 and 4 of the CAAU, and in particular to study all legal matters related to the promotion of peace and security in the African continent, the demarcation and delineation of African borders as well as legal matters relating to the political and socio-economic integration of the Continent." In 2014, the AUCIL had an approved budget of $619,016 out of which the donors were expected to fund 82 percent.

Other APSA structures are African Union Border Programme, CISSA and the African Committee of Experts on the Rights and Welfare of the Child. CISSA was established in Abuja, Nigeria, on August 26, 2004, to provide security and intelligence information to the AU and African countries that can be used to promote security by identifying threats, analyzing them and proffering possible intervention measures. It serves as a platform for African state security and intelligence agencies to cooperate and collaborate in intelligence and security information gathering. In the process, this intelligence and information is supposed to be shared with the AUC chairperson. Unfortunately, CISSA has not been integrated in APSA and the Peace and Security Department (PSD) under whose umbrella are the CEWS, and the divisions of defense and security and conflict prevention. During its 10th Annual conference held in Harare, Zimbabwe, in May 2013, under the theme "The Nexus between Africa's Natural Resources, Development and Security," CISSA indicated its interest to focus on sources of conflicts such as the failure to address poverty, cross-border crimes, terrorism, drug trafficking, cyber-crime, pornography, cyber terrorism, online financial fraud and cyber espionage. Although poverty is an issue on which the CEWS is supposed to be focusing, it is notable that CISSA has identified these other security issues that are not on the radar screen of the PSD.[24]

The most recent structure is the African Capacity for Immediate Response to Crisis (ACIRC), which could be added to APSA. When the Malian crisis developed in early 2013, the AU was faced with the reality that ASF is far from reaching its RDC. Consequently, at its 22nd session of the AU Assembly, held in Addis Ababa in May 2013, the Assembly established the ACIRC. The proposal for this arrangement did not define how ACIRC would relate to the ASF. Despite assurances from the AU leadership and countries that have pledged to contribute troops to ACIRC that it is a temporary (interim) measure, it appears that the ASF and ACIRC are being developed on different tracks.[25]

APSA legal instruments

The international legal instruments shown in Table 4.1, dating back to 1945, provide the legal basis for the operation of APSA.

APSA guiding principles

Coordination and cooperation

The PSC Protocol acknowledges in its Preamble the importance of maintaining security "within the framework of increased and well coordinated continental cooperation." It also acknowledges "the need" for the AU "to forge closer cooperation" with the UN and other international organizations, and "to develop formal coordination and cooperation arrangements" with "Regional Mechanisms" "in the promotion and maintenance of peace, security and stability in Africa." In particular, the Protocol calls for cooperation with RMs through establishment of "liaison offices to the Regional Mechanisms" and concluding "a Memorandum of Understanding on Cooperation." The Commission is expected, according to Article 13 [16], to work with the UN Secretariat "in the co-ordination of external initiatives in support

Table 4.1 APSA legal instruments

Instrument	Year of adoption
United Nations Charter	1945
OAU Charter	1963
Convention for the Elimination of Mercenarism in Africa	1977
African Charter on Human and Peoples' Rights	1981
Declaration of the Assembly of Heads of State and Government of the OAU on the Political and Socio-Economic Situation in Africa and the Fundamental Changes Taking place in the World	1990
African Charter on the Rights and Welfare of the Child	1990
Bamako Convention on the Ban of the Import in Africa and the Control of Trans-boundary Movement and Management of Hazardous Waste within Africa	1991
Treaty Establishing the African Economic Community (Abuja Treaty)	1991
Declaration on the establishment within the OAU of a Mechanism for Conflict Prevention, Management, and Resolution	1993
The African Nuclear-Weapons-Free Zone Treaty (Pelindaba Treaty)	1996
Declaration and Plan of Action on Drug Abuse and Illicit Trafficking Control in Africa	1996
Plan of Action of the 1st Continental Conference of African Experts on Landmines on a Landmine Free Africa	1997
African Nuclear Weapon Free Zone Treaty (The Pelindaba Treaty)	1998
OAU Convention on the Prevention and Combating of Terrorism	1999
The Solemn Declaration on the Conference on Security, Stability, Development, and Cooperation in Africa (CSSDCA)	2000
Bamako Declaration on an African Common Position on the Illicit Proliferation, Circulation, and Trafficking of Small Arms and Light Weapons	2000
Constitutive Act of the African Union	2000
Declaration on the Framework for an OAU Response to Unconstitutional Changes of Government	2000
The New Partnership for Africa's Development (NEPAD)	2001
Protocol to the Treaty Establishing the African Economic Community Relating to the Pan-African Parliament	2001
Protocol Relating to the Establishment of the Peace and Security Council	2002
Protocol to the African Charter on Human and Peoples' Rights on the Rights of Women in Africa	2003
Protocol of the Court of Justice of the African Union	2003
Protocol on Amendments to the Constitutive Act of the African Union	2003

Table 4.1 (cont.)

Instrument	Year of adoption
African Union Convention on Preventing and Combating Corruption	2003
Policy Framework for the Establishment of the African Standby Force and the Military Staff Committee	2003
Protocol to the OAU Convention on the Prevention and Combating of Terrorism	2004
Common African Position on Anti-Personnel Landmines	2004
Solemn Declaration on a Common African Defence and Security Policy	2004
The African Union Non-Aggression and Common Defence Pact	2005
Policy on Post-Conflict Reconstruction and Development (PCRD)	2006
Declaration on the African Union Border Programme and its Implementation Modalities as Adopted by the Conference of African Ministers in Charge of Border Issues	2007
Memorandum of Understanding on Cooperation in the Area of Peace and Security between the African Union, the Regional Economic Communities and the Coordinating Mechanisms of the Regional Standby Brigades	2007
African Charter on Democracy, Elections, and Governance	2007
Protocol on the Statute of the African Court of Justice and Human Rights	2008
Ezulwini Framework for the Enhancement of the Implementation of Measures of the African Union in Situations of Unconstitutional Changes of Government in Africa	2009
African Union Convention for the Protection and Assistance of Internally Displaced Persons in Africa (Kampala Convention)	2009
Statute of the African Union Commission on International Law	2009
African Union Policy Framework on Security Sector Reform	2013
African Union's 50th Anniversary Solemn Declaration	2013

of the African Standby Force capacity-building in training, logistics, equipment, communications and funding." It also calls on member states to "extend full cooperation to, and facilitate action by the Peace and Security Council for the prevention, management and resolution of crises and conflicts" and for the PSC to work in "close cooperation with the African Commission on Human and Peoples' Rights in all matters relevant to its objectives and mandate."

Consultations

Another principle on which the AU places a premium is that of consulting with the partners. While acknowledging, in the PSC Protocol Preamble, the primacy of the UN Security Council in maintaining "international peace and security, as well as the provisions of the Charter on the role of regional arrangements or agencies in the maintenance of international peace and security," the AU recognizes "the need to forge closer cooperation and partnership between the United Nations, other international organizations and the African Union, in the promotion and maintenance of peace, security and stability in Africa." International partnerships are elaborated in Chapter 5.

The chairperson of the Commission, according to Article 12 [7] of the protocol, is expected to consult with "Member States, the Regional Mechanisms, the United Nations and other relevant institutions" on "the practical details for the establishment of the Early Warning System" and "the steps required for its effective functioning." The chairperson of the Commission is also expected, "under the authority of the Peace and Security Council," to consult "with all parties involved in a conflict" before undertaking efforts and taking "all initiatives deemed appropriate to prevent, manage and resolve" the conflict. Moreover, in deploying the ASF, the Commission, according to Article 13 [16], is expected to hold "consultation with the United Nations Secretariat, assist in the co-ordination of external initiatives in support of the African Standby Force capacity-building in training, logistics, equipment, communications and funding."

It is also in recognition of their role in the implementation of the peace and security agenda that the AU seeks to coordinate its activities with those of the RMs. In Article 16 [2] the AU commits to consult RMs to "promote initiatives aimed at anticipating and preventing conflicts and, in circumstances where conflicts have occurred, peace-making and peace-building functions." In Article 17 [3] the PSC commits itself and the chairperson of the AUC to "maintain close and continued interaction with the United Nations Security Council, its African members, as well as with the Secretary-General, including holding periodic meetings and regular consultations on questions of peace, security and stability in Africa."

Additionally, the PSC can (according to Article 8 [11] of the Protocol) "hold informal consultations" with "parties concerned by or interested in a conflict or a situation under its consideration." The chairperson of the AUC, according to Article 11 [2], is also expected to consult "with the Member States concerned" when selecting members of the PoW. For its part, according to Article 11 [6], the Panel is expected to consult the chairperson if it has to hold its meetings outside AU headquarters.

Partnerships

The implementation of the ambitious peace and security agenda requires partnerships between different actors who have a stake in the agenda. The PSC Protocol recognizes the importance of partnerships in a number of ways. Drawing on UN Charter Chapter VIII, which recognizes the importance of partnerships in meeting its objective of maintaining international security, the PSC Protocol endorses the "partnership between the United Nations, other international organizations and the African Union, in the promotion and maintenance of peace, security and stability in Africa." The Protocol also calls for an "effective partnership" between RMs and the PSC "in the promotion and maintenance of peace, security and stability." Based on a strong belief in the principle of partnerships, the Protocol (Article 7 [k]) gives the PSC the power to "promote and develop a strong 'partnership for peace and security' between the Union and the United Nations and its agencies, as well as with other relevant international organizations."

African ownership

Bearing in mind that the motivation for establishing APSA was to apply "African solutions to African problems," it is understandable that APSA is based on the principle of African ownership of the solutions to African peace and security problems. While acknowledging in the Preamble and in Article 17 of the PSC Protocol that the UN Security Council "has the primary responsibility for the maintenance of international peace and security," Article 16 of the Protocol establishes the AU's "primary responsibility for promoting peace, security and stability in Africa." African ownership entails defining, redefining, and refining the peace and security agenda. So far there is no evidence that the AU has done this. The conceptualization of APSA has slipped from its grip and it has, subsequently, been reconceptualized by external partners who are paying for its "operationalization." Moreover, the AU has been keen to include issues favored by donors – such as piracy, weapons of mass destruction, and support for Africa Command (AFRICOM).[26] As will be explained in Chapter 6, understanding African problems requires an African paradigm and African-generated knowledge to define and implement the African solutions. So far the AU has not taken a lead in adopting an African paradigm to guide the identification of Africa's peace and security problems, or to generate African solutions to address them. Conversely, the AU also seems to have taken this principle to the extreme by claiming exclusive "African ownership", even to the dismay of African partners such as RMs and CSOs. The AU application of the principle has been a source of friction in its cooperation and coordination with the UN.

Notwithstanding this friction, the German government has demonstrated its own understanding of the African peace and security agenda, and the architecture for implementing it. According to the German ministry of foreign affairs, the AU "has evolved as an African peace and security architecture aimed at finding African solutions to African problems."[27] Accordingly, the German government has committed finances to construct a building to house the AU Peace and Security Department, delimit and demarcate African borders, and build the capacity of the AU police force.

Comparative advantage

The AU is well aware that all the different actors have particular endowments and specialized contributions to make in the implementation of the peace and security agenda. This principle is simply based on an understanding that the actors identified in the architecture have the ability to contribute to the implementation of the peace and security agenda in ways that are specific to their respective resources, abilities, and capabilities. Hence, Article 16 specifically calls for laying down "modalities" of partnerships "determined by the comparative advantage of each and the prevailing circumstances." The AU has recognized the fact that the RMs are closer to the conflicts and have the advantage of having the knowledge to intervene in timely and appropriate ways, particularly in the early stages of conflict until it is ready to complement or partner with them. This principle was put to use in the Darfur region and in Kenya in 2008. When the AU was called upon to respond to the crisis in Darfur its partners offered various forms of assistance that ranged from logistical support to the supply of equipment and other assets that it needed to operate the African Union Mission in Sudan (AMIS), which was later transformed into a hybrid force – UNAMID. Although partnership has not worked as expected, it contains a number of elements that point to how the principle works.

The 2008 Kenyan situation is probably the clearest demonstration of the AU undertaking initial intervention to manage the post-election violence. The AU appointed a panel of eminent personalities, headed by former UN Secretary-General Kofi Annan, to resolve the crisis under its mandate. The UN for its part provided secretarial support, while the EU and other international partners provided financial resources. Civil society was also tapped for expertise, while regional organizations such as the EAC, and foreign powers such as the US and China, provided moral support and full backing of the Annan-led effort. However, it should be cautioned that this principle, if overemphasized, could distort and undermine the development of Africa's self-reliance and independence in establishing and managing the peace and security architecture. There is a concern that Africans are already bearing the heavier burden in managing African conflicts – by supplying the necessary soldiers – while the international community supplies their equipment and pays for them.

Supporting Africans to directly address violent conflicts has many benefits. First, it gives the Europeans a feel-good sense of coming to the aid of the needy. It is morally uplifting to do something about the "scar of humanity." This looks even better if it appears that one is actually supporting the victims to find and implement their own solutions.

Second, it is costly to deploy European or American forces to remote parts of the globe where their vital interests are not clearly defined. Governments from abroad have a hard time explaining such deployments to their own voters and taxpayers. For instance, the maintenance of a Swedish contingent in the European Battle Group cost 300 million euros per year.[28] Compare this with the annual cost of $200 million to maintain the AU Mission in Somalia (AMISOM) in Somalia, or the $100 million that was spent supporting AMIS over a two-year period.

Third, an African life is cheaper than an American or European one, both financially and politically. It would be very difficult for Western governments to explain to their populations how and why they had to lose more than 3,000 soldiers over six years in Somalia, compared to the UN's losses over six decades. So the support that Western countries have provided presents a win-win situation: the West has provided some assistance to Africa when it needed it most, and may rightly claim the moral high ground; while Africans, however, have been provided with resources without which the problems would have deteriorated or taken longer to solve; and the international community is saved an embarrassing situation since the richer developed countries have utilized their resources to rescue those unable to help themselves.

Subsidiarity

The AU thinking implies that the Union knows the African condition better than international organizations, while the RMs know more about conflicts and security issues in their respective regions by virtue of their proximity to them. Hence, the AU expects the UN to allow it to handle African peace and security issues just like it allows the RMs to handle those issues at their level. It was only after efforts at this level failed that the international community was called in to give complementary support. The AU was cognizant of the importance of this principle, as well as that of comparative advantage, when it identified other players such as the CSOs and member states in the architecture. The PSC Protocol has recognized the importance of this principle by including other actors in the implementation of its agenda. For instance, it wants to ensure that CSOs also contribute to the promotion of peace and security in Africa. Although this principle calls for the devolution of decisions to the lowest possible level, our analysis in Chapter 2 showed that the AU is still run on a top-down basis with all powers either reserved to the supreme organ – the Assembly – or to the Commission's headquarters in Addis Ababa.

Complementarity

The AU also subscribes to the principle of complementarity, which envisions relationships or situations in which the actors involved in implementing the peace and security agenda support each other regardless of their strengths and weaknesses. For instance, if an RM responds and takes a lead in responding to a conflict, the AU will support it and expect the UN also to contribute to the effort. This principle, together with those of subsidiarity and African ownership, have caused some friction with the UN – which prefers to take the lead role itself and apply its own rules and standard operating procedures in peacekeeping operations.

If this principle were to apply in an ideal situation, each of the actors in APSA would perform specific functions but at the same time would all be joined together to achieve desired outcomes. The structure of the body into parts allows performance of certain functions. It is in recognition of this responsibility, and out of respect for each other's roles, that the Protocol calls for setting up the "modalities of partnership" to determine "the comparative advantage of each and the prevailing circumstances."

Lessons learned and best practices

A review of the AU's implementation of its peace and security agenda would probably conclude that it has tried to "reinvent the wheel" several times in the last ten years. A keen observer of the performance of the AU in preventing, managing, and resolving conflicts in a number of member countries would likely conclude that it got involved in each of them as if they were happening for the very first time. This is the consequence of a lack of learning from accumulated experience, and of failure to extract best or good practice for use in the future. The AU has not explored and adopted best practice when implementing the peace and security agenda. It has a poor institutional memory leading to an over-reliance on European experts to generate the ideas and knowledge needed to establish the necessary architecture, and to undertake appropriate activities to prevent, manage and resolve conflicts. This lack of retention of best practice has meant that the AU takes longer, and spends more, when responding to conflicts and other security challenges. The AU needs to have sets of guidelines, ethics or ideas to guide it in taking the most efficient or prudent courses of action whenever faced by conflicts and security challenges.

For example, the AU does not have a unit for "lessons learned." There is also no effective process for evaluating those initiatives and activities that are undertaken as part of efforts to promote peace and security – either concurrently, or after the event. Furthermore, the AU does not debrief personnel returning from missions, and has no institutional memory on the peace missions it has been involved in. None of its activities are undertaken with the requirement that there will be end-of-mission assessments, exit interviews, debriefings, mid-mission assessments, documentation, and archiving of information.

These principles should not only be applied in the working relationships between the AU and its partners, but also within the PSC structures, the PSD, and the AUC. As was pointed out in Chapter 2, there is a noticeable lack of coordination and cooperation between the PSC and other APSA arrangements such as the CEWS, the Commission, and the MSC. The unanswered question is how APSA might apply these principles vis-à-vis the AGA, whose greatest potential contribution could come in the form of addressing the root causes of African conflicts.

The role of member states

Although the AU is a body of member states, it is important to note that individual members are given specific peace and security responsibilities in the CAAU and in the Protocol.

The AU member states are expected to respect the principles articulated in Article 4, particularly those related to the promotion of peace and security on the continent. Additionally, member states are expected to:

- cooperate with the ASF when it is executing its functions
- pay their dues and other financial obligations to the AU
- implement AU decisions
- behave in a manner that promotes peace and security, i.e. maintaining a peaceful co-existence, settling disputes when they arise, avoiding the use of force, and respecting the sovereignty and independence of each other.

In Article 7 of the Protocol member states are expected to contribute to the implementation of the APSA in the following ways:

- recognize that while carrying out its "duties," the PSC "acts on their behalf"
- "agree to accept and implement the decisions of the Peace and Security Council, in accordance with the Constitutive Act"
- "extend full cooperation to, and facilitate action by the Peace and Security Council for the prevention, management and resolution of crises and conflicts, pursuant to the duties entrusted to it under the present Protocol"
- shoulder their duties and responsibilities of promoting peace and security, particularly those with memberships on the PSC, including the defraying of "additional expenses incurred by the Commission" when they host its meetings
- "extend full cooperation to, and facilitate action by the Peace and Security Council for the prevention, management and resolution of crises and conflicts."

The role of the Regional Mechanisms

The inclusion of the RMs[29] in its peace and security architecture is another example of how the AU can utilize the complex relations between globalization, security, and governance in pursuit of its objectives. Before the PSC Protocol was signed at the AU summit in Durban in 2002, a meeting had been convened in Addis Ababa in May 2002 to review the state of the RMs and their experiences in conflict prevention, management, and resolution. This meeting examined experiences and hindrances to cooperation under the OAU, as well as the underlying objectives and modalities of cooperation between the RMs and the proposed PSC. It subsequently recommended the formalization of relations between the AU and the RMs, and suggested a Memorandum of Understanding (MoU) to specify the context and content of this relationship.

The PSC Protocol acknowledges the contribution of the RMs in the maintenance of peace, security, and stability, and the need to develop formal coordination and cooperation between them and the AU. For example, Article 7 [j] of the Protocol calls for "close harmonization, co-ordination and co-operation between Regional Mechanisms and the Union in the promotion and maintenance of peace, security and stability in Africa."

Moreover, Article 16 of the PSC Protocol states that "Regional Mechanisms are part of the overall security architecture of the Union." It suggests the harmonization and coordination of activities with these Mechanisms to ensure effective partnership, taking account of "the comparative advantage of each and the prevailing circumstances." Since its operationalization in 2004, the PSD has worked closely with RECs by:

- consulting on initiatives aimed at anticipating and preventing conflicts and in circumstances where conflicts have occurred, and in peacemaking and peace building functions
- harmonizing and coordinating efforts
- regularly exchanging information
- involving the RMs in the CEWS and the ASF
- allowing the RMs to participate in PSC deliberations
- establishing liaison offices in the RMs, and vice versa.

In January 2008 the AU and the RMs signed a MoU with the main objective of institutionalizing and strengthening their cooperation and closely coordinating "their activities toward their shared goal of ridding the continent of the scourge of conflicts and laying the foundation for sustainable peace, security and stability."[30] They also committed to "contribute to the full operationalization and effective functioning" of APSA. The MoU strongly affirms APSA principles of partnership, coordination, cooperation, subsidiarity, complementarity and comparative advantage in the following areas: operationalization and functioning of APSA; the prevention, management and resolution of conflicts; humanitarian action and disaster response; post-conflict reconstruction and development; arms control and disarmament; preventing and combating counter-terrorism and transnational organized crime; managing borders; sharing knowledge; and mobilizing resources.

It is notable that the MoU narrowly defines APSA to include the CEWS, the ASF and the PoW,[31] and identifies border management as part of the peace and security agenda. Also worth noting is the detailed description of the cooperation arrangement in the form of information exchange, meetings, institutional presence and joint activities and field coordination. The signatory organizations also commit themselves to harmonizing and coordinating their relations with those of international organizations – particularly the UN – as well as civil society.

Despite the frequent reference to partnership, complementarity between the AU and the RM has not been easy. The AU and the RMs have experienced a tumultuous relationship when addressing threats or situations of conflict and insecurity. Examples are the "rocky" relations between SADC and the AU in addressing the Madagascar crisis; between ECOWAS and the AU in Côte d'Ivoire; between the AU and ECOWAS in Niger; between the AU and ECOWAS in Togo; and between the AU and IGAD in South Sudan, which was characterized by a lack of cooperation and coordination.

There has been an improvement in communications since the appointment of REC/RM Liaison Officers (LOs) to the AU and to the RECs, although their mandates are still obscure. Some of the RECs have deployed LOs with backgrounds that do not fit the responsibilities of their offices. Currently, apart from the responsibility to attend meetings, the LOs are little more than couriers transmitting documents back and forth – a function that could easily be carried out via electronic communication. The duties of the LOs are still unclear since the RECs and the RMs continue to send their representatives to meetings organized by the AUC, despite having representatives in the Commission.

Coordination has been complicated by proliferation, overlapping, and multiple memberships of the RECs, as noted in Figure 4.3. Overlapping mandates promote competition and rivalry instead of interaction and cooperation, while multiple membership is a burden to those countries who must stretch their resources in order to contribute to the objectives of the various overlapping organizations. It is curious that an organization such as COMESA – which is well prepared to promote economic integration – would want to veer into the realm of peace and security. The experience the AU has had of dealing with these issues demonstrates that they can easily derail or undercut development and integration agendas.

Through donor encouragement and support, some RECs have made attempts to coordinate their activities. For instance, COMESA, EAC, and IGAD are working together on addressing the proliferation

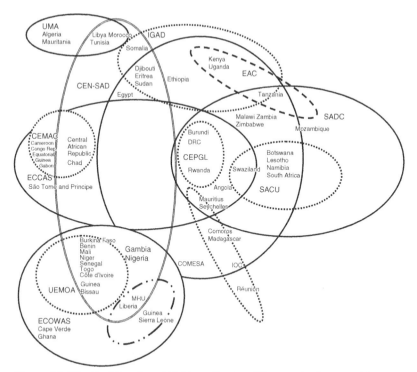

Figure 4.3 The Proliferation of African Regional Economic Communities
Source: United Nations Economic Commission for Africa

of small arms and light weapons, transhumance and pastoralist conflicts, piracy, and terrorism in the eastern Africa region. ECCAS and ECOWAS have also made attempts to cooperate on curbing human trafficking and piracy in the central and west Africa region, and in the Gulf of Guinea.

For the first time, in 2013, the AU collaborated with the RECs, ECOWAS and ECCAS, to deploy missions in Mali and the CAR. Additionally, the AU mandated its largest peacekeeping operation so far when it increased AMISOM's force strength to 22,126. A surge of violent armed conflicts in 2013 saw an increase in AU and RM deployments of PKOs. The RMs also proved in 2013 that they are crucial in the implementation of the AU's peace and security agenda. Solomon Dersso notes how the RM's buy-in and support were critical in the implementation of the PSC decisions. For instance, when ECCAS failed to abide by its "decision to isolate the new leadership of the CAR," the PSC could not force it to comply. A review of the PSC's responses to conflict "situations in Madagascar, the eastern DRC, Mali, Guinea Bissau, the CAR, Somalia, Sudan and South Sudan" in 2013 shows that they were significantly shaped by SADC, the ICGLR, ECOWAS, ECCAS and IGAD.[32]

In terms of mediating conflicts, SADC took a lead role in Madagascar, ECOWAS in Guinea Bissau and Mali, the ICGLR and ECCAS in the CAR and the DRC, and IGAD in South Sudan. In these situations their proximity to the theatres of conflict made them "the natural first points of recourse to those in conflict."[33] The best illustration of the application of the principles of comparative advantage and complementarity can be observed in the partnership of the AU and SADC in Madagascar, when, in early 2013, they worked closely to ensure the return of the country to democratic rule.[34] Nevertheless, as the case of the CAR showed, there is a lack of clarity in the relationship between the AU and the REC/RMs on whether the former is the key partner that directs the others, an implementing agency, or an equal partner.

Challenges to the harmonization of the AU-REC mechanisms

The contributions of the RMs in implementing Africa's peace and security agenda are undermined by a number of factors. A lack of capacity and resources to develop and follow through on promising initiatives remains a major barrier to the role of the RMs in effective conflict prevention, management, and resolution. They lack the capacity to fully engage and positively contribute to the implementation of the peace and security agenda. Most of the RECs are poorly run, with poor leadership which lacks an overall vision or plan of action. The personnel, particularly in the fields of peace and security, lack the right training, education, and experience to perform the duties they are assigned. Like the AU, the RECs are heavily dependent upon "international partners" – particularly the G8 countries – which in turn hinders their development into independent organizations. There are serious concerns about whether the RECs can effectively contribute to the implementation of the peace and security agenda without external support.

Additionally, RECs operate in environments that lack the sort of common regional values that are crucial for binding members of the RECs together and reducing competition among them. The EAC provides the best example of how to go about building common regional values through the creation of political will among regional leaders, the establishment of political solidarity, and the development of common political values, systems, and institutions.[35] All these are needed to sustain and deepen the desire for regional integration.

The contributions of civil society to peace and security

Article 20 of the PSC Protocol states that "non-governmental organizations, community-based and other civil society organizations, particularly women's organizations," will be encouraged "to participate actively in the efforts aimed at promoting peace, security and stability in Africa," and "may be invited to address the Peace and Security Council" when "required." When such organizations are invited to appear the PSC (Article 8) they can participate "in the discussion relating to that conflict or situation," but "without the right to vote." The PSC may also consult such CSOs "involved and/or interested in a conflict or a situation" when discharging "its responsibilities." Furthermore, the CSO is expected, under Article 12, "to facilitate the effective functioning of the Early Warning System" and to cooperate with the ASF – in accordance with Article 13 – when it undertakes its functions. CSOs are also expected, according to Article 21 of the PSC Protocol, to contribute to the Peace Fund.

One area in which civil society was expected to play a significant role in the promotion of the peace and security agenda is through the African Peer Review Mechanism (APRM) process, which was designed to be inclusive at national level. In those countries that have undergone the reviews, civil society has played the active and significant role of critiquing government performance with respect to governance, the promotion of democracy, respect of human rights, tackling poverty, and delivering services. Undoubtedly, civil society could make a major contribution through this process, if only governments would allow it to fully participate instead of excluding and treating it as an enemy of the state. Indeed the role of civil society in the APRM should not be confined to the review stage – it should be extended to include the monitoring and evaluation of the countries' implementation plans of action.

Although the PSC Protocol calls for the PSC to collaborate and partner with civil society to promote peace and maintain security on the continent there is little evidence to show how this has been done successfully in practice. The situation is such that even research institutes, thinktanks, universities, and African scholars are rarely approached to contribute. The only partnership that is visible is that between the Addis Ababa University and the PSD through the German-funded Institute for Peace and Security Studies, which claims to be the latter's thinktank.

The AU prefers to use a limited pool of mostly European consultants as its "experts," and it is they who generate ideas, write key documents, review projects and programs, and produce implementation reports. The most active CSOs engaging the AU in peace and security matters are either foreign ones with liaison offices to the AU, or foreign-funded ones such as the South Africa-based Institute for Security Studies. African CSOs lack the funds or the necessary government support to enable them to fully engage with the AU, as demanded by the organization's various instruments.

Conclusions

The AU has formulated a broad approach to peace and security that incorporates military and non-military factors. However, Africa continues to experience wars, conflicts, crises, and terrorist attacks partly because the AU's peace and security architecture has been poorly implemented, thereby rendering it incapable of adequately handling its primary tasks. The Union's PSC is poorly run, the relationships between the AU and the RECs are far from smooth, and Africa's capacity to deploy Peace Support Operations (PSOs) is weak. Thus, without a peace and security architecture that is capable of addressing Africa's numerous problems effectively, peace and security will remain elusive. Moreover, despite the rhetoric surrounding self-pacification, ownership of the agenda, and "African solutions for African problems," APSA is wholly dependent on outside funding, a situation that enables outsiders to define, shape, and drive Africa's peace and security agenda.[36]

There is a need for the AU to clarify several relationships if its APSA is to succeed. At the first level, the relationships between key organs that have responsibility for peace and security need to be re-examined. These organs include the AUC, the PSC, the PAP, and the ACHPR. At the second level, the AU relationships with the RECs/RMs and the CSOs need to be made much clearer. The third level involves relationships between the AU and international actors, including the UN and Africa's international partners (see Chapter 5). It is these relationships that will enable APSA to function to its optimal level.

Besides relationships, the AU ought to demonstrate that it has learned from its previous mistakes. A number of lessons have come out of the AU deployments in Burundi, Darfur, Mali, and Somalia. First, the difficulties in deploying AU forces are related to the military capabilities of its participating member states – very few of them have specialized units for PSOs. These few are also overstretched since they have deployed in almost all the PSOs on the continent, including the UN's. Second, the

AU has very limited peace mission planning, deployment, and operational capabilities.

As security and peace remain scarce on the continent, there is a need for the AU, as well as the PSC and other organs with responsibility for security, to re-examine their objectives, modalities, and resources. The AU needs to do more to normalize relations with the RECs, compel or persuade its members to pay their dues on time, and involve the CSOs more broadly in its security and peace building activities. Without such measures its idea of finding "African solutions to African problems" will, ironically, continue to be driven and underwritten by Africa's international partners.

Notes

1 The United Nations Organization Stabilization Mission in the Democratic Republic of the Congo, with a strength of 26,700 personnel, took over from the United Nations Organization Mission in the Democratic Republic of the Congo on July 1, 2010. The latter was established in November 1999.
2 See OAU, CSSDCA Solemn Declaration, AHG/Decl.4 (XXXVI) 2000. Available at: www.peaceau.org/uploads/ahg-decl-4-xxxvi-e.pdf (last accessed March 20, 2015).
3 Peter Vale, *Security and Politics in South Africa: The Regional Dimension* (Boulder, CO: Lynne Rienner) (2003): 7–27.
4 See, for instance, Heidi Hudson, "'Doing' Security as Though Humans Matter: a Feminist Perspective on Gender and the Politics of Human Security," *Security Dialogue*, vol. 36, no. 2 (2005): 155–74.
5 These organizations were: African Security Dialogue and Research, the African Peace Forum, the Institute for Human Rights and Development in Africa, the Institute for Security Studies, the Southern Africa Human Rights Trust, the Southern Africa Institute for International Affairs, and the West African Network for Peace. The initiative folded in 2012 when donor funding ran out.
6 Ali A. Mazrui, *Towards a Pax Africana: A Study of Ideology and Ambition* (London: Weidenfeld and Nicolson) (1967): 3–20.
7 Statement of the Chairperson of the Commission on the Occasion of the Solemn Launching of the Peace and Security Council, Addis Ababa, May 25, 2004: 8. Hereafter referred to as the chairperson's statement.
8 Kwame Nkrumah, *Africa Must Unite* (London: Panaf Books) (1963): 203.
9 For a critical study of the genesis, organization, and achievements of the G8, see Hugo Dobson, *The Group of 7/8* (London: Routledge) (2006).
10 Boutros Boutros-Ghali, *An Agenda for Peace* (New York: United Nations) (1992).
11 See President Jimmy Carter, "A Foreign Policy Based on America's Essential Character," *Department of State Bulletin*, vol. 76, no. 1981 (June 13, 1977): 622.
12 For a useful analysis of the work and processes of the UN Security Council, see Edward C. Luck, *UN Security Council: Practice and Promise* (London: Routledge) (2006).

13 See, for instance, Samuel M. Makinda, "Terrorism, counter-terrorism and norms in Africa," *African Security Review*, vol. 15, no. 3 (2006): 19–31; and Samuel M. Makinda, "The History and Root Causes of Terrorism in Africa" in Wafula Okumu and Anneli Botha (eds) *Understanding Terrorism in Africa: In Search of an African Voice* (Pretoria: Institute for Security Studies) (2006): 15–21.

14 For insightful analyses of terrorism in Africa since September 2001, see, for example, Wafula Okumu and Anneli Botha (eds) *Understanding Terrorism in Africa: In Search of an African Voice* (Pretoria: Institute for Security Studies) (2006); and by the same authors, *Understanding Terrorism in Africa: Building Bridges and Overcoming the Gaps* (Pretoria: Institute for Security Studies) (2007).

15 For more details on the characteristics of armed violence in Africa, see Stephen Ellis, "Liberia 1989–1994: A Study of Ethnic and Spiritual Violence," *African Affairs*, vol. 94, no. 375 (1995): 165–97; D. Keen, *The Economic Functions of Violence in Civil Wars* (London: Oxford University Press) (1998); Christopher Clapham, *Guerrillas* (Oxford: James Currey) (1998); A. Clayton, *Frontiersmen: Warfare in Africa Since 1950* (London: UCL Press) (1999); Human Rights Watch, *Divide and Rule: State-Sponsored Ethnic Violence in Kenya* (New York: HRW) (1993); Human Rights Watch, *Easy Prey: Child Soldiers in Liberia* (New York: HRW) (1994); and Human Rights Watch, *Leave None to Tell the Story: Genocide in Rwanda* (New York: HRW) (1999).

16 See IANSA, Oxfam and Saferworld, "Africa's Missing Billions – International Arms Flows and the Cost of Conflict," *Briefing Paper* (October 2007).

17 For a perceptive analysis of internally displaced persons, see Thomas G. Weiss and David A. Korn, *International Displacement: Conceptualization and Its Consequences* (London: Routledge, 2006).

18 See Article 12 of the PSC Protocol.

19 Current PoW members are Mary Chinery-Hesse (West Africa), Salim Ahmed Salim (East Africa), Marie-Madeleine Kalala (Central Africa), and Kenneth Kaunda (South Africa). As of this writing, Ahmed Ben Bella, who passed away in 2012, had not been replaced.

20 These "friends of the panel" are Elisabeth K. Pognon (West), Miguel Trovoada (Central) and Brigalia Bam (South). As of this writing, the East and North regions did not have "friends of the panel."

21 See modalities for the functioning of the Panel of the Wise as adopted by the Peace and Security Council at its 100th meeting held on November 12, 2007.

22 See African Union Independent Panel of Experts, "Assessment of the African Standby Force and Plan of Action for Achieving Full Operational Capability by 2015" (October 2013).

23 For reports on corruption in peacekeeping missions, see Benon Herbert Oluka, "UPDF Suspends 15 for Selling Amisom Slots," *The Observer*, November 4, 2014. Available at: www.observer.ug/index. php?option=com_content&view=article&id=34764:-updf-suspends-15-for-selling-amisom-slots&catid=78:topstories&Itemid=116 (last accessed March 18, 2015); Rodney Muhumuza, "Uganda Arrests Somalia Peacekeepers over Theft," Associated Press, October 29, 2013. Available at: bigstory.ap.org/article/uganda-arrests-somalia-peacekeepers-over-theft (last accessed March 18, 2015); Timothy Nsubuga, "Corruption: State

House Cited in Multi-million Dollar Theft," *Uganda Correspondent*, March 26, 2012. Available at: www.ugandacorrespondent.com/articles/2012/03/state-house-cited-in-multi-million-dollar-corruption/ (last accessed March 18, 2015); Transparency International UK, "Corruption and Peacekeeping," available at: www.transparency-se.org/130925-PK-report.pdf (last accessed March 18, 2015); "UN Lifts Lid on Incompetent, Abusive and Corrupt Peacekeepers," available at: www.timeslive.co.za/world/2013/04/19/un-lifts-lid-on-incompetent-abusive-and-corrupt-peacekeepers (last accessed March 18, 2015); and Paul D. Williams, "Peace Operations in Africa: Lessons Learned Since 2000," *Africa Security Brief no. 25* (July 2013). Available at: http://africacenter.org/2013/07/peace-operations-in-africa-lessons-learned-since-2000/ (last accessed March 20, 2015)

24 Isdore Guvamombe, "CISSA: When the Ides of March Woke up a Continent," *The Zimbabwe Herald*, April 23, 2013. Available at: http://www.herald.co.zw/cissa-when-the-ides-of-march-woke-up-a-continent/ (last accessed March 18, 2015).

25 The AU has increasingly relied on "high-level panels" to undertake missions such as: facilitating peace in Darfur and between Sudan and South Sudan; investigating human rights violations in South Sudan; assessing APSA institutions, etc. The AU High-level Implementation Panel on Sudan, headed by former South African president, Thabo Mbeki, is the most prominent such panel, having lasted since 2008.

26 See, for example, Samuel M. Makinda, "Why AFRICOM Has Not Won Over Africans," *Africa Policy Forum* (Washington DC: Center for Strategic and International Studies), (November 2007). Available at: http://csis.org/publication/why-africom-has-not-won-over-africans (last accessed March 18, 2015).

27 See "Support for the African Peace and Security Architecture," German Ministry of Foreign Affairs. Available at: www.gicafrica.diplo.de/Vertretung/suedafrika-dz/en/02-Content/01__GA/Partnership/Germany-AU-G8.html (last accessed March 18, 2015).

28 See "EU Battlegroup," available at: www.globalsecurity.org/military/world/europe/eu-battlegroups.htm (last accessed March 18, 2015).

29 The term "Regional Mechanisms" in this book refers to Regional Economic Communities, and arrangements that are involved in promoting peace and security. The latter includes the International Conference on the Great Lakes Region and the ASF's Coordination Mechanisms – the Eastern Africa Standby Force Coordination Mechanism and the North African Regional Capability.

30 The RECs that signed the MoU were CEN-SAD, COMESA, EAC, ECCAS, ECOWAS, IGAD, SADC, and Union of Arab Maghreb (UMA), and the coordinating mechanisms were EASBRICOM and the North African Regional Capability.

31 This narrow understanding of APSA was reiterated at the third meeting of chief executives of the AU and RECs for "Conflict Prevention, Management and Resolution" that took place in Zanzibar on November 8, 2010.

32 See Solomon A. Dersso, *Annual Review of the African Union Peace and Security Council 2013/2014* (Pretoria: Institute for Security Studies): 42.

33 See Report of OAU/Regional Organizations Meeting on Cooperation in Conflict Prevention, Management and Resolution, held on May 20–21, 2002, in Addis Ababa.
34 See Bah A. Sarjoh, "Consolidating Regional Mediation Approaches: Addressing the Question of Partnerships: Remarks at the Fourth AU High-Level Retreat on the Promotion of Peace, Security and Stability in Africa: The AU's 2013 Golden Jubilee Retreat," October 29–30, 2013, Abidjan, Côte d'Ivoire.
35 See Wafula Okumu, "A Charter for Social Development and Governance: The Political Economy of 'Regional Goods'" in Rok Ajulu (ed.) *A Region in Transition: Towards a New Integration Agenda in East Africa* (Midrand: Institute for Global Dialogue) (2010).
36 See Samuel M. Makinda, "African Thinkers and the Global Security Agenda" in Makumi Mwagiru and Okello Oculli (eds) *Rethinking Global Security: An African Perspective?* (Nairobi: Heinrich Böll Foundation) (2006): 21–37.

5   The African Union's international partners

As demonstrated in previous chapters, the African Union's (AU) agenda is unlikely to be realized in the foreseeable future without outside assistance. The issue is not about whether outsiders should participate in Africa's pursuit of its goals or not. The AU and its member states are part of international society and as such they derive many of their own norms, values, and rules from this wider global society. This is partly why Article 3 [e] of the Constitutive Act of the African Union (CAAU) states that one of the AU's objectives is to "encourage international cooperation, taking due account" of the United Nations (UN) Charter and the Universal Declaration of Human Rights (UDHR). What counts most in such cooperation is the terms of engagement. This chapter is concerned with international partnerships that relate to the operation of the AU organs, arrangements, and structures.

Not surprisingly, in the past decade the AU has entered into partnerships with a number of international actors ranging from multilateral organizations – such as the UN and the European Union (EU) – to individual countries, with a view to promoting its peace, security, and governance agendas. These partnerships, mostly defined in agreements, are designed, directed, and based on the kind of financial and technical support given to the AU's peace and security architecture. The level and strength of the partnerships is also determined by the amount of financial support the AU receives. The questions raised by keen observers of the AU's engagements with its international partners concern the level and depth of any negative impact they have – not only on the definition and understanding of the "African problems," but also on "African ownership" of the "African solution." Has the way the AU entered and managed these partnerships enabled external actors to redefine Africa's peace, security, and governance agendas, and the architectures for implementing them? Can the contributions of these partners to the implementation of these agendas be measured? What is the long-term impact of these partnerships on Africa's quest for self-reliance and ownership of its own initiatives to address its peace, security, and governance challenges? Have these external relations conformed to the values of African Peace and Security Architecture (APSA), including partnership, cooperation, coordination, complementarity, subsidiarity, and comparative advantage?

After locating the aims and provisions for entering into partnerships with external actors in the AU's formal instruments, this chapter critically examines the roles played by a number of key external actors in the implementation of Africa's peace, security, and governance agendas. These include the UN, the EU, the US, and China.[1] It should be noted that there are a range of non-state and transnational interactions between Africans and peoples outside the continent; and, while not the focus here, they also play an important role in implementing APSA and African Governance Architecture (AGA).[2] The rest of this chapter is divided into three parts. The first examines the nature and pattern of international partners established to support APSA. The second provides an overview of the AU's relations with key external actors. The third, which is the conclusion, evaluates the AU's management of its external engagements.

Forging external partnerships for peace, security, and governance

As stated in Chapter 4, "partnership" is one of the most important values that underpin APSA. One of the original aims of the Organization of African Unity (OAU) was to bring African states together to collectively militate against unwanted external influence and interference on the continent, including the rejection of forms of neo-colonialism that might arise following the achievement of independence. Of course, after formal decolonization a range of external interests remained in Africa, including Cold War geostrategic interests, the continuing management of ex-colonial relationships and interests, and other vested economic and political interests. In more recent times, new external (as well as intra-African) pressures covering various issues – including protecting civilians during violent conflict, overcoming poverty and disease, mitigating climate change, and countering transnational terrorism and organized crime – have required the AU to find ways to manage external interests and pressures in ways that balance them with the interests, values, and norms of the continent's governments and peoples. Moreover, during the last decade the African resources boom – particularly in hydrocarbons, precious minerals, and arable land – has created what some have described as a "new scramble for Africa,"[3] with the continent's wealth in raw materials becoming an important facilitator of global economic growth. After a period of relative global neglect during the 1990s, Africa became a theater for major (and emerging) power competition, with some predicting that current efforts to unlock the economic potential of the continent might mean that we are entering the "African Century."[4]

Kwame Nkrumah was weary of external actors' intentions to use multiple means to undermine Africa's independence and sovereignty. In the book, *Dark Days in Ghana*, Nkrumah warned:

> We must be constantly vigilant. Imperialist intelligence organisations are hard at work in Africa, manipulating political pressures internally and externally within developing, independent states. Evidence of their activities may be seen in the conspiracies, subversions, coups and assassinations hitherto virtually outside our political experience, but in recent years a painful reminder that we are not yet masters in our own house.[5]

It appears this fear was widely held by African leaders during the OAU First Ordinary Session of the Assembly of Heads of State and Government, held in Cairo, Egypt, in July 1964, when they adopted Resolution AHG/Res.16 (1) to express their "conscious[ness] of the existence of extra-African manoeuvres aimed at dividing African States." The Assembly was informed by the fact that "extra-African" forces and interests would manipulate border problems inherited from the colonial era to destabilize the newly independent states. African leaders were caught in a catch-22. On the one hand, they were weary of past negative relations Africa had had with foreign powers, while on the other hand they were conscious of the need to establish and maintain partnerships with them in the implementation of the peace, security, and governance agendas.

It was this understanding that influenced their decision to transform the OAU into the AU, which was regarded as a Pan-Africanist organization that would "take up the multifaceted challenges that confront our continent and peoples in the light of the social, economic and political changes taking place in the world." To achieve this, the AU was given the following objectives as articulated in Article 3 of the CAAU:

- encourage international cooperation between Africa and the rest of the world (3 [e])

- establish the necessary conditions which would enable the continent to play its rightful role in the global economy and in international negotiations (3 [i]), and
- work with "relevant international partners" to enhance human security of the African people (3 [n]).

The AU, which holds primary responsibility for promoting peace, security, and governance on the continent, has committed itself to achieving these goals through partnerships with both continental and external actors. As pointed out in Chapter 2, one of the driving motivations for the formation of the AU was the traumatic experiences in the aftermath of the collapse of the Somali state in 1991 and the Rwanda genocide of 1994, which displayed the indecisiveness and inability of the international community to intervene in complex emergency situations in Africa. The CAAU not only contains clauses that anchor the AU on the principle of "self-reliance" but also identify the importance of partnerships in meeting the organization's objectives.

For the AU, taking up this challenge was to be achieved through the establishment of common "institutions … with the necessary powers and resources to enable them to discharge their respective mandates effectively." In part, this was to be accomplished by reforming the OAU into a more proactive body that owned "African solutions" and determined how they were to be implemented with both internal and external partners. External actors would have to come up with other, or better, arguments for their interference and intervention if the continental body was performing this role effectively. Yet while this proactivity might result in some mitigation, it could not prevent all unwarranted interference and intervention on the continent: not all outsiders are interested in African solutions, and some external interests are in tension with Africa's own interests and values, particularly when it comes to natural resources extraction.[6] Therefore, the AU has been required to actively manage – at a continental level – the African engagement of a growing number of outside actors offering to contribute to the promotion and maintenance of its peace, security, and governance agendas.

The Preamble of the CAAU recalls the important role played by the OAU in providing a "unique framework" for Africa's relations with the rest of the world.[7] The AU is now charged with promoting and defending "African common positions on issues of interest to the continent and its peoples."[8] A 2003 amendment to the CAAU, Article 3 [p], inserted a new objective: to "develop and promote common policies on trade, defence and foreign relations to ensure the defence of the Continent and the strengthening of negotiating positions."[9] A further 2003 amendment,

Article 4 [q], calls for the addition of the principle of "restraint by any Member State from entering into any treaty or alliance that is incompatible with the principles and objectives of the Union."[10] Similarly, the AU's Peace and Security Council (PSC) is charged with ensuring that "any external initiative in the field of peace and security on the continent takes place within the framework of the Union's objectives and priorities."[11] These provisions indicate, on paper, a limited form of central AU management – or gatekeeping – of the external relations of the continent. Yet while the AU seeks some alignment of negotiating positions and central coordination, it has experienced difficulties in conceiving, generating, adopting, and implementing "common positions" – as witnessed in its handling of UN Security Council reforms, the establishment of the US Africa military command (AFRICOM), and the role of the International Criminal Court (ICC) in tackling impunity in Africa.

Other elements of the AU's governance system outline an important role for pursuing forms of cooperation and collaboration with external actors. For example, one of the objectives of the CAAU, Article 3 [n], is to "work with relevant international partners" to eradicate "preventable diseases" and "promote good health on the continent." The Protocol establishing the Peace and Security Council is much more explicit about the dynamics of the relationship between the organization and external actors. For example, in its Preamble, the Protocol states the AU is "mindful" of the UN Security Council's primary responsibility for maintaining "international peace and security" and the Charter's "provisions" that recognize "the role of regional arrangements or agencies in the maintenance of international peace and security." Consequently, this lays the foundation for the AU to forge "closer cooperation and partnership" with the UN and "other international organizations" to promote and maintain "peace, security and stability in Africa." Article 7 [k] of the PSC Protocol gives the Council the power to "promote and develop a strong 'partnership for peace and security' between the Union and the United Nations and its agencies, as well as with other relevant international organizations." Such cooperation is envisaged in preventing, managing, and resolving conflicts.[12] The formal relationship between the AU and the UN, which was touched on in Chapter 4 and will be discussed further below, is explicitly set out in Article 17 of the PSC Protocol.

The AU has also set out what it characterizes as "Africa's Strategic Partnerships," which are "ground breaking partnerships with the rest of the world [that are] aimed at enhancing cooperation and consolidating growth of the continent."[13] Meanwhile, cooperation between Africa and its existing, traditional partners was being "re-defined, invigorated and strengthened."[14] The principal partnerships are identified as being with the EU, Brazil, China, Japan, the US, Kuwait, Saudi Arabia, India, Turkey, South Korea, and with international organizations including the UN, the League of Arab States, the Organization of American States, the Organization of Islamic Cooperation, the Commonwealth, the International Committee of the Red Cross, and Organisation Internationale de la Francophonie (OIF).[15] Also listed are "Partnerships in Prospect" with the Caribbean, Iran, and Australasia.[16] In justifying and explaining the strategic nature of these partnerships, the AU states:

> The philosophy underpinning Africa's new partnerships is predicated on specific objectives with pre-determined "Win-Win" outcomes for the mutual benefits of the parties involved. It is based on the principle of trust, equality and mutual respect. It aims at obliterating the age-long pattern of donor-recipient relationship, to one founded on reciprocal obligations and responsibilities. These partnerships are consistent with the clearly defined vision and development strategy of the African Union …[17]

This indicates that the AU is attempting to set the parameters for external engagement with the continent, in line with continental interests, values, and norms. As Okumu and Makinda argue, while there are "many contexts through which African states and organizations engage with the rest of the world,"[18] three key ones can be identified. First, perceptions – i.e whether external actors view Africa principally as a source of opportunity ("Afro-optimists") or as a source of problems ("Afro-pessimists"). This, in turn, shapes the framework for how commercial activities, aid, security, and other relations are pursued, and how much credibility is afforded to continental governance institutions like the AU. Second, and related, is the level of genuine respect shown by external actors to core values and mutual interests, including equality, joint-ownership, and reciprocal treatment and support. How these interests and values are recognized and acted upon is crucial to the nature and sustainability of the AU's external relations. Third, the level of competition by external actors in the pursuit of their interests and influence across Africa.[19] Not only is the African resources boom again positioning the continent as a theater for major power competition (following the original "Scramble" and again during the Cold War), the level of external interest in Africa over the past decade has made management of external relations difficult, especially given the AU's limited human and financial resources.

In attempting to manage these relations, the AU Permanent Representative Committee (PRC) maintains a Sub-Committee on Multilateral Cooperation – which reports on Africa's strategic partnerships. At the January 2012 AU summit, the Executive Council (EC) endorsed the recommendations of the Sub-Committee's global review of Africa's strategic partnerships, which sought to manage within a clearer and more strategic framework the set of existing and potential new external relations. The EC endorsed recommendations relating to:

• the principles governing the establishment of strategic partnerships
• the categories and classification of Africa's strategic partnerships
• the criteria proposed for establishing strategic partnerships between Africa and other parts of the world.

The EC also indicated that any new partnerships "should be based on decisions of the organs of the Union and should also be aligned to the needs of the respective regions of Africa," and asserted the "need to promote continent-wide approach and the African Union vision in the conduct of such partnerships, rather than the bilateral cooperation dimensions."[20] The EC also requested that the Commission establish a Partnerships Management and Coordination Division (PMCD). Despite this framework for AU engagement with external partners, there is deep concern that these relations could be negatively contributing to the efforts to meet other AU objectives. This was the message African Union Commission (AUC) chairperson Nkosazana Dlamini-Zuma delivered to the EC in January 2013 when she stated:

> We will continue to work with our cooperating partners, on the agenda set by the continent. Furthermore, work is on the way on the global review of our partnerships. To this end, we must consider putting a moratorium on the establishment of new partnerships. Especially continent-country partnerships, until we have reviewed the existing ones.[21]

The EC did indeed set a moratorium on new partnerships in January 2013.[22] At the January 2014 AU summit, in the context of the AU's Agenda 2063, it requested the AUC, working with the Sub-Committee on Multilateral Cooperation as well as a Panel of African Experts, to "undertake a comprehensive evaluation of all Africa's Strategic Partnerships" and prepare a report for the mid-2014 summit.[23] How the AU manages its international relations will be crucial for the ongoing legitimacy and effectiveness of the organization. If it is unable to shape external influences and pressures in ways that are more in the interests of Africa – or at least mitigate their worst effects – it may be bypassed or ignored by African peoples and governments. If it is able to play a form of gatekeeping role for the continent, it will gain credibility as an important medium between the world of external interests and the wealth of human and natural resources of the continent. An understanding of the AU's formal relations with some key external actors might give an indication of the Union's future extra-continental engagements.

Overview of the AU's key external relations

The United Nations

The starting point for the formal relationship between the UN and the AU is found in the UN Charter, and especially its principles, objectives, and normative values. Chapter VIII sets out the mechanism through which the world body may cooperate with "Regional Arrangements," although this relationship is envisaged in the Charter as one pertaining principally to peace and security matters rather than governance more generally. The main purposes of this section of the Charter are, first, to establish a legal place within the UN Charter system for regional security governance mechanisms, and in fact to encourage collaboration between the UN and regional bodies in pursuit of peace and security.[24] Second, the Charter makes clear that the relationship is one of subsidiarity – the UN Security Council is the final arbiter on any enforcement action at the regional level, and must be kept aware of what regional bodies are doing; while the actions of regional bodies in managing peace and security must always be consistent with the UN Charter.[25] These provisions therefore establish a relationship – and indeed actively promote cooperation – between the UN and the AU, but this is within the context of a formal hierarchy in which the AU is a junior partner. Despite the AU recognizing the UN's primacy in maintaining international security, it has assigned itself the primacy of promoting and maintaining peace and security on the African continent. Herein lies the inherent source of checkered and tense relations between these two international organizations.

Although cooperation between the UN and the AU has "greatly intensified in recent years," this should also be seen as part of a more general process by which the UN has been enhancing its interactions and collaborations with a range of regional and sub-regional bodies, helping to build their capacities as well as establishing more effective divisions of labor.[26] For instance, a Regional Consultative Mechanism, established when the AU came into existence, is convened and chaired by the executive secretary of the UN Economic Commission for Africa (ECA), based in Addis Ababa.[27] The Department of Political Affairs also established the UN Liaison Office to the African Union in November 2006. In June 2013 the UN Office to the AU (UNOAU), also based in Addis Ababa, signed a Host Country Agreement with the Ethiopian government, providing a legal mandate for its operation. The Office, which was established in 2010, is managed by the Special Representative of the UN Secretary-General to the African Union.[28]

The current framework underpinning UN-AU relations is the Ten-Year Capacity-Building Programme for the African Union, stemming from the 2005 UN World Summit. It was developed in 2006, and was the product of "extensive consultations" between the AUC and UN agencies and departments.[29] The Declaration establishing this program indicated that its aim was to develop a "stronger relationship" between the two organizations and that it was broadly conceived to cover a wide range of issues, including peace, security, governance, institution building, elections, human rights, the rule of law, humanitarian response and recovery, food security, socio-cultural and health issues, and the environment.[30] According to the UN Secretary-General, the UN "as a family considers the reinforcement of its cooperation with the AU as an important step towards strengthening the capacity of the continental body."[31]

The AU-UN relationship has been the subject of great attention by the world body in subsequent years. Attempts were made to delineate the nature of the relationship to ensure coordination, support, and effectiveness while minimizing the potential for friction and duplication. In March 2008 the Security-General reported on the relationship in terms of the maintenance of international peace and security, noting that:

> When the African Union undertakes peace and security interventions, it perceives its actions as a contribution to the international community and therefore needs the support of external actors. Understanding and appreciating how such partnerships should be framed is crucial as there is the potential for misunderstanding and misperception concerning the meaning and scope of such a partnership.[32]

Following the Secretary-General's report, the UN Security Council – through its adoption of Resolution 1809 – welcomed and encouraged

Table 5.1 Trust Fund and UN assessed contributions to AMISOM ($ million)

Year	Trust Fund income*	Trust Fund expenditure	Assessed funding expenditure	Total annual expenditure
2009	28.7	5.5	71.9	77.4
2010	4	8.1	160.2	168.3
2011	13.2	20.8	210	230.8
2012	30.3	22.8	287.5	310.3
Total	76.2	57.2	729.6	786.8

* Contributors to the Trust Fund have been Australia, Canada, the Czech Republic, Denmark, Germany, India, Japan, Korea, Malta, Saudi Arabia, Sweden, Turkey, and the UK.

Sources: United Nations Support Office to AMISOM (UNSOA); M. Freear and C. de Coning, "Lessons from the African Union Mission for Somalia (AMISOM) for Peace Operations in Mali" in *Stability: International Journal of Security & Development*, vol. 2, no. 2 (2013): 1–11, available at: http://dx.doi.org/10.5334/sta.bj

greater cooperation between the UN and the AU on a range of key elements, indicating its own determination to develop the relationship.[33]

The AU and the UN have developed a clear set of guidelines to foster greater cooperation and partnership, as outlined in the above discussion. This has been particularly evident in the peace and security sector, where there is frequent collaboration – including a joint peace operation in Darfur (African Union-United Nations Hybrid Operation in Darfur – UNAMID).[34] Other notable examples of AU-UN cooperation in the promotion of peace and security are Somalia, Sudan, and South Sudan.

One of the areas where partner support is prominently pronounced is in the Peace Support Operations (PSOs). AU Mission in Somalia (AMISOM), as another AU-mandated PSO, would not have been possible without external support as shown in Table 5.1.

Tensions have emerged in a number of cases. For example, there were clear divisions between the positions of the AU and the UN Security Council regarding the UN-authorized North Atlantic Treaty Organization-led (NATO) military intervention in Libya in 2011. Although all three African members of the UN Security Council – Nigeria, South Africa, and Gabon – voted for Resolution 1973 authorizing the enforcement of a no-fly zone over Libya, the AU was against the use of force.

In its relations with external partners the AU usually demands that they be underpinned by the principle of "respect of African Ownership and Priority Setting." The AU has always demanded that its partnership with the UN, especially the Security Council, should be defined and built on its terms – which include the lead role of setting up priorities and implementing the "African solutions to African problems." For instance, the PSC Protocol recognizes that the UN Security Council has the primary responsibility for maintaining international security, but insists that the AU has primary responsibility for maintaining peace and security in Africa.

AU relations with the UN concerning the promotion of its peace, security, and governance agendas hinge on the latter's legitimization of the former's actions. Without such an endorsement the AU would have difficulty in garnering the necessary political and financial support that it needs to undertake PSOs. The modus operandi that was established in Burundi in 2004 is that in cases where the UN is restrained by its own rules, the AU intervenes to secure peace and the UN steps in to keep it. In situations such as that in Somalia, where peace is elusive, the AU continues to play the lead role with the support of the UN and other international partners. The AU has benefited immensely from the UN's vast experience in mission support through these arrangements.

The AU-UN relationship has been characterized by a superiority syndrome, as well as often a lack of consultation. For example, in the case of Mali there was little consultation between the UN Security Council and the PSC on the transition from the African-led International Support Mission in Mali (AFISMA) to the UN Multidimensional Integrated Stabilization Mission in Mali (MINUSMA). According to Bar A. Sarjor, "the AU's request for closer consultation on the transformation from AFISMA to MINUSMA and the use of assessed contributions to provide logistics support to AFISMA was not heeded by the UN."[35] It is notable that the UN took over AFISMA as if there were no similar past experiences.[36] Indeed, Thomas Weiss and Martin Welz have concluded that the "AU-UN cooperation in Mali is disconcerting."[37]

The lack of complementarity and mutual respect between the UN and the AU in Libya and Mali suggests that the partnership between these international organizations might develop negative tendencies that could have long-term consequences for the implementation of the peace, security, and governance agendas in Africa. The Libya and Mali cases demonstrated that the AU and the UN had different "solutions" to "African problems." Indeed, had the UN listened to the AU's position that taking out Gaddafi would have far-reaching consequences, the Sahel region might not be swarming with radical militants heavily armed with weapons left over from the Libyan conflict.

The AU-UN relationship is a work-in-progress that has been characterized by frustrations, contestations over the meaning of the partnership, division of labor, and the sharing of responsibilities. In this relationship the UN does not regard itself as a donor, but more as "an important provider of technical assistance and [a] source of conceptual inspiration for the AU."[38] In this role the UN would prefer to determine how peacekeeping is planned and carried out in view of its long experience in this field. However, the AU believes that the UN should pay for those missions for which it does not want to commit international boots on the ground. In cases where the UN has troops on African soil, the AU believes the UN should follow the Union's script that is reflective of its "African ownership principle." For its part, the UN appears to have a low regard for AU capabilities to plan, fund, and manage a PSO. The UN's intentions to build the AU's capacities in the fields of "training, military, police, logistics, finance, and communication" has not produced the desired results despite the establishment of an office to the AU headed by an under-secretary-general.

For a number of reasons the AU-UN relationship is markedly different from the AU's relations with other major partners – especially the EU, the US, and China.

The European Union EU

Broader engagements between the EU and Africa are, to a large extent, underpinned by past colonial relationships as well as specific frameworks that have reflected the changing norms of global governance. Relations with France, the UK, and Portugal, former colonial powers on the continent, and their multilateral offshoots – the OIF, the Commonwealth, and the Community of Portuguese Language Countries – have further enhanced AU-EU relations. These relations have developed on two tracks. Initially, in the AU's nascent period, individual European countries including Belgium, Denmark, Sweden, Spain, and the UK, provided bilateral support to the Conflict Management Centre as it morphed into the Peace and Security Department (PSD). This arrangement was found to be untenable since it required individual reporting for each donation. It also encouraged unhealthy competition between donors who wanted to be identified with specific outcomes. The donors eventually reached an agreement through which they could put their money in a basket to support program activities and to pay for its staff. At the same time the Group of Eight (G8) was considering the "Africa Action Plan," which was subsequently taken over by the EU.

In the post-independence period, the first arrangement facilitating relations between Africa and Europe was the EU's African, Caribbean and Pacific framework, which was established through the 1975 Lomé

Convention and updated in the 2000 Cotonou Agreement. Specific relations were further developed through Africa-EU summits in 2000 (Cairo), 2007 (Lisbon), 2010 (Tripoli), and 2014 (Brussels). At the Lisbon summit, the Joint Africa-EU Strategy (JAES) and its Action Plan were adopted as a new Strategic Partnership, which set the parameters of the "partnership" and redefined the "shared values" between the two continents.[39] According to the EU, the JAES represented its new "continental approach" to Africa and would take their relationship to "a new level." As such, the AU and the EU "agreed to pursue common interests and strategic objectives together, beyond the focus of traditional development policy. The two continents started cooperating as equal partners."[40] The EU claims that the AU is a "key international partner" and a "strategic player in managing crises and promoting peace, stability, democracy, human rights and development on the continent."[41] Indicating the AU's coordinating role in the continent's external relations, the EU suggests that in certain policy areas the AU "acts as a standard setter," and in other areas the AU "increasingly acts as a spokesperson for Africa."[42] Finally, the EU argues that under the JAES it was "working towards Africa-led and -owned approaches, strengthening the primary responsibility of African governments for the issues in question."[43]

Relations between the AU and the EU are maintained by the Africa-EU summits, biennial ministerial-level meetings (comprised of AU foreign ministries, the AUC, EU foreign ministries, the European Commission, and the European Council), annual "consultations" with the AU PSC, and meetings of the Joint Task Force and Joint Expert Groups.[44] The AU also maintains a Mission to the EU in Brussels, while the EU does likewise in Addis Ababa.[45]

In implementing the peace and security pillar, the EU adopted a "Concept for strengthening African capabilities for the prevention, management and resolution of conflicts" in 2006, and the JAES in 2007. The JAES identified peace, security, and governance among the four areas for the EU partnership with Africa.[46] Besides making a commitment to support the full implementation of APSA, the strategy also endorsed the principles of

> equality, based on mutual recognition and respect for institutions and the definition of mutual collective interests; partnership, i.e. developing links based on political and commercial cooperation; (and) ownership, i.e. strategies and development policies being country-owned and not imposed from the outside.[47]

The EU has been particularly heavily involved in supporting APSA. Since the establishment of its African Peace Facility (APF) in 2004, the EU has emerged as the AU's leading partner in the implementation of its peace, security, and governance agendas, and has provided 740 million euros in funding to this end. From 2007 the range of activities of the Facility were expanded, and funding goes towards capacity building, PSOs, and early response mechanisms.[48] In practical terms, the EU has supported the AU peacemaking efforts in Darfur, Somalia, Guinea Bissau, Mali, the Central African Republic (CAR), and the operationalization of APSA through the APF. In its first phase (2003–07), the EU disbursed 250 million euros, which mostly went to support AMIS. In the second phase (2008–10), 300 million euros were sent directly to the AU so as to promote the principles of African "ownership," African "solidarity," and the creation of "conditions" for African development.[49] Additionally, the EU has funded the "Instrument for Stability (IfS)," which has been supporting AU mediation efforts and the strengthening of the regional capacities for peacekeeping. The EU has also channeled funds to support the implementation of the Common African Defence and Security Policy (CADSP) and the establishment of the African Standby Force (ASF) and peacekeeping operations in Sudan and Somalia.

An evaluation of the APF carried out in 2013 found that if it were not for this European funding, APSA "might ... not have occurred due to African resource constraints and variable commitment by African states to the APSA project."[50] However, the APF's support of APSA seems to have mainly concentrated on its peacekeeping objective by spending 90 percent of its funds on PSOs in the Comoros, the CAR, Mali, Somalia,[51] and Sudan.[52] The remaining funds were spent on supporting the "operationalization of APSA," the AU-Regional Economic Communities/Regional Mechanism (RECs/RM) Liaison Offices (LOs),[53] the AU Liaison Offices in post-conflict countries, early warning, mediation efforts, AU PSD salaries,[54] and the Peace Academy. The APF assessment team pointed out that this clearly showed that the APF has yet to identify its "comparative advantage." Nonetheless, it is obvious that it has a keen interest in areas that allow the EU to collect information (Early and Response Mechanism), and to be noticed in action (PSOs).

The EU has faced a number of challenges while supporting APSA through the APF. Among these is "a serious dilemma" of either (1) continuing to disburse financial assistance to African partners (the AU and the RMs) to support the so-called "African solutions" under the principle of "African ownership" – despite their serious capacity challenges in utilizing the funds, or (2) deploying its own personnel to build a bureaucracy "to effectively manage APF activities and monitor the use of APF funding, tasks which require a presence both in Brussels and in Africa."[55]

As a result of competition from other partners – such as the US, which has a keen but somewhat different interest in an African security agenda – the EU has to tread carefully since the AU, the RECs, and the RMs are now constantly being encouraged from abroad to pay more attention to issues such as piracy, terrorism, weapons of mass destruction, security sector reform, and radicalization. Indeed, there is usually tension among donors over which issue or agenda should be given top priority.

The EU has not been able to measure the effectiveness of its support over the years since the institutional base of the AU/RECs/RMs has proved too weak to provide a solid base upon which to carry out an assessment. While aware that the PSD has failed to clearly articulate the AU's peace and security agenda, and provide strategic planning for APSA, the EU has not only glossed over these weaknesses, it has continued to sustain this state of affairs by claiming it respects the principle of "African ownership."

What might be the basis of this apparent EU generosity? The evaluation team noted that the APF has "enhanced political credibility and influence" of the EU in Africa. Supporting Africans in directly addressing their own violent conflicts has many benefits. As was explained in Chapter 4, this strategic disposition is underpinned by numerous factors, including the fact that it is cheaper to pay for an African life than a European one, both financially and politically. Some of the EU calculations, including its generosity to Africa, are shared by the US.

The United States

The life of the AU has coincided with an important period in the reassessment of US global strategy. As the AU was in the process of being founded, New York and Washington experienced, in September 2001, the most devastating terrorist attack carried out by the al-Qaida network. As a result, the AU-US relationship could be summarized in two words: terrorism and AFRICOM. Counter-terrorism calculations shaped the initial US approach to the AU, while AFRICOM has largely shaped US answers to all AU and African problems. Even the US response to the Ebola epidemic in West Africa in late 2014 was handled by AFRICOM. For this reason it is plausible to argue that the US relationship with the AU has, to a great extent, been shaped and driven by American strategic interests defined by its global War on Terror. The US has come to regard and treat the AU as an important instrument for waging this war.

This is not to suggest that the US has no other goals in Africa. Indeed, since the establishment of the AU one could argue that the US has had four principal and, in some ways, overlapping interests on the continent, namely: (1) countering Muslim militancy and terrorist threats to its security and geostrategic goals; (2) securing access to vital natural resources; (3) creating better opportunities for US companies to do business in a rising Africa; and (4) countering rapidly developing Chinese influence on the continent.[56]

The first interest has been pursued using bilateral programs as well as some contributions to APSA. The second has largely been pursued bilaterally, while the other two have involved competing for influence both bilaterally and through the AU. The US has identified the AU and APSA as a means of enhancing its bilateral relations with African countries by maintaining or giving the impression that it is backing "African solutions to African problems." The US government has used the AU to blunt opposition to AFRICOM, as well as to legitimize and to effectively stamp it on the continent. When AFRICOM was launched in 2007 there was widespread opposition across the continent; no country offered to host it.[57] Consequently, it was headquartered in Stuttgart, Germany, but it aims to use African proxies to deter and defeat "transnational threats" to "US national interests."[58]

In fact, key Bush and Obama administration national security policy documents have identified the need to "embrace effective partnerships" with the AU and African states to counter common security threats.[59] The Obama administration's belated June 2012 US Strategy Towards Sub-Saharan Africa, suggested that the US-Africa relationship would be based upon the principles of mutual responsibility and mutual respect, while indicating that in its view the AU "serves as an important leader on political, diplomatic, and peacekeeping issues across the continent."[60] The AU-US partnership is also driven partly by its cost-efficiency: "In an era of declining defense budgets, working with African countries in addressing security challenges on the continent is an effort to prevent conflict and share the cost of global security."[61] It is, however, sold to Africa as an instrument for promoting its "security, stability and prosperity."

Through AFRICOM, the US has supported elements of APSA, including the establishment of the ASF and training the personnel in the Peace Support Operations Division. It has also provided over $250 million in funding to AMISOM.[62] However, AFRICOM's first major military operation, Operation Odyssey Dawn, was the attack on Libyan government positions in March 2011 as part of the UN-sanctioned no-fly zone,[63] an intervention that was opposed and criticized by the AU.[64] In the Libyan case, the US and its international allies privileged their partnerships with more compliant regional organizations – the Arab League and the Gulf Cooperation Council – over their partnership with the AU.

US-AU relations have evolved over the years and taken different forms. In October 1996 the Bill Clinton administration established the Africa Crisis Response Initiative (ACRI), which was designed to facilitate the training of up to 12,000 African troops who would participate in humanitarian crises on the continent. In 2004 ACRI was changed to the African Contingency Operations Training and Assistance (ACOTA), and to the Global Peace Operations Initiative (GPOI) in 2005. Since 2007 AFRICOM has been the vehicle for delivering most training, equipment, logistical, and technical assistance. As of 2014 AFRICOM was active in more than 40 African countries.

US diplomatic cables released by Wikileaks reveal the very intricate plan of using the AU and its top leadership to give AFRICOM an African foothold, despite opposition such as the 2007 Pan-African Parliament (PAP) vote that rejected the establishment of American military bases on African soil.[65] In a clear illustration of how the AU lacks common positions within its organs, the Commission chairperson, Alpha Konare, informed the Americans on November 8, 2007, that he was pleased with their "decision to establish AFRICOM" since it would act as a check on a Europe that was steering Africa off "the course." He then asserted that despite Africa's historical ties to Europe, it was in dire need of "US assistance." He advised the Americans to overlook those opposing AFRICOM on the basis that it could be used to enhance US interests in Africa such as securing strategic resources and checking the influence of China. While urging the establishment of AFRICOM headquarters in Africa in order to serve the interests of the US "better," Konare cautioned against some countries – in particular Liberia – that were campaigning to host it for financial motivations. The Americans also got Konare to commit the AU to establish the ASF using "a mixing of EU, UN, and US models," and to request assistance from the US to implement "a common defense policy."

After Konare was replaced in January 2008, the Americans established a similar relationship with his successor, Jean Ping. In a meeting between Ping and the then AFRICOM commander, General William Ward, at the AU's headquarters on August 20, 2008, the discussion focused on how AFRICOM and the AU could collaborate "in combating narco-trafficking through Africa" and in preventing and resolving African conflicts. While offering to assist the AU to deal with security threats such as narco-trafficking, terrorism, illegal fishing, and piracy, the US insisted that the AU approach its member states to seek direct US assistance. The US also heavily relied on the AUC leadership to identify countries which would be ideal for AFRICOM to work with, and how to address some of the security threats. For instance, Ping suggested to General Ward that former Angolan foreign, minister Joao Bernardo de Miranda – the AU's envoy to Guinea Bissau – should "brief AFRICOM on the narco-trafficking issue" since he knew which elements within the Guinea Bissau government "might be willing to cooperate with the international community." He told the Americans: "[T]he AU lacks the capacity to fend off these illicit activities," and requested their assistance. While underscoring AFRICOM's willingness to assist countries that were subject to security threats, General Ward stressed AFRICOM's willingness to directly help nations that sought US aid to take "action against smugglers, pirates, and illegal fishermen." His predecessor, Konare, had also on November 8, 2007, shared with the Americans "his concern about the growing influence of Islam in Africa, noting that seventeen percent of the total current Muslim population in the continent is of Middle Eastern origin," and warned "that what [was then] ... happening in the UK could happen in Africa if Africans do not" get support from external partners such as the US.

Through manipulation of the AUC leadership, AFRICOM was able to set up a Command, Control, and Communication Information System for the AU by selling it as a "communication package" that would boost its integration and communications capacity in PSOs. This was to be achieved by providing a High Frequency radio voice network, with a follow-on Very Small Aperture Terminal capability. The AU was told the system would facilitate interoperability and information sharing between the AU headquarters in Addis Ababa, the five headquarters of the regional ASF brigades, and other units and facilities related to the ASF, by linking them through "voice, data, and fax." The system was also to be used "to support regional peacekeeping and counter-narcotics efforts through Global Peace Operations Initiative (GPOI) funding." Additionally, AFRICOM and Mitre Corporation collaborated to take control of the previously bought communications gear by shipping it to Stuttgart to be reconfigured before being handed over to the AU. AFRICOM has plans to establish an operations center on AU premises in a German-constructed building that will house the peace and security department.[66] In Somalia, AFRICOM has procured "airtime cards for the AMISOM Commanders' satellite phones" and contracted EMC Corporation "to reset" the modems and repair the VSAT. AFRICOM has also embedded its "technical and military advisers" in the AU PSD to directly monitor its peace and security activities and to generate "technical" documents and reports on APSA.[67]

AFRICOM seems to have deeply penetrated the psyche of the AU's leaders. It has proved able to extract from them a commitment to resolve Africa's peace, security, and governance challenges. In one instance, Ping complained that Africans suffered from problems of "internalizing universal values" such as "democracy, respect for human rights, good governance, and the rule of law;" pointed out the hopelessness of countries such as Guinea, where "everything is possible;" and criticized Gaddafi for complicating AU actions in places such as Mauritania, while assuring the US that the AU shared its position that "al-Qaida" is a key "threat" to international security. Whenever such laundry lists were presented, the Americans always offered AFRICOM as the "solution" to Africa's peace and security challenges.[68]

Despite widespread protestations and warnings that AFRICOM would be used to get rid of leaders who the West did not like, such as Gaddafi, the Americans have been able to establish it with the encouragement of the AU. In fact, AFRICOM is well entrenched in the AU and its representatives actively take part in the execution of its security agenda – particularly on matters relating to Muslim terrorism and nuclear proliferation. In one of its high-profile operations, AFRICOM is supposedly working closely with the AU to catch the elusive and mysterious Joseph Kony of the Lord's Resistance Army. AFRICOM has also set up drone stations and joint operations with many African states, including Somalia, Ethiopia, the Seychelles, South Sudan, Uganda, the CAR, the Democratic Republic of Congo (DRC), Egypt, and Ghana. In December 2012 the Obama administration announced that it was dispatching 3,500 Special Forces and military trainers to 35 African states as part of its counter-terrorism efforts. AFRICOM's most significant operations so far have been the ousting from power of Gaddafi – which led to his summary execution by Libyan rebels – and the special operations in Somalia against Al-Shabaab militants.

So far, the US has utilized its relations with the AU to pursue transnational terrorists and to ensure that AFRICOM provides answers to most of the problems that Africans face, but it is also concerned about the growing influence of China and other emerging countries in Africa.

China

While Beijing highlights Chinese solidarity with African governments during the decolonization period, it has been over the last 15 years that Chinese engagement with Africa has developed into one of the most significant of the continent's external relationships – one that has changed the dynamics of existing Western influence and strategies. China's global rise has been well documented and Africa has been, and will continue to be, an important element of Chinese economic growth as well as a region in which Beijing can continue to demonstrate China's growing global power and status. China has sought, in particular, to gain greater access to African natural resources to fuel its own industrialization program. Its principal method for doing this has been to exchange the extraction and exportation of African resources to China, in return for Chinese-funded (and often Chinese-built) critical infrastructure projects. China has also recently become more involved in Africa's peace and security affairs, including the deployment of Chinese peacekeepers.[69] Most symbolically, the Chinese government provided a grant of $200 million to build a glitzy, ultra-modern, AU Conference office building – which was opened in January 2012.[70]

The AU has indicated that there is a "need to align the partnership" to the AU's strategic objectives, while Chinese funding of the "magnificent" new AU headquarters is seen as "testimony to the real value this partnership brings to Africa."[71] According to one view, Chinese investments in Africa

> generate multiple layers of benefits for China, including contracts for Chinese service companies, the relocation of labour-intensive, heavy-pollution industries from China, political favours extracted from African governments on foreign policy issues at multilateral forums, such as the UN, and a positive international image of China being a "responsible stakeholder."[72]

Regular high-level meetings are held between the Chinese government and African governments. Most prominently, the ministerial-level Forum on China-Africa Cooperation (FOCAC) was established in Beijing in 2000 "for collective consultation and dialogue and as a cooperation mechanism among developing countries."[73] After the initial Beijing meeting, four subsequent FOCAC meetings have been held: Addis Ababa (2003), Beijing (2006, at summit level), Sharm el-Sheikh (2009), and Beijing (2012).[74] These summits have resulted in massive Chinese investment in Africa, and since 2012 China has been its largest trading partner.[75]

The Chinese have designed a specific mode of engaging the AU that is reflective of their understanding of the African realities and the prevailing opportunities on the continent. For instance, the Chinese stay out of African affairs and do not present themselves as saviors of desperate African souls or being in possession of the elixir that will wipe out African problems. They know what they want and communicate that directly to the Africans. They present their interests as being mutually beneficial. These interests are presented in strictly economic terms and the relations that are forged thereafter are mainly economic. They do not proselytize, lecture, or impose religious, ideological, or economic views or models on Africans. However, it can be argued that the Chinese approach also has important implications for human security in Africa. While an approach emphasizing the sovereignty of African governments is a welcome one in the context of a history of colonial and Cold War interference in African affairs, the extent to which this has translated to a privileging of regime security over the human security of African peoples may ultimately undermine the AU's stated aims of advancing peace, security, and good governance. An approach that reinforces the practice of "responsible sovereignty" by African governments (and by extension, the AU) is perhaps the best hope of achieving these important aims in the face of growing external engagement with the continent by China and other major powers.

Conclusion: evaluating the AU's management of key external relations

The deformed establishment of APSA is partly to blame for the lack of coherence in the way the international partners support it. There is usually a bazaar-like atmosphere during meetings that are called to pledge support to APSA, with partners freely "picking and choosing" activities that best enhance their own national interests. During these meetings the representatives of the AU partners compete with each other to take ownership of activities that will give their respective countries high visibility in Africa and in their home countries. In the final analysis, the partners do not coordinate their assistance efforts and the AU is consequently overwhelmed by an outpouring of support. The AU not only lacks the capacity to coordinate external support, it has also been unable to define the appropriateness of such support or target its priority areas. The AU also lacks the capacity to utilize these funds effectively, and instead prefers to use them to fund day-to-day activities such as meetings and travel expenses. While the partners know that the AU is incapable of efficiently utilizing such funds, they have established their own parallel programs and activities in the name of the AU.[76] This means it is not possible to measure the impact of this funding on the prevention, management, and resolution of conflicts since their assessments are tailored to prove to the donor countries' own populations and policy makers that their funds are not being wasted. As such, it is very difficult to measure the effectiveness of partner support to the implementation of the AU peace and security agenda. Most of the "assessment reports" have been produced by European consultants who have become de facto AU staffers by virtue of being contracted since 2005 to carry out various "studies." These consultants have completely changed the meaning and conceptualization of APSA, while also redefining what the peace and security agenda should be and what the partners should fund.

In many cases the donors and the AU pretend to each other that they have a common understanding of both African "problems" and "solutions." While the AU passionately insists on "owning" the "African solution," the partners offer no objection to this and promptly set about deciding how this "solution" should be conceived and implemented. If the high-level statements of African leaders endorsing the "African solutions to African problems" mantra are used to measure "African ownership," then there is no doubt that it has a clear rhetorical ownership. But the practical picture is that high-sounding statements extolling African solutions are not financially backed by continental sources. The burden of financing these "African solutions" has been handed over to external partners. While giving Africans a false psychological feeling of ownership, the partners have redefined and driven the "solutions" to "African problems" by imposing stringent funding conditions and by deploying their own technical experts to the AU. In other words, APSA is conceptually and technically not African. The implementation of the APSA is led and financed by foreigners, and it is not fully reflective of Africa's peace and security agenda.

The record so far indicates that the AU is not yet able to forge and manage partnerships in ways that genuinely promote its peace, security, and governance agendas, but it is also unable to effect any change in this engagement for various reasons. One of these is the lack of funds. Another is the lack of appropriate knowledge. It is through the construction of its own knowledge base that the AU might, in the future, realize the ultimate dream of "African solutions to African problems."

Notes

1 There are other international actors, such as the International Committee of the Red Cross and Oxfam, which have entered into deals with the AU to promote their own specific agendas. This chapter does not consider such actors, as well as the African diaspora, even though the AU has designated the diaspora as its sixth region. The potential for the African diaspora to influence the bilateral relations with Africa of the states in which they are living remains, but such influence is difficult to document directly. See, for example, Melissa Phillips, "Migration and Australian Foreign Policy Towards Africa: The Place of Australia's African Transnational Communities" in David Mickler and Tanya Lyons (eds) *New Engagement: Contemporary Australian Foreign Policy Towards Africa* (Melbourne: Melbourne University Press) (2013).

2 In this context, Ian Taylor wisely reminds us to be wary of making firm distinctions between non-state actors and states, and between Africa and "the world." See Ian Taylor, *The International Relations of Sub-Saharan Africa* (New York and London: Continuum) (2010): 1–2.

3 See Pedraig Carmody, *The New Scramble for Africa* (Cambridge, UK, and Malden, MA: Polity) (2011). In 2011, in the face of China's rapid expansion into Africa, the then-US secretary of state, Hillary Clinton, warned of a "new colonialism" sweeping the continent. See "Clinton Warns Against 'New Colonialism' in Africa", *Reuters*, June 11, 2011. Available at: www.reuters.com/article/2011/06/11/us-clinton-africa-idUSTRE75A0RI20110611 (last accessed March 18, 2015).

4 See, for example, Bob Carr, "Africa Down Under," speech by Australian foreign minister, Perth, August 29, 2012. Available at: http://foreignminister.gov.au/speeches/2012/bc_sp_120829.html (last accessed March 18, 2015).

5 Kwame Nkrumah, *Dark Days in Ghana* (London: Panaf Books) (1968): 157–8.

6 Again, we should be careful to distinguish between the interests of African citizens and the interests of their governments, which too often are in tension.

7 CAAU, Preamble.

8 CAAU, Article 3 [d].

9 Protocol on amendments to the CAAU, Article 3 [p].

10 Protocol on amendments to the CAAU, Article 4 [q].

11 Protocol Relating to the Establishment of the Peace and Security Council of the African Union, Article 7 [l].

12 Protocol Relating to the Establishment of the Peace and Security Council, Articles 12 [3]; 13 [4], [15], [16]; 21 [3].

13 African Union, "Africa's Strategic Partnerships," available at: www.au.int/en/partnerships (last accessed March 18, 2015).

14 Ibid.: 1.

15 Ibid.

16 Ibid.

17 Ibid.

18 F. Wafula Okumu and Samuel M. Makinda, "Engaging with Contemporary Africa: Key Contexts for External Actors" in Mickler and Lyons (eds) *New Engagement*: 18–19.

19 Ibid.

20 African Union Executive Council, "Decisions", EX.CL/Dec.668–695 (XX), Twentieth Ordinary Session, January 23–27, 2012, Addis Ababa, Ethiopia.

21 African Union, "Welcome Remarks by HE Dr. Nkosazana Damini Zuma Chairperson of the African Union Commission at the Opening Session of the 22nd Ordinary Session of the Executive Council," Addis Ababa, January 24, 2013. Available at: http://summits.au.int/en/20thsummit/speeches/welcome-remarks-he-dr-nkosazana-dlamini-zuma-chairperson-african-union-commiss-0 (last accessed March 18, 2015).

22 African Union Executive Council, "Decisions", EX.CL/Dec.726–766 (XXII), Twenty-Second Ordinary Session, January 21–25, 2013, Addis Ababa, Ethiopia.

23 African Union Executive Council, "Decision on the Report of the PRC Sub-Committee on Multilateral Cooperation with Respect to Africa's Strategic Partnerships," Doc. ECX.CL/802 (XXIV) iv, Twenty-Fourth Ordinary Session, January 21–28, 2014, Addis Ababa, Ethiopia. Available at:http://au.int/en/content/addis-ababa-21-28-january-2014-executive-council-twenty-fourth-ordinary-session (last accessed March 18, 2015).

24 Charter of the United Nations, Article 52.

25 Ibid., Articles 52, 53, 54.

26 United Nations Department of Political Affairs, "United Nations – African Union Cooperation," available at: www.un.org/wcm/content/site/undpa/main/activities_by_region/africa/unlo (last accessed March 18, 2015).

27 UN Security Council, "Report of the Secretary-General on the Relationship between the United Nations and Regional Organizations, in Particular the African Union, in the Maintenance of International Peace and Security," S/2008/186 (April 7, 2008): 2.

28 Zeryhun Kassa, "Ethiopia, UNOAU Signs Host Country Agreement," *all Africa*, June 14, 2013. Available at: http://allafrica.com/stories/201306170755.html (last accessed March 18, 2015); United Nations Secretary-General, "Secretary-General Appoints Haile Menkerios of South Africa as Special Representative to the African Union," SG/A/1406, press release, UN Department of Public Information, May 17, 2013. Available at: www.un.org/News/Press/docs/2013/sga1406.doc.htm. Last accessed on May 8, 2015.

29 United Nations General Assembly, "Letter Dated 11 December 2006 from the Secretary-General Addressed to the President of the General Assembly," A/61/630 (December 12, 2006). Available at: www.un.org/ga/search/view_doc.asp?symbol=A/61/630 (last accessed March 18, 2015).

30 Ibid.

31 United Nations General Assembly, "Cooperation Between the United Nations and Regional and other Organizations: Report of the Secretary-General," A/61/256 (August 26, 2006): 5. Available at: www.un.org/ga/search/view_doc.asp?symbol=A/61/256 (last accessed March 18, 2015).

32 UN Security Council, "Report of the Secretary-General on the Relationship between the United Nations and Regional Organizations, in Particular the African Union, in the Maintenance of International Peace and Security," S/2008/186 (April 7, 2008): 2.

33 UN Security Council, Resolution 1809 (2008), S/RES/1809 (April 16, 2008).

34 See David Mickler, "UNAMID: A Hybrid Solution to a Human Security Problem in Darfur?" *Conflict, Security and Development*, vol. 13, no. 5 (2013): 487–511.

35 See Bah A. Sarjoh, "Consolidating Regional Mediation Approaches: Addressing the Question of Partnerships: Remarks at the Fourth AU High-Level Retreat on the Promotion of Peace, Security and Stability in Africa: The AU's 2013 Golden Jubilee Retreat", October 29–30, 2013, Abidjan, Côte d'Ivoire.

36 However, the renaming of the AU Mission in Burundi (AMIB) as the UN Mission in Burundi (UNMIB) stands out as an example of a smooth transition with many useful lessons for similar transitions in the future.

37 Thomas G. Weiss and Martin Welz, "The UN and the African Union in Mali and beyond: A Shotgun Wedding?" *International Affairs*, vol. 90, no. 4 (2014): 904.

38 See Olaf Bachmann, "The African Standby Force: External Support to an 'African Solution to African Problems'?" *IDS Research Report*, no. 67 (April 2011): 17.

39 African Union, "Africa's Strategic Partnerships": 1–2; European Union, "The Continental Approach," available at: www.eeas.europa.eu/africa/continental/index_en.htm (last accessed March 18, 2015).

40 European Union, "The Continental Approach."

41 Africa-EU Partnership, "European Union," available at: www.africa-eu-partnership.org/about-us/partners/european-union (last accessed March 18, 2015).

42 Ibid.

43 Ibid.

44 Africa-EU Partnership, "How it Works," available at: www.africa-eu-partnership.org/about-us/how-it-works (last accessed March 18, 2015).

45 African Union, "Permanent Mission to the European Union and the ACP – Brussels Office," available at: http://au.int/en/commission/permanent-mission-european-union-and-acp-brussels-office (last accessed March 18, 2015); Delegation of the European Union to the African Union, "Delegation to the African Union," available at: http://eeas.europa.eu/delegations/african_union/index_en.htm (last accessed March 18, 2015).

46 The other areas were trade and regional integration, and MDG issues.

47 See EU Strategy for Africa, available at: http://europa.eu/legislation_summaries/development/african_caribbean_pacific_states/r12540_en.htm (last accessed March 18, 2015).

48 European Commission, "African Peace Facility," available at: http://ec.europa.eu/europeaid/where/acp/regional-cooperation/peace/index_en.htm (link no longer accessible).

49 See "The African Peace Facility," available at: http://ec.europa.eu/world/peace/geographical_themes/africa/african_peace/index_en.htm (last accessed March 18, 2015).

50 See the following report: "African Peace Facility Evaluation: Reviewing the Overall Implementation of the APF as an Instrument for African Efforts to Manage Conflicts on the Continent," November 2013. Available at: www.africa-eu-partnership.org/sites/default/files/documents/apf_evaluation_final_report.pdf (last accessed March 18, 2015).

51 The APF has contributed 443.9 million euros since 2007. This amount covered troop allowances (military and police), a mission subsistence allowance

of \$90/day, civilian salaries, travel costs, running and administrative costs, and compensation for death and injury. See APF Assessment Annex: 61.

52 The APF pays the allowances of troops serving in these peace missions.

53 These are the REC/RM Liaison Offices to the AU, and the AU Liaison Offices to the RECs/RMs.

54 It is notable that the ASF financed almost half of the PSD staff (the Peace Support Operations Division; conflict prevention and early warning; the post-conflict reconstruction development unit; the defense and security division; and the PSC), 80 percent of which are externally funded.

55 "African Peace Facility Evaluation."

56 See Alexis Habiyaremye, "CHINAFRIQUE, AFRICOM, and African Natural Resources: A Modern Scramble for Africa?" *Whitehead Journal of Diplomacy and International Relations* (Winter/Spring 2011).

57 For a discussion of the initial African skepticism over AFRICOM, see Samuel M. Makinda, "Why AFRICOM Has Not Won Over Africans," Center for Strategic & International Studies, Washington DC (November 2007). Available at: http://csis.org/publication/why-africom-has-not-won-o ver-africans (last accessed March 18, 2015); and Wafula Okumu, "Africa Command: Opportunity for Enhanced Engagement or the Militarization of US-Africa Relations?" Testimony before the US House of Representatives, Committee on Foreign Affairs, Subcommittee on Africa and Global Health (August 2, 2007).

58 United States Africa Command, "About the Command," available at: www. africom.mil/about-the-command (last accessed March 18, 2015).

59 Lauren Ploch, "Africa Command: U.S. Strategic Interests and the Role of the U.S. Military in Africa," Congressional Research Service, Report for US Congress, RL34004 (July 22, 2011): 14–15. The quotation cited is from the 2010 National Security Strategy of the United States.

60 The White House, *U.S. Strategy Towards Sub-Saharan Africa* (Washington DC) (June 2012): 1.

61 Lesley Ann Warner, "Advancing Peace and Security in Africa" in Africa Growth Initiative, *Top Five Reasons Why Africa Should be a Priority for the United States* (Washington DC: The Brookings Institution) (2013): 3–4.

62 US Department of State, "The United States and the African Union."

63 Ploch, "Africa Command": 1.

64 "AU's Opposition to Military Intervention Ignored by UNSC, Obama" in *Sudan Tribune*, March 18, 2011. Available at: www.sudantribune.com/spip. php?article38332 (last accessed March 18, 2015).

65 Ploch, "Africa Command": 25.

66 According to leaked US cables, AFRICOM has already ensured "that the blueprints contain proper specifications to accommodate a large enough space and wiring needed for the new Operations Center room" that it will be setting up. See www.wikileaks.org/plusd/cables/09ADDISABABA1242. html. Last accessed on May 8, 2015.

67 All equipment purchased and donated to the AU is shipped to Stuttgart for reconfiguration before being handed over.

68 On March 25, 2008, Mary Yates also met with Ramtane Lamamra – the AU Commissioner for Peace and Security at AU headquarters – to discuss AFRICOM's plans to extend into North Africa through military cooperation arrangements, and the AU's North African Standby Brigade, and in addressing maritime security challenges facing Africa. The Americans then

went ahead to offer Lamamra "assistance in" developing: a "maritime strategy"; writing a white paper on maritime security needs, and possible programs to present at an upcoming meeting of ministers and chiefs of defense; and to rally other partners to cooperate with it in enhancing Africa's maritime security.

69 Wu Zhengyu and Ian Taylor, "From Refusal to Engagement: Chinese Contributions to Peacekeeping in Africa," *Journal of Contemporary African Studies*, vol. 29, no. 2 (2011): 137–54.

70 Yara Bayoumi, "Glitzy New AU Headquarters a Symbol of China-Africa Ties," Reuters, Addis Ababa, January 29, 2012. Available at: www.reuters.com/article/2012/01/29/ozatp-africa-china-idAFJO E80S00K20120129 (last accessed March 18, 2015). The Chinese building was designed in China and built by Chinese workers using Chinese materials. The only African contribution came from the Ethiopian government, which donated the land it stands on. Although the building has been handed over to the AU, the Chinese still maintain it. The fear is that it will be too expensive to maintain once it is wholly handed over to the AU.

71 African Union, "Africa's Strategic Partnerships": 3.

72 Yun Sun, "China in Africa: Implications for U.S. Competition and Diplomacy" in Africa Growth Initiative, *Top Five Reasons Why Africa Should be a Priority for the United States* (Washington DC: The Brookings Institution) (2013): 6.

73 African Union, "Africa's Strategic Partnerships": 3.

74 The AUC moved from observer status to full member status of the FOCAC in October 2011.

75 See Chantelle Benjamin, "Africa Isn't a Big Bull in China's Shop" in *Mail & Guardian*, June 21, 2013. Available at: http://mg.co.za/article/2013-06-21-00-africa-isnt-a-big-bull-in-chinas-shop (last accessed March 18, 2015). Africa-China relations revolve around trade in minerals, oil and gas, finance, processing, manufacturing, trade-related services, agriculture, transportation, information communications technology, and pharmaceuticals. Sino-African trade amounted to nearly $200 billion in 2012, compared to $166.3 billion in 2011.

76 The best example is the German Gesellschaft für Internationale Zusammenarbeit (GIZ), which used the AU Border Programme as cover for establishing its own program on borders in Africa.

6   Knowledge and development[1]

Knowledge is central to Africa's peace, security, development, and good governance. It is knowledge that drives globalization, stock markets, changes in information technology, and strategies to tackle the Ebola virus and HIV/AIDS. The successful pursuit of democratization, gender equality, environmental management, and sustainable development is predicated upon the rejection of obsolescent knowledge and the promotion of a knowledge renaissance. Without certain types of knowledge, Africa would stagnate economically, remain insecure, and be unable to formulate effective and progressive governance strategies.

Therefore, it is appropriate that one of the objectives of the African Union (AU), as articulated in Article 3(m) of the Constitutive Act, is to advance "the development of the continent by promoting research in all fields, in particular in science and technology." The Constitutive Act also requires the Executive Council (EC) to coordinate and take decisions on "education, culture, health and human resource development" and on "science and technology." Moreover, the Constitutive Act established two Specialized Technical Committees (STCs) to deal with knowledge and innovation: the Committee on Industry, Science and Technology, Energy, Natural Resources, and the Environment; and the Committee on Education, Culture, and Human Resources. In addition, the Science and Technology department within the Commission deals with ideas, knowledge, and innovation. Thus, knowledge and its application in development activities are at the core of the Union's objectives.

There is a correlation between knowledge, development, peace, and global influence. If the AU were to exercise influence in world affairs, its member states would need to participate in the control of the fountains of knowledge. Africa's abject poverty and the lack of global influence appear to stem in part from its weak knowledge base in science, technology, and innovation. According to the World Bank's knowledge economy index (2012), the highest-ranking African country was Mauritius at 62 out of 144, followed by South Africa (67), and Tunisia (80). In terms of world regions, Africa came last of eight, after South Asia (seven) and the Middle East (six).

Ali Mazrui succinctly underlined the power of knowledge and ideas when he observed: "The entire international system of stratification has come to be based not on 'who owns what' but on 'who knows what.'"[2] Urging African policy makers to pay more attention to innovation and science and technology, Calestous Juma has argued: "Much of the reference to Africa in international forums has focused on the continent's natural wealth. However, natural resource endowment is not a sufficient basis for economic growth; it must be accompanied by investments in science and technology."[3] Investment in science and technology implies innovation as well as the establishment of foundations for knowledge production.

For the purposes of this chapter, the term "knowledge" includes, but is not limited to, formal and informal education and scientific know-how. It may be acquired through many sources, including books, journals, the internet, educational institutions, research centers, internships, workshops, and conferences. It is no wonder that the World Bank's knowledge economy index rests on four pillars: economic incentive, innovation, education, and information and communications technology (ICT) infrastructure. However, these pillars cannot always be taken for granted. For example, in a 2014 study of the knowledge economy and financial sector competition in Africa, Simplice Asongu found that "education and innovation in terms of scientific and technical publications broadly bear an inverse nexus with financial development."[4] The study also concluded that "ICT generally has a positive incidence on all financial sectors but increases the non-formal sector to the detriment of the formal sector."[5]

Thus, knowledge is a double-edged sword that can be used for destruction or for construction. This is because knowledge comes in various forms and shapes. For example, there is forward-looking and backward-looking knowledge; there is knowledge that reinforces ethical and moral values, and knowledge that disrupts them; there is knowledge that encourages individualism and one that emphasizes communal identity; there is knowledge that encourages gender equality and one that discourages it. All forms of knowledge have been generated or invented for a reason.

There is also an intimate relationship between knowledge and the variables that underpin the argument in this book, namely: peace, security, and governance. Without these variables it would be hard to transmit and apply new ideas in Africa. Therefore, the AU's chance of tapping into global knowledge flows depends upon its ability to exploit the benefits of peace, globalization, security, and governance.

This chapter proceeds on the assumption that a strong knowledge base is a prerequisite for the attainment of the AU's goals in peace, security, and good governance. This is largely because knowledge leads to emancipation and empowerment. The rest of this chapter is divided into four sections. The first explores the global structure of knowledge and claims that Africa remains on the scientific, technological, economic, political, and military margins of the world largely because it is a net consumer – rather than a producer – of usable knowledge. The second examines the meaning of development in Africa. The third section discusses how African states could acquire a larger share in the benefits of global knowledge if they established a political and legal atmosphere that permitted innovations in science and technology, flexible working conditions, and respect for fundamental freedoms. The fourth discusses why African states might find it easier to build knowledge economies if they paid adequate attention to capacity building.

The global structure of knowledge

Africa's opportunities to benefit from global knowledge flows lie partly with the international community, and partly with Africa itself. Africa is rich in natural resources, but to turn them into consumable wealth requires a capacity to engage in appropriate knowledge-intensive processes. This can be obtained through education, social learning, and the strategic partnerships that the AU, African states, and universities could establish with institutions abroad. Through strategic partnerships Africa might build its pool of expertise in a range of disciplines such as law, medicine, policy studies, and science and technology. Africa needs to seek knowledge that can facilitate the positive aspects of globalization, sustainable development, democratic governance, and peace building. It is the AU and its members that should come up with initiatives on how they can tap into appropriate sources of knowledge. However, the donor community would need to provide training facilities and financial resources which the AU and its members can tap into. This is the way to create what a former director-general of United Nations Educational, Scientific, and Cultural Organization (UNESCO), Koichiro Matsuura, described as "societies of shared knowledge."[6]

One of the starting points for a discussion of the role of knowledge in Africa in a globalizing world is the global structure of knowledge, which is a major determinant of Africa's share of new ideas and innovations. The Western world dominates the global structure of knowledge through various means, including journals, books, conferences, and seminars that promote Western-generated forms of knowledge. For example, the refereeing process in journals is a policing exercise which ensures that only knowledge that is framed in certain ways – i.e. that which reflects American or Western standards – is accepted for publication. Even within the West, North American and western European journals differ as to what they seek. They prefer articles that utilize particular epistemological lenses and/or research methods, with a view to ensuring that only certain forms of knowledge are produced.

North American and Western domination of knowledge is also achieved through citations, which are considered a measure of the impact of publications. Whereas African scholars often cite sources from all parts of the world, North Americans and, to a certain extent, western Europeans, mainly cite fellow Westerners – even on African issues where credible African sources exist. Even textbooks written by Africans for fellow Africans rely heavily on Western-generated epistemological and methodological perspectives and fail to question the normative and political dimensions of the paradigms that they utilize. A good example is the 1999 edition of *Power, Wealth and Global Order: An International Relations Textbook for Africa.*[7] This is a very good book from the point of view of orthodox International Relations theories. However, it makes no effort to explore the perceptions of us/ them, self/other and outside/inside in African traditions. Its bibliography includes one item by Kwame Nkrumah, but it lists no publication by other African thinkers who played important roles in shaping Africa's perceptions of its relations with the rest of the world – such as Frantz Fanon, Julius Nyerere, Leopold Senghor, and Sekou Toure.

As a net consumer rather than a net producer of knowledge, Africa suffers several disadvantages. First, the AU and its members apply knowledge that was shaped by non-African contexts, which might have little or no relevance for African conditions. Knowledge production is a social and political process that reflects the historical, cultural, and institutional milieu of its producers. Knowledge is constructed for a social, scientific, or political purpose, and for a community of scholars or policy makers. In interpreting data, researchers are often influenced by their cultural, ideological, or ethical values. In disseminating the findings of research, scholars emphasize some of the facts but ignore others, depending on their audience and preferences. What Robert Cox said about theory equally applies to knowledge. He argued: "Theory is always for someone and for some purpose. All theories have a perspective. Perspectives derive from a position in time and space, specifically social and political time and space."[8]

Moreover, when researchers convey their findings, they do so in language which cannot be value-neutral. In Sub-Saharan Africa this linguistic factor assumes an extra dimension because the language for the transmission of ideas is often a borrowed one: English, French, and Portuguese. As knowledge construction is a social and political process, it has to be recognized that while scholars may engage in serious research and may treat all evidence consistently, they cannot provide value-free knowledge.

Second, all knowledge is contestable and, in some cases, transient, and Africa is disadvantaged because it plays no role in the adjudication of knowledge claims. The transient character of knowledge suggests that while society may accept today's scientific findings, it should not lose sight of the possibility that these findings may be challenged tomorrow.

A good recent example of a successful contestation of established knowledge was the challenge to the claim by medical science that peptic ulcers were caused by excessive acidity in the stomach. For many years antacids were prescribed, and are still prescribed in many African countries. But in the early 1980s a study in Western Australia found that the cause of stomach ulcers was not acidity, but rather the bacteria *helicobacter pylori*. Excessive acidity was a symptom, not a cause. The study established that "100 percent of patients with duodenal ulcer and 80 percent of those with gastric ulcer" had *helicobacter pylori*.[9] This was a big threat to the pharmaceutical companies – which manufactured antacids – and they initially challenged the study using other gastro-enterologists and histopathologists to try to discredit the two medical researchers, Barry J. Marshall and J. Robin Warren, who had discovered *helicobacter pylori*. However, it is now generally accepted that *helicobacter pylori* "is the cause of most gastric and duodenal ulcers, with elimination of the organism leading to healing of the ulcers and a significant reduction in the incidence of recurrence."[10] The implication of such knowledge contestations is that Africa, as a net consumer, receives only that knowledge which the knowledge brokers in the developed world consider to be socially and politically palatable.

As Andrea Useem argues:

> Research, one of the few tools – or weapons – available to professional intellectuals, is also tangled in a global political economy that tends to marginalize Africa. Public universities on the continent have minuscule research budgets, so professors must raise funds from one of the few sources of money in Africa – donor organizations like the US Agency for International Development

or the World Bank, which often promote the very orthodoxies that researchers seek to question. Intellectuals also blame their own governments for choosing foreign ideas over local ones. But ideas from the West often come with powerful incentives – the cash to put them into effect.[11]

To participate effectively in the contestation of knowledge, African researchers need excellent facilities for investigation and experimentation. Unfortunately, African states have few research facilities and centers that can challenge North American and Western intellectual dominance of various disciplines, from science, technology, and innovation, to humanities and social sciences. For instance, in security matters the South African-based Institute for Security Studies – which has offices in several other African states – is the only outfit with a continental presence. However, the dominance of the Institute for Security Studies is due to its ability to attract foreign funding for production of reports that affirm existing Euro-centric paradigms.

Robert Cox has argued that a problem-solving formula "takes the world as it finds it, with the prevailing social and power relationships and the institutions into which they are organized, as the given framework for action."[12] This approach can be useful in some circumstances, especially because it can "fix limits or parameters to a problem area." However, it is not appropriate for critiquing the Western dominance of the global security agenda.[13] To participate effectively in the global security debates, African researchers would need to combine insights from problem-solving and critical approaches. A critical approach, according to Cox, "does not take institutions and social and power relations for granted but calls them into question by concerning itself with their origins and how and whether they might be in the process of changing."[14]

Third, Africa's marginal socio-economic position vis-à-vis other parts of the world is, in large part, due to the fact that it is a net consumer of knowledge and technology. More than 150 years ago Karl Marx argued that it was the economic base that determined the prevalent ideas and institutions of a society. If this was the case during his time, it is no longer so. The global structure of knowledge and ideas plays a very important role in determining the structure of political and economic power and influence. Societies that are rich in natural resources but poor in knowledge and modern technology, like many African states, may not succeed as well as those that have both knowledge and resources. Indeed, those states that are rich in knowledge and modern technology are likely to have greater global influence, even if they are poor in natural resources. This is one of the reasons why a natural resource poor country like Japan is wealthier and globally more influential than a natural resource rich country like the Democratic Republic of Congo (DRC), which is poor in knowledge.

The current global structure of knowledge disadvantages Africa and demands that African researchers endeavor to produce knowledge that has the potential for global application. To move in this direction the AU and its members need to design strategies and mechanisms through which African researchers on the continent, and in the diaspora, can utilize globalization processes to generate new knowledge for the continent on a continuing basis.

Globalization, as we have stated, implies universalization, harmonization, and homogeneity – which ultimately result in the marginalization of African values, institutions, and norms. With regard to knowledge, globalization has been associated with according priority to "Western rational scientific knowledge ... at the expense of local knowledge."[15] It has been criticized for offering "legitimacy to the dominant liberal agenda," thereby undermining "the value of local diversity."[16] While it is true that globalization – and especially the information or digital society – has undermined indigenous and religious bases of knowledge, it has not been totally negative. In fact, some aspects of globalization have provided great opportunities that the AU and its members can exploit, but only if African governments invest in science, technology, and innovation, as well as in the humanities and social sciences. In other words, globalization has the potential to bring Africa in from the cold.

For AU and its members to make greater use of the forces of globalization, they will have to invest in the knowledge sector. With the right policies, strategies, and mechanisms, African states and their people would find that they were not absolute losers in the globalization processes. In 2006 the High-Level African Panel on Modern Biotechnology (hereafter African Panel on Biotechnology), co-chaired by Calestous Juma and Ismail Serageldin, argued that "Africa's 'distance' from the centers of technological origin is a source of creativity in applying existing technologies to new uses and therefore expands the prospects for international cooperation."[17] The 1999 United Nations Development Programme (UNDP) *Human Development Report* discussed what it called "globalization with a human face," namely a form of globalization that was predicated on ethics, equity, inclusion, human security, sustainability, and development.[18]

The challenge for the AU and African policy makers is to utilize African researchers and specialists in such a way as to construct a strong knowledge base. It is within this context that the AU can achieve its goal of development which, in turn, has an impact upon peace, security, and good governance.

What does development entail?

Development, whether sustainable or otherwise, has always carried normative and ethical connotations. It has both qualitative and quantitative aspects, meaning that it is both about the fulfilment of basic material needs and the achievement of human dignity – including meaningful participation in the affairs of the community. In terms of physical needs, development is about improvement in people's living conditions. This includes, but is not limited to, the provision of food, shelter, education, and health. However, development is also about governance – i.e. people's capacity to control their own lives and manage their own affairs. It includes capacity building, thereby implying the introduction of new ideas, standards, institutions, norms, and techniques of overcoming obstacles to human progress. All African governments claim that they should be judged on their ability to bring about development. Development, therefore, should serve as a legitimating norm for African governments.

The meaning of development has not always been as broad as it is today. After World War Two, for example, development was associated with self-sustained economic growth and the reduction of poverty, and was measured in terms of the gross domestic product (GDP). It was further assumed that the former colonial powers, and other rich countries, had a moral responsibility to provide development assistance to the newly independent African states. After all, as Walter Rodney argued, the development of Europe in the nineteenth and early twentieth centuries was part of the dialectical process through which Africa was underdeveloped and impoverished.[19]

During the course of the 1960s and 1970s, some analysts started to argue that the term development described not only attempts to redistribute resources between countries, but also the equitable redistribution of wealth *within* states. The idea of equitable development emanated from the ethical view that all people are equal and therefore entitled to the same opportunities for development. Even then, development was understood in narrow economic terms. Whenever the rich countries provided assistance to African states, it was largely in relation to major economic projects and with a view to improving GDP. But in some African states GDP was growing even as some sections of the population were living in squalid conditions. This form of development was criticized by those who argued that while growth was purely economic and vertical, development was horizontal and should be measured, in part, by the level and intensity of social services such as health, education, housing, and water.

Since the 1980s development has come to mean much more than economic progress. Policy makers and scholars now talk of development that has human, social, political, and economic dimensions. At first, this move away from the narrow economic-oriented definition of development included the provision of basic needs such as shelter, water, and sanitation, as well as education and health. This expanded definition has been reflected in the UNDP's *Human Development Report*, which, since 1990, has listed as indicators of a country's development a number of factors, including: maternal and infant mortality rates; engagement in research and development; and the bridging of the gender gap. In this sense, development describes many of the activities and processes that are encompassed in knowledge creation, human security, and peace building.

Rights and empowerment

In what way could it be argued that development is also a human right? The 1948 Universal Declaration of Human Rights (UDHR), as well as the 1966 International Covenant on Economic, Social and Cultural Rights, regarded development as a human right. Accordingly, African scholars and policy makers have argued for decades that development is a human right.

However, Western countries did not accept this until the 1990s. Indeed, the US government voted against the 1986 UN Declaration on the Right to Development. Several other Western countries abstained. More recently, the West has caught up with Africa and now considers development to be a human right. Following the 1993 World Conference on Human Rights in Vienna, the Vienna Declaration and Programme of Action stated that "democracy, development and respect for human rights and fundamental freedoms are interdependent and mutually reinforcing."[20] This has various implications for African governments. As the global norm of development is predicated on the understanding that richer countries have a moral obligation to provide assistance to poorer ones, Africa's poverty can be blamed partly on the whole world.

As the 1993 Vienna Declaration and Programme of Action stated, there is a close relationship between development and democracy. In fact, since the 1990s it has been increasingly recognized that democracy, social progress, education, and people's participation in determining their own destinies, are integral to development. The reason development and democracy are closely interrelated is that it is difficult to describe a people as "developed" unless they participate meaningfully in the management of their own community. That community may be a village, a clan, an ethnic network, a grassroots organization, a local council, or even the country as a whole. The term development has expanded to include democratization, an independent judiciary, and an open, responsible, and accountable government.

This brings into focus the relationship between knowledge, empowerment, and development. Former United Nations (UN) Secretary-General, Boutros Boutros-Ghali, appears to have had this in mind when he emphasized in 1995 that development "can only succeed if it responds to the needs of the people, and if it articulates these needs into a coherent policy framework."[21] Through capacity building seminars and workshops, knowledge can be disseminated. This will, in turn, sensitize people to liberal democratic ideas and encourage them to participate more effectively in the development process.

There is also a close relationship between development and human security. Indeed, various analysts have defined development and human security in similar terms. Like development, human security is primarily about the quality of life for individuals as well as for their communities. For example, Caroline Thomas posits that human security "has both qualitative and quantitative aspects," and that it is "pursued for the majority of humankind as part of a collective, most commonly the household, sometimes the village or the community defined along other criteria such as religion or caste."[22] Thomas further argues: "At one level, [human security] is about the fulfillment of basic material needs, and at another it is about the achievement of human dignity, which incorporates personal autonomy, control over one's life, and unhindered participation in the life of the community."[23] She observes that human security requires emancipation "from oppressive structures – be they global, national or local."[24] Thus, human security and the broad definition of development refer to the same type of activities, processes, and achievements.

This discussion has highlighted the fact that development is propelled by globalization processes, and that it is also intimately related to human security, peace building, and good governance. This means that the tools through which the AU can pursue peace, security, gender equality, good governance, respect for the rule of law, and development, are similar. To be sustained, such tools need to be reinforced by the progressive political and legal mechanisms of the member states.

The political and legal climate

Political and legal mechanisms or governance structures are crucial for innovation and the generation of knowledge. Any country's intellectual capital is only as strong as the political and legal climate permits. It is the governance structures of African states that have, in part, determined the poor shape of their knowledge bases. Calls for greater investment in science, technology, and innovation cannot be heeded by African states unless they restructure their political and legal systems. Just as foreign direct investment requires supportive governance structures, investment in knowledge creation needs an accommodating politico-legal climate, and the AU has the potential to facilitate it.

There are several obstacles to the efficient production of knowledge in Africa. The first is the low premium placed on knowledge in policy formulation. In most African countries, governments have treated knowledge producers with hostility, and have totally disregarded scientifically produced knowledge as a mechanism for informing policy-making. Even the AU has heavily relied on knowledge generated by non-Africans in formulating its policies, as well as in conceptualizing, establishing, and running its structures. The second obstacle is the low remuneration for researchers and university lecturers in many states. South Africa is the exception, but even there lecturers' salaries have been falling behind those of other professions. The third obstacle is the lack of flexibility in employment conditions. There are no incentives for hardworking researchers and lecturers, and no funds available for hiring the best researchers. The fourth is the constraints under which scholars carry out research. In developed countries, researchers simply need funds to conduct research. Ethics committees in their universities may insist on following certain ethical rules, but they do not hold them back. However, in many African states, researchers need research clearance certificates, and obtaining them can often take many months in some states. The fifth obstacle is the unwillingness of the political elite to recognize that competent researchers can provide useful input into the policy process.

If African states were to make use of the knowledge produced in Africa and elsewhere, the policy establishments would need to take a number of steps to reconfigure their governance structures. The first would be to make conditions for carrying out research more flexible and attractive by redesigning political and legal mechanisms that would accommodate innovation in the social sciences, humanities, science and technology, and in other fields. The donor community could play the important role of encouraging African states to take such initiatives, by funding them. It is through such measures that Africa might benefit from a highly skilled and mobile workforce and develop appropriate knowledge economies. The knowledge-friendly governance structures required for African states to share in the benefits of the global knowledge economy may vary from one state to another, and from one sub-region to another. Appropriate structures and mechanisms should be able to tackle the need for flexibility in the workforce, should accommodate innovations in the arts, sciences, and in technology, and should reform taxation rules – especially those relating to the importation of equipment associated with knowledge creation. They also need to address human rights, gender relations, environmental issues, and participatory democracy.

The second step would be to provide a mechanism for integrating science, technology, and innovation adequately into development plans. Many African states are interested in the benefits of science, technology, and innovation, but some of them lack the basic policy infrastructures to integrate them sufficiently into development objectives. This may be blamed partly on the lack of strategic leadership, the shortage of skilled personnel, and the nature of governance structures. Some critics have raised legitimate questions about genetic engineering, which, in its present form, is relatively new and may be fraught with danger and uncertainty. This issue needs to be addressed by the scientific community – including biotechnologists, ethicists, and environmental specialists – but without a proper governance climate this is not possible. It is through new governance structures and processes that African states might meaningfully integrate science, technology, and innovation into their development plans and develop appropriate knowledge economies.

The third step would be to design governance frameworks that take account of both global forces and indigenous contributions. African countries are part of international society, so their political and legal structures are partly derived from the rules, institutions, values, and norms that underpin life in other countries. For example, establishing knowledge-friendly governance frameworks in Africa would need to take into account the revolution in biotechnology and biomedical research, global knowledge flows, and agricultural innovations. This would help African states take advantage of the latest technology to improve crops, enable farming in semi-arid areas, and exploit biodiversity resources. It would also facilitate the development of strategic partnerships between African universities and research centers, and their counterparts abroad. Therefore, it is imperative that African policy makers recast their governance structures in order to tap into knowledge that reflects the changes in global norms while at the same time serving local needs.

However, foreign institutions cannot be transplanted root, stem, and branch into Africa without taking account of African practices. The structural adjustment programs, which the International Monetary Fund (IMF) and the World Bank promoted from the 1980s, did not take into account the positive aspects of existing practices. As a result, structural adjustment programs were partly responsible for eroding the accumulated technological capacity in several sectors. The new structures need to reflect as much as possible the progressive values, norms, and standards in Africa. Indigenous Africans have knowledge about medicine, environmental management, and agriculture, which may be of use in the future. In this regard African universities have an important role to play in setting the breadth and depth of indigenous values that are to be incorporated into the knowledge bank. Knowledge production demands that African policy makers promote and experiment with policies that incorporate social learning. Social learning encourages borrowing from other countries, but it also requires a greater understanding of the evolving social, cultural, economic, and scientific contexts within which African universities and research centers operate.

Thus, one of the priorities of the AU and its members should be to redesign governance structures to embody incentives and flexibility in workplace relations, provide room for the input of indigenous knowledge, and reflect the changing global norms and best practices. Policy makers need to recognize that universities and research centers have the capacity to play useful roles in policy making by identifying problems and suggesting solutions to them.

Capacity building

Africa has the least scientific capacity of any region in the world. According to the 1998 UNESCO World Science Report, Africa was virtually a bystander in most international science issues. It has not only failed to make an impact on the development of new materials and products, it has played no major role in the fast-moving, far-reaching information technology and communications industry.[25] The UNESCO report claims that in a 1992 survey, Africa counted a total of 20,000 scientists and engineers, representing just 0.36 percent of the world total. These scientists were responsible for only 0.8 percent of the total world scientific publications. Africa's share of patents is "close to zero," and the continent has produced only six Nobel laureates in medicine and chemistry.[26] Africa has produced very few "patents, scientific publications and technological innovations, the common yardsticks for science and technology output." Between 2000 and 2004, Africans were awarded 633 patents by the US Patents and Trademarks Office, and its researchers produced "only 1.8 percent of the world's total scholarly publications."[27]

There are several internal politico-economic reasons for Africa's fragile capacity in science, technology, and innovation. The first is the lack of political support for indigenous efforts in science and technology. A good illustration of the lack of devotion to scientific work is provided by an Ethiopian scientist who, in the 1990s, tried to isolate a soap ingredient for commercial exploitation from a soap berry plant, but gave up due to lack of government support and left for an American university. The American researchers he was working with not only discovered that the ingredient had other potentials, they deliberately failed to share their findings with the Ethiopian scientist. They then went on to develop the ingredient into a very rich anti-bilharzia treatment, patented their discovery, and sold it to a pharmaceutical company for millions of dollars. If the Ethiopian government had supported its scholar, the scientific and financial benefits would have accrued to Ethiopia and its scientists.

The second reason, which is related to the first, is the minuscule expenditure on science education, research, and development in universities and research institutes.[28] Indeed, some African universities and training institutes have been mismanaged, starved of research funds, and neglected to the extent that they offer few answers to Africa's knowledge needs. According to the 2014 UNDP *Human Development Report*, only six African states spend more than 0.5 percent of their GDP on research and development: Tunisia (1.1 percent), South Africa (0.9), Gabon (0.6), Morocco (0.6), Botswana (0.5), and the DRC (0.6). Another 14 African states spend between 0.1 and 0.4 percent on research and development, while more than 30 countries allocate no money to it at all.[29] Due to the lack of funding from their own national governments, African research institutes are almost totally reliant on foreign donations. This has the effect of making them producers of knowledge that serves the interests of donors. But without such foreign support, African research institutes could not survive. Although such support might be seen as a lifesaver for African research institutes, it also means that African scientists have to promote the research agenda of those that are funding them. As a result of this, such institutes rarely produce new knowledge that serves African interests. In fact, the African Panel on Biotechnology has underlined the "need to shift from dependence on relief models to a new emphasis on competence-building."[30]

The third reason is the migration of scientists from Africa to other parts of the world, which is sometimes called the "brain drain." As most research institutes are poorly funded and lack modern research equipment, most scientists have left the continent for greener pastures in Europe and North America. Since the 1960s, Africa has been losing a high percentage of its scientists due to poor remuneration, research equipment, and other factors.

The volume and cost of the African brain drain is colossal. By 2006 it was estimated that the continent was losing 20,000 skilled professionals every year.[31] Most of these were highly trained professionals such as doctors, engineers, and other scientists. Since 1992 Algeria has lost an estimated 45,000 of its academics and researchers as a result of the civil war, and because of a poor scientific environment at home. The brain drain produces a two-pronged "brain strain" on development by depriving Africa's weak economies of their best human resources, while at the same time forcing the hiring of expatriates to fill the gap at an estimated cost of $5.6 billion a year.[32]

To address these and similar problems, in 2006 the African Panel on Biotechnology called for the creation of African Regional Innovation Communities.[33] This approach has merit because the production of scientific knowledge in Africa is severely hampered by the lack of, or obsolete and dilapidated, infrastructure. This situation has compelled African scientists to operate in environments in which they merely perform routine tasks that contribute little or nothing to scientific innovation. This type of condition needs to be reversed through the introduction of calibrated capacity building programs.

The term "capacity building" is often used to refer to a wide range of activities related to learning and the acquisition and use of knowledge. For example, the United Nations Environment Programme (UNEP) has defined capacity building as

> the strengthening and/or development of human resources and institutional capacities. It involves the transfer of know-how, the development of appropriate facilities, and training in sciences related to safety in biotechnology and in the use of risk-assessment and risk-management.[34]

In UNESCO's *Science Report 2010*, the term "capacity building" is used to refer to the training of highly qualified human resources to work in particular fields.[35] Similarly, in this chapter the term "capacity building" is used in a limited sense to refer to the building of human resources and societal structures and mechanisms that are necessary to perform specific tasks – namely, the creation of knowledge using indigenous and global sources. It is employed to describe the creation of conditions and organizational structures through which African societies can achieve human welfare, participatory democracy, peace, and socio-economic justice.

As a process of acquiring and applying knowledge, capacity building legitimizes imitation. This implies that through capacity building, individuals are encouraged to adopt the skills, techniques, and methods of those whom they perceive as "successful," and apply them to address problems in their own situations.

Capacity building is crucial for development and for the application of appropriate science, technology, and innovation. Unfortunately, at this stage of Africa's development, there are still very few appropriate organizational structures and outfits to support capacity building. For this reason, developing institutional capacity remains a high priority for Africa.

Successful Asian states like Japan, Malaysia, Singapore, South Korea, and Taiwan care more about capacity building than do their African counterparts. The problem with this example, however, is that these Asian states have built their intellectual capital under authoritarian or semi-authoritarian regimes, under a form of governance that African states must avoid. Nevertheless, there are aspects of these countries' development that African states may need to emulate, namely adequate investment in capacity building. If African states do not do this they are unlikely to succeed in creating the sort of infrastructure that will help remove them from the poverty cycle.

Donor countries insist upon thinktanks and research centers playing a role, but critics have raised doubts about the neo-liberal-based epistemological and methodological straitjackets that bind such organizations. Besides the Institute for Security Studies, which was mentioned earlier, there are several reputable research centers in Africa. These include the African Centre for the Constructive Resolution of Disputes, the African Centre for Technology Studies, the African Economic Research Consortium, the Council for the Development of Social Sciences Research in Africa, the Kenya Institute of Public Policy Research and Analysis, and the UN University Institute for Natural Resources in Africa. The ambitions, competencies, and effectiveness of these and similar organizations vary enormously. They also face different financial, political, and legal constraints, depending on where they are based. Some of these research centers carry out rigorous policy analysis and have influenced state policies. However, unless some of them are freed from their neo-liberal straitjackets, they are unlikely to support, consistently, policies that are predominantly geared towards human welfare, participatory democracy, and socio-economic justice.

In the long term, African states will have to look for alternative ways of capacity building. The richer African states, like South Africa, may prove able to train their own personnel in most disciplines, and with minimal outside assistance. The poorer states, however, face a daunting task in this regard. They need to restructure their universities, fund them appropriately, and encourage strategic leadership of them. If they cannot afford to understake such measures then policy makers in such states need to explore opportunities for establishing regional institutes to help develop the capacity they need to enhance their knowledge bases. As part of its proposal for regional innovation centers the African Panel on Biotechnology has suggested a model based on the five African sub-regions: central Africa, eastern Africa, north Africa, southern Africa, and west Africa.[36] The Pan-African University (PAU), a recent AU initiative to provide opportunities for postgraduate training to African students, is based on this decentralized model.

One of the priorities for African policy makers is to ensure that high quality research moves out of university campuses into the government ministries. In addition, African policy makers and educational leaders need to broaden and deepen research partnerships with industry, as well as with developed and other developing countries. Through such partnerships they may acquire part of the knowledge and funding they need to help their societies establish strong knowledge bases. It is these measures that will pave the way for the creation of competitive knowledge economies in Africa.

Conclusions

Compared to other parts of the world, Africa remains scientifically, economically, politically, and militarily marginalized as a result of its weak knowledge base. This situation presents four major challenges to the AU and African policy makers in general. First, African policy makers should define the type of knowledge they need. Knowledge has been used for different purposes, including the creation of profit for corporations at the expense of workers, as well as for waging war on other societies. African policy makers have to identify the knowledge they need to attain human welfare, participatory democracy, peace, and socio-economic justice. As Peter Vale has argued: "[S]ound policy options often follow new understandings."[37]

The second challenge is to facilitate the emergence, nurturing, and training of strategic leaders. Whether it is political, business, or educational leaders, or leaders in science, technology, and innovation, it is people with strategic vision who will find the way out of Africa's marginalized position. The donor community will need to play a role by providing training and exposing such leaders to best practice.

The third challenge is to build governance structures through which the AU and its members can more effectively address their problems in a globalizing environment. It is through an accommodating politico-legal climate that the African people can use new technologies, as well as indigenous knowledge, to participate meaningfully in development. Without this transformation of their governance structures, African states will have very limited chances to create the sort of appropriate knowledge that will enable them to address some of the main causes of poverty.

The final challenge is to pay more attention to research and development. As the UNDP *Human Development Report 2014* has pointed out, "research and development policies can promote technology innovation to develop new sources of employment, increase workforce education and provide more training and retraining."[38] Moreover, adopting such policies might help as part of a process of revamping the universities and other centers of learning, establishing regional research centers, and deepening strategic partnerships with successful countries. Thus, it is important that the AU and African states take capacity building more seriously as part of their efforts to create appropriate knowledge bases. Such knowledge bases could, in turn, enhance conditions for peace, security, and good governance.

Notes

1 Some parts of this chapter are derived from Samuel M. Makinda, "African Thinkers and the Global Security Agenda" in Makumi Mwagiru and Okello Oculli (eds) *Rethinking Global Security: An African Perspective?* (Nairobi: Heinrich Bo' ll Foundation) (2006): 21–37; and Samuel M. Makinda, "How Africa Can Benefit from Knowledge," *Futures*, vol. 39, no. 8 (2007): 973–85.
2 Ali A. Mazrui, "Technological Underdevelopment in the South: The Continuing Cold War" in Paul Wapner and Lester E. J. Ruiz (eds) *Principled World Politics: The Challenge of Normative International Relations* (Lanham, MD: Rowman and Littlefield) (2000): 275.
3 Calestous Juma, *Science, Technology and Economic Growth: Africa's Bio-policy Agenda in the Twenty-first Century*, UNU/INRA Annual Lectures on Natural Resources Conservation and Management in Africa (Tokyo and Accra: UNU/INRA) (2000): 49.

4 Simplice A. Asongu, "Knowledge Economy and Financial Sector Competition in African Countries," *African Development Review*, vol. 26, no. 2 (2014): 333.
5 Ibid.: 338.
6 UNESCO World Report, *Towards Knowledge Societies* (Paris: UNESCO Publishing) (2005): 5.
7 Philip Nel and Patrick J. McGowan (eds) *Power, Wealth and Global Order: An International Relations Textbook for Africa* (Rondebosch, Cape Town: University of Cape Town Press) (1999).
8 Robert Cox, "Social Forces, States and World Orders: Beyond International Relations Theory" in Robert O. Keohane (ed.) *Neorealism and Its Critics* (New York: Columbia University Press) (1986): 207.
9 Charles S. Goodwin, "Helicobacter Pylori: 10th Anniversary of its Culture in April 1982," *Gut: An International Journal of Gastroenterology and Hepatology*, vol. 34, no. 3 (1993): 293.
10 Patrick R. Murray, Ken S. Rosenthal, George S. Kobayashi and Michael A. Pfaller, *Medical Microbiology*, 3rd edition (St. Louis: Mosby) (1998): 256. On the basis of their discovery, Marshall and Warren won the Nobel Prize for medicine in 2005.
11 See Andrea Useem, "An Era of Painful Self-Examination for Many Intellectuals in Africa," *The Chronicle of Higher Education* (October 10, 1997): A47.
12 Cox, "Social Forces, States and World Orders": 208.
13 Ibid.
14 Ibid.
15 Caroline Thomas, "Introduction" in Caroline Thomas and Peter Wilkin (eds) *Globalization, Human Security and the African Experience* (Boulder, CO: Lynne Rienner) (1999): 2.
16 Ibid.: 2.
17 *Freedom to Innovate: Biotechnology and Africa's Development.* Draft Report of the High-Level African Panel on Modern Biotechnology of the African Union and the New Partnership for Africa's Development (July 14, 2006): 2.
18 UNDP, *Human Development Report 1999* (New York: United Nations) (1999): 1–13.
19 Walter Rodney, *How Europe Underdeveloped Africa* (Dar es Salaam: Tanzania Publishing House) (1972): 103–61.
20 United Nations General Assembly, "Vienna Declaration and Programme of Action," Doc. A/CONF. (1993): 5.
21 Boutros Boutros-Ghali, *An Agenda for Development* (New York: United Nations) (1995): 2.
22 Thomas, "Introduction": 3.
23 Ibid.
24 Ibid.
25 See: www.unesco.org/new/en/natural-sciences/science-technology/prospective-studies/unesco-science-report/world-science-report-1998/ (last accessed March 27, 2015).
26 These were five South Africans who won prizes in medicine and chemistry, and one Egyptian who won a chemistry prize.
27 See Anastassios Pouris and Anthipi Pouris, "The State of Science and Technology in Africa (2000–2004): A Scientometric Assessment,"

available at: www.repository.up.ac.za/bitstream/handle/2263/14593/Pouris_
State(2009).pdf?sequence=1 (last accessed March 18, 2015).

28 Out of the less than 0.5 percent of gross national product (GNP) spent on
science research, 47 percent goes to research in agriculture, forestry, and
fisheries.

29 UNDP, *Human Development Report 2014* (New York: United Nations)
(2014): 196–9.

30 *Freedom to Innovate*: 44–5.

31 See *Daily Nation* (Nairobi), May 19, 2006.

32 Although skilled workers make up only four percent of the total workforce in Africa, they comprise more than 40 percent of the migrants. Some
African countries, such as Cape Verde, Gambia, the Seychelles, Mauritius,
and Sierra Leone, have lost more than 50 percent of their skilled workers
through migration. For more on the issue of the African brain drain, see,
for example, Amy Hagopian, Matthew J. Thompson, Meredith Fordyce,
Karin E. Johnson, and L. Gary Hart, "The Migration of Physicians from
Sub-Saharan Africa to the United States of America: Measures of the
African Brain Drain," available at: www.human-resources-health.com/con-
tent/2/1/17 (last accessed March 28, 2015).

33 *Freedom to Innovate*: 59–60.

34 I. Virgin, R. J. Frederick and S. Ramachandran, "Biosafety Training
Programs and Their Importance in Capacity Building and Technology
Assessment" in Sivramish Shantharam and Jane F. Montgomery (eds)
*Biotechnology, Biosafety and Biodiversity: Scientific and Ethical Issues for
Sustainable Development* (Enfield, NH: Science Publishers) (1999): 6.

35 UNESCO, *Science Report 2010* (Paris: UNESCO Publishing) (2010): 130.

36 *Freedom to Innovate*: 59–60.

37 Peter Vale, *Security and Politics in South Africa: The Regional Dimension*
(Boulder, CO: Lynne Rienner) (2003): 5.

38 UNDP, *Human Development Report 2014*: 95.

7 Addressing the challenges of peace, security, and governance

During the 50th anniversary of the founding of the Organization of African Unity (OAU) in May 2013, the African Union (AU) came up with a new blueprint called Agenda 2063. In explaining the vision and priorities of Agenda 2063, the AU claims this new design

> is an approach to how the continent should effectively learn from the lessons of the past, build on the progress now underway and strategically exploit all possible opportunities available in the immediate- and medium- terms, so as to ensure positive socio-economic transformation within the next 50 years.[1]

If this new guide for Africa's development in the next five decades was accompanied by concrete proposals – especially on how to build and sustain institutions that address the challenges of peace, security, and governance – it could demonstrate that the AU and its member states have found a formula through which they would meet the needs, interests, and aspirations of the African people. Without such proposals Agenda 2063 might just remain a slogan.

As we have argued throughout this book, the AU is expected to undertake several political, economic, social, and technological measures if it is to help the African people and their respective states improve their conditions in this globalizing world. At the forefront of these are the challenges of peace, security, and governance. These challenges, in turn, require paying adequate attention to several important issues, including knowledge production, development, environmental management, affordable healthcare, and individual liberties. In his final report to the United Nations (UN) General Assembly on September 19, 2006, Kofi Annan referred to three major challenges that the world faced: "[T]he security challenge; the development challenge; and the challenge of human rights and the rule of law."[2] These challenges are similar to those that the AU and its member states face, and they call for a creative understanding and application of the processes of globalization.

As was pointed out in the first edition of this book, the impacts of globalization are patchy in an Africa where large sections of the population have only limited access to information and communications technology (ICT), and where there is also widespread poverty, rampant corruption, random violence, gender inequality, autocratic rule, preventable disease, hunger, and a lack of access to education, proper sanitary conditions, and adequate shelter. These are development issues, but they also have significant peace, security, and governance dimensions.

The aforementioned problems are exacerbated by the fact that some of the political leaders in the AU Assembly are dictators who control their own countries as if they were their own personal fiefdoms, and who have no clear plans for relinquishing power through peaceful means. This situation runs counter to what Ben Kioko, a former legal counsel to the AU, described as "the philosophical bases for cooperation" in the AU. These bases require that all member states "observe certain fundamental values and standards, including respect for human rights, democratic governance, and the condemnation of unconstitutional changes of government."[3] Thus, despite the euphoria that greeted the AU when it was established in 2002, and the celebrations that marked the 50th anniversary of the founding of the OAU in 2013, little has been done to make the AU a people's organization.

The pursuit of people-centered security remains a forlorn hope, civil society organizations (CSOs) have been marginalized, and power struggles among some regional players continue. The AU, which remains a work-in-progress, appears to be held back by some of the negative politics, cronyism, and other administrative malpractices that dogged the OAU. The rest of this chapter summarizes the peace, security, and governance challenges for the AU going forward.

The peace challenge

Peace in Africa is supposed to serve as a foundation for human solidarity and progress. This is partly why some of the objectives, principles, and structures of the AU suggest that peace is considered a central goal of the Union. For example, the preamble of the Constitutive Act of the African Union (CAAU) states that the AU founders were

> conscious of the fact that the scourge of conflicts in Africa constitutes a major impediment to the socio-economic development of the continent and of the need to promote peace, security and

stability as a prerequisite for the implementation of our development and integration agenda.

In addition, the 2004–07 Strategic Plan proclaims that one of the AU's goals is a "peaceful, integrated and prosperous Africa, driven by its own people and a dynamic force in the global community."[4]

In the 1994 UN annual report, the UN Secretary-General Boutros Boutros-Ghali argued: "Peace, the economy, the environment, society and democracy are interlinked dimensions of development."[5] Boutros-Ghali sought to emphasize peace building and peace maintenance rather then conflict resolution and conflict management. In *An Agenda for Peace*, Boutros-Ghali employed the term "peace building" to refer to capacity building, societal transformation, and reconciliation among the parties in dispute.[6] By focusing on peace building, societies could undermine the root causes of war and conflict. Utilizing Boutros-Ghali's insights, one can view peace as a necessary condition for globalization, political stability, industrialization, and good governance. Peace is also important for knowledge creation, healthcare, agriculture, transport, and critical infrastructure.[7] It is by addressing the challenge of peace – which effectively means tackling the above issues – that the AU might promote "sustainable development at the economic, social and cultural levels as well as the integration of African economies" (Article 4 [j]).

Just as peace is crucial for attaining the above goals, knowledge is the key to many of Africa's political, economic, social, environmental, and technological problems. However, there are various types of knowledge, which suggests that African policy makers have to make choices. Some types of knowledge can bring about freedom, development, and empowerment; while others might only succeed in generating war, conflict, and poverty. Therefore, the AU needs to identify the types of knowledge needed and devise appropriate strategies for obtaining it. Without strategies to utilize innovations for exploiting Africa's resources, globalization might pass Africa by, and prospects for peace, development, and human emancipation could remain bleak.

To pursue peace and exploit the processes of globalization, African states would need to invest in knowledge production by considering the options below:

• engaging the expertise of home-based scientists and scholars with a view to incorporating their ideas into development plans
• involving the expertise of African scientists and scholars in the diaspora, who may use their experiences abroad to benefit the continent

- seeking the expertise of other scientists and scholars around the world with a view to building Africa's future capacity
- exploring the possibility of combining insights from traditional knowledge, with ideas from global sources.

The CAAU (Article 3 [n]) has pledged that the Union will work "with relevant international partners in the eradication of preventable diseases and the promotion of good health on the continent." The promotion of basic health is a prerequisite for sustained economic growth, education, procreation, security, and development. Some of the indicators of development are improvements in life expectancy, reductions in infant mortality rates, and access to proper sanitary conditions. These goals are hard to realize without peace. It is peace that provides conditions through which the AU and African policy makers can address the HIV/AIDS pandemic, tackle women's and children's health issues, and deal with other common but devastating diseases such as malaria, tuberculosis, asthma, intestinal parasites, and related tropical ailments. However, to do so they need to invest in health – and especially in the training and retention of doctors, nurses, and other health specialists. They also need to devise strategies through which governments, CSOs, and international partners can work together in the delivery of high quality and affordable health services throughout the continent.

If peace creates conditions that are crucial for the provision of health services, it is an equally vital ingredient for successful agriculture. In turn, agriculture is crucial for the production of food and cash crops, for poverty alleviation, employment, development, and foreign exchange earnings. Indeed, a large portion of Africa's international trade is based on agriculture and forestry products. The challenge for African policy makers is to explore ways of investing more in agriculture and ensuring that there is enough food for the people while also producing cash crops for export. They also need to create an environment in which African scientists, in collaboration with international partners, experiment with crops that can be farmed in arid areas. Moreover, given the low levels of protein in the diets of many African families, policy makers need to consider whether they should provide an environment that enables African scientists to experiment with crops such as rice, millet, and maize – which are all richer in protein.

If agriculture is crucial to the stability, development, and international trade of African states, this can only be so if agricultural commodities can be transported from one point to another on roads, railways, aircraft, or ships. The transport networks and other infrastructures are essential for development and human emancipation, but they cannot be sustained without peace. Unfortunately, as a result of corruption, cronyism, nepotism, misguided policies, and the lack of appropriate knowledge, much of Africa has extremely poor transport infrastructure, antiquated energy and water supply facilities, and limited access to ICT. This situation increases the cost of commodities, reduces the competitiveness of some economies, discourages foreign investment, and holds back human emancipation and empowerment processes.

The AU was created to address the peace challenge and to foster African integration, which means investing in the construction and maintenance of transport networks and critical infrastructure. Transport networks and ICT can have various types of use, but they should be geared towards facilitating the transformation of rural areas, stimulating agricultural production, promoting gender equality, encouraging small- and medium-sized enterprises, attracting foreign investment, and aiding regional integration. It is through such measures that African governments can construct genuine platforms for peace and security that are necessary for emancipation and empowerment.

The security challenge

As stated earlier, one of the objectives of the AU is to promote peace, security, and stability as a prerequisite for the implementation of the development and integration agenda. The Union established a Peace and Security Department (PSD) within the Commission, as well as the Peace and Security Council (PSC). These were discussed extensively in Chapter 4. In addition, the AU established the African Peace and Security Architecture (APSA), which was designed to operationalize its security objectives. In addition, the AU's Common African Defence and Security Policy (CADSP) defines security broadly to include human rights, the right to participate fully in the process of governance, the right to development, education, and health, and the right to protection against poverty, marginalization, and natural disaster. At face value this definition points in the direction of emancipation and empowerment.

However, an increasing incidence of terrorism – especially in Algeria, Egypt, Kenya, Nigeria, and Somalia – as well as the continuing conflicts in the Central African Republic (CAR), the Democratic Republic of Congo (DRC), Mali, Somalia, South Sudan, and Sudan's Darfur region, suggest a failure of the AU to meet its own security objectives. Its early warning system has not performed as expected, the Standby Force has been ineffective, and the other APSA structures have failed. The continuing security issues raise question marks over the Union's commitment and approach to security.

One of the biggest challenges that the AU faces in deploying its peace support operations (PSOs) missions is the lack of resources, particularly human and financial. Although countries contributing units to AU missions have provided infantry battalions with modest assets, there is over-dependence on external assistance to deploy and remain operational. It has become clear from the experiences of Burundi, Darfur, Mali, and Somalia that the AU cannot deploy a mission without funds from the donor community. For example, while pledges of support for the African Union Mission in Sudan (AMIS) in Darfur were pouring in from the US, Canada, Australia, the European Union (EU), Japan, and China, pledges from African countries were negligible, with Botswana categorically stating that it would not send troops. The absence of financial support has severely undermined the ability of AU missions to function effectively, and once deployed the troops have faced difficulties in command and control, logistics, and resupply. To meet the challenges of security adequately, African states need to invest in the training of their personnel in PSOs, sensitize them to gender issues, and establish a fund from which the AU can draw money expeditiously whenever PSOs are mounted.

The AU also faces a major problem stemming from its concept of self-pacification, which has been undermined by a lack of political will to intervene decisively in situations where lives are threatened. Attempts to make the search for a solution to the Darfur conflict an international effort were thwarted when African countries insisted that it was an "African problem" that needed an "African solution." This not only saw AU member states leading the way in opposing a UN Security Council resolution that called for immediate sanctions against Sudan, it also saw them refusing to acknowledge that the atrocities taking place in Darfur amounted to genocide, war crimes, and crimes against humanity. Moreover, when the then US secretary of state, Colin Powell, stated before the US Senate Foreign Relations Committee in September 2004 that genocide had been committed in Darfur, the AU challenged him to back up his claims. The AU claimed that although its observer teams had found mass graves, this did not necessarily constitute genocide. In addition, the AU did little to put pressure on Sudan in 2006–07 to accept the proposal for a joint UN/AU peacekeeping force in Darfur. The challenge for the AU is to acknowledge that the idea of applying African solutions to African problems may work in some circumstances, but not in others. It needs also to accept that this concept runs counter to the Union's position that security is universal, global, and indivisible. In fact, it would not be reasonable for the AU to insist on the idea of African solutions for

African problems when African states themselves are not willing or able to fund attempts to find solutions. Those who fund the AU's security program would want to see an immediate end to war crimes and human rights abuses.

It was generally expected that after the AU had erected APSA, it would make the key structures of the PSC operational, and render the process of attaining security much easier. However, after the construction of APSA, other weaknesses emerged. APSA structure does not reflect the African ownership that was expected of it. Moreover, although there have been a number of collaborations between the AU, the Regional Economic Communities (RECs), and international organizations on matters relating to responding, managing, and resolving conflicts in Africa, there has yet to emerge a true partnership between the AU, the RECs, the UN, and the CSOs in promoting peace and security in Africa. A related problem with regard to the AU peace and security processes concerns decision-making. The unclear rules of procedure within the AU system have led to delayed action or inaction. The Rules of Procedure of the Assembly, the Executive Council (EC), and the PSC did not stipulate how decisions on intervention under Articles 4 [j] and 4 [h] would be made.

For the AU to succeed in implementing its enormous peace and security agenda, it first needs to address the challenges of building its administrative and operational capacity, running its organs and mechanisms well, and adequately funding its activities. It also requires the forging of close partnerships with the RECs, the CSOs, the UN, the EU, and other organizations. In addition it requires the streamlining of the decision-making process, and the garnering of the necessary political will, to enable the "right" decisions to be fully implemented.

The governance challenge

The governance challenge for the AU manifests itself at two levels, which are interrelated. The first level concerns governance within the AU itself, especially the relationships between different organs and structures, the rules of procedure, and the level of commitment to the Union's objectives and principles. The second level of governance concerns the capacity of the AU to serve as a role model for its member states and the RECs, and having the strategies in place to share the Union's values and norms with the rest of the continent. Success at the first level can have a recognizable impact on the second level. Both levels require a clear understanding of the governance structure or architecture, and a solid commitment to implement it.

It was for this reason that the AU Assembly adopted the African Governance Architecture (AGA) at its 16th ordinary session in January 2011. On paper, AGA is the overall political and institutional framework for the promotion of good governance. It seeks to achieve its aims by enhancing interactions and synergies between the decision-making AU organs and structures. Based on three pillars – norms, institutional framework, and interactions – AGA also intends to encourage the generation of shared governance values and visions on the continent. It is also critical that AGA and APSA are harmonized to work in ways that enhance, rather than weaken, each other's opportunities for success. The success of AGA will greatly benefit the implementation of the peace and security agenda, particularly the prevention of conflict.

Achieving these objectives requires collaboration among various agents: the AU, the RECs, African states, CSOs, and the international partners. A crucial element in this process is the recognition that the African people need to be consulted and to participate in the pursuit of the AU's objectives and principles. Theoretically, this represents a normative jump from the state-centrism of the OAU, to processes and activities that are more people-centered. However, as was explained in Chapter 3, AGA has not successfully resolved the problems of governance within the AU itself. Until this has been achieved the AU will not be in a strong position to tackle governance problems continent-wide.

Indeed, the AU's compliance with its own principles, objectives, and decisions would have been much easier to accomplish, and more realistic, had there been oversight mechanisms provided for in the CAAU. Presently the African Union Commission (AUC) is extremely powerful and controls virtually the entire organization – to the detriment of other organs. The most prominent tussle for power has been between the Commission's Peace PSD and the PSC. Since its creation in 2004, the PSC has heavily relied on the PSD for secretarial support and expertise. Nevertheless, over time PSC members have realized that they have merely been endorsing the agenda and decisions of the PSD. Given the significance of the PSC in the attainment of the Union's goals, it is imperative that the PSC be provided with sufficient resources to conduct its business independently and effectively.

Although the CAAU clearly identifies the component organs of the Union, it is silent on the powers and duties of most of these structures, as well as the sequencing of their establishment. The operationalization of these organs has proceeded without attention being paid to the core goals of the Union. Besides establishing the Assembly, the EC, the PRC, and the Commission, the organ that has received most attention is the PSC. Nonetheless, organs such as the Economic, Social, and Cultural Council (ECOSOCC), the Specialized Technical Committees (STCs), and the financial structures, have not performed as expected. There has also been apathy towards the establishment and running of the Pan-African Parliament (PAP) and the judicial and human rights organs – structures that are key to the promotion of security, governance, democracy, and justice. The sequencing and operationalization of these organs also reveal power struggles among member states and reflect the interests of particular African leaders. The level of such power struggles, and of outside influence over the sequencing of organs, is determined by the nature of the issues involved and how much benefit the competing African leaders anticipate being able to derive from them. Hence, it appears much easier to garner support for the setting up of mechanisms that deal with relatively "soft" issues – such as knowledge, the environment, and ICT – than it is to deal with the "hard" issues such as the peer review process and performance monitoring.

The AU has also faced the daunting task of designing the organs and management systems required, and of acquiring the technical assistance needed to build them. The Union had an exceedingly shallow pool of expertise to draw from to build the new complex structures stipulated by the Constitutive Act. Since it could not attract qualified expertise from international organizations such as the UN, the AU was faced with the choice of either poaching personnel from the RECs – and thereby draining their much-needed human resources – or retaining the "seasoned" OAU staff. In retaining the OAU staff, the AU took a gamble and lost the opportunity to assemble a highly professional staff that had no, or limited, association with the OAU. Currently the AU heavily relies on foreign consultants offered by its international partners.

Although the AU and New Partnership for Africa's Development (NEPAD) place great emphasis on good governance and the transparency of member states, they remain silent on how their financial structures and other organs of the AU will be held accountable and monitored within a framework of good governance and corporate responsibility. However, these oversights are merely a reflection of the historical fact that institution building, at both national and regional levels, has been one of Africa's weakest points. The lack of an African standard for building and sustaining institutions has led to the creation of structures and mechanisms that serve as impediments to economic development, democratization, and the implantation of justice values.[8]

Conclusions

The peace, security, and governance challenges that the AU, its member states, and the African people face are daunting – but they are not insurmountable. The key to most of the problems rests with having the right paradigm and generating appropriate knowledge. The tasks for the Union and its member states are to identify the right type of knowledge, for specific projects, and at particular times. It is always important for all concerned to bear in mind the fact that knowledge is always created for a specific purpose and for a particular policy community or academic community. The AU and its member states need to search for knowledge that is likely to help them achieve human welfare, participatory democracy, peace, security, and socio-economic justice. Most importantly, they should seek knowledge that will lead to human emancipation and empowerment.

Notes

1 See Agenda 2063, available at: http://agenda2063.au.int/ (last accessed March 23, 2015).
2 UN Secretary-General, "Address to the General Assembly," September 19, 2006: 1.
3 Ben Kioko, "The Right of Intervention under the African Union's Constitutive Act: From Non-Interference to Non-Intervention," *International Review of the Red Cross*, vol. 85, no. 852 (2003): 807.
4 See *High Level Panel of the Audit of the African Union*, chaired by Adebayo Adedeji (also known as the Adedeji report) (December 2007): 64.
5 Boutros Boutros-Ghali, *Building Peace and Development: Annual Report of the Work of the Organization* (New York: United Nations) (1994): 3.
6 Boutros Boutros-Ghali, *An Agenda for Peace* (New York: United Nations) (1992).
7 Critical infrastructure generally includes communications networks, banking, health services, energy and water supplies, emergency services, and transport networks. It comprises facilities, supply chains, and information technologies that are crucial to the social, economic, and political wellbeing of any society.
8 For different perspectives on this issue, see, for example, Rorden Wilkinson and Steve Hughes (eds) *Global Governance: Critical Perspectives* (London: Routledge) (2002).

Select bibliography

Books

Akokpari, John, Angela Ndinga-Muvumba and Tim Murithi (eds) *The African Union and its Institutions* (Johannesburg: Jacana) (2009). Provides an assessment of the AU's aims and institutions, and includes contributions by scholars, civil society representatives, and practitioners with AU experience.

Edozie, Rita Kiki, *The African Union's Africa: New Pan-African Initiatives in Global Governance* (East Lansing: Michigan State University Press) (2014). Examines the "African Union phenomenon" and how the AU is impacting on African politics at different levels.

Engel, Ulf and Joao Gomes Porto (eds) *Towards an African Peace and Security Regime: Continental Embeddedness, Transnational Linkages, Strategic Relevance* (Surrey, UK, and Burlington, VT: Ashgate) (2013). Examines and evaluates the emerging African Peace and Security Architecture, including norms, institutions, and relationships.

Francis, David, *Uniting Africa: Building Regional Peace and Security Systems* (Aldershot, UK, and Burlington, VT: Ashgate) (2006). Examines how regional and continental peace and security systems can address African conflicts, with chapters on the AU as well as Africa's different regional systems.

Jeng, Abou, *Peacebuilding in the African Union: Law, Philosophy and Practice* (Cambridge and New York: Cambridge University Press) (2012). Drawing on insights from different disciplines, this book examines the AU's attempts to build and sustain peace on the continent. It includes case studies of Somalia and Burundi.

Murithi, Timothy, *The African Union: Pan-Africanism, Peacebuilding and Development* (Burlington, VT: Ashgate) (2005). Examines the basis and working of the AU, and how it is tackling peace and development challenges.

Murithi, Timothy and Hallelujah Lulie (eds) *The African Union Peace and Security Council: A Five-Year Appraisal*. ISS Monograph Series, no. 187 (Pretoria: Institute for Security Studies) (2013). Examines and evaluates the formative period of the AU's main decision-making organ on matters of peace and security.

Murray, Rachel, *Human Rights in Africa: From the OAU to the African Union* (Cambridge: Cambridge University Press) (2004). Provides an overview of the evolution of human rights from OAU to AU structures.

Welz, Martin, *Integrating Africa: Decolonization's Legacies, Sovereignty, and the African Union* (London: Routledge) (2013). Uses a comparative analytical framework to examine a selection of cases of African countries and evaluate their level of support for pursuing deeper political integration. It explains the level of variation between the cases and how, in turn, this impacts upon the nature of the AU.

Articles

Baimu, Evarist, "The African Union: Hope for Better Protection of Human Rights in Africa?" *African Human Rights Law Journal*, vol. 1, no. 2 (2001): 299–326. Examines the place of human rights in economic and political integration efforts on the African continent, particularly in the AU.

Demeke, Tsegaye, "The New Pan-African Parliament: Prospects and Challenges in View of the Experience of the European Parliament," *African Human Rights Law Journal*, vol. 4, no. 1 (2004): 53–73. Examines the salient features of the Pan-African Parliament with a focus on its composition, functions, and powers as they are enshrined in the provisions of the protocol, and compares the PAP to its European equivalent.

Franke, Benedikt and Stefan Ganzle, "How 'African' is the African Peace and Security Architecture? Conceptual and Practical Constraints of Regional Security Cooperation in Africa," *African Security*, vol. 5 (2012): 88–104. Assesses the influence and outcomes of external actors on the "Africanness" of the African peace and security architecture.

Kindiki, Kithure, "The Normative and Institutional Framework of the African Union Relating to the Protection of Human Rights and the Maintenance of International Peace and Security: A Critical Appraisal," *African Human Rights Law Journal*, vol. 3, no. 1 (2003): 97–117. Examines norms and institutions dealing with human rights challenges on the continent as developed under the AU framework.

Makoa, Francis K., "African Union: New Organization, Old Ideological Framework," *Strategic Review for Southern Africa*, vol. 26, no. 1 (2004): 14. Argues that the OAU's ideological framework that guides the AU constitutes a hurdle that the latter needs to overcome if it is to transform the African continent.

Mwanasali, Musifiki, "The African Union, the United Nations, and the Responsibility to Protect: Towards an African Intervention Doctrine," *Global Responsibility to Protect*, vol. 2 (2010): 388–413. Examines how the Responsibility to Protect doctrine has been interpreted and applied under the AU framework.

Okumu, Wafula, "The African Union: Pitfalls and Prospects for Uniting Africa," *Journal of International Affairs*, vol. 62, no. 2 (2009): 93–111. Critically assesses the performance of the AU since its inception.

Stefiszen, Karen, "The African Union: Challenges and Opportunities for Women," *African Human Rights Law Journal*, vol. 5, no. 2 (2005): 358–86. Examines AU structures in terms of the challenges and opportunities they present for women's rights advocacy.

Weiss, Thomas and Martin Welz, "The UN and African Union in Mali and Beyond: A Shotgun Wedding?" *International Affairs*, vol. 19, no. 4 (2014): 889–905. Examines the evolving relationship and areas of emerging tension between the UN and AU in peace operations, with a focus on Mali.

Welz, Martin, "The African Union Beyond Africa: Explaining the Limited Impact of Africa's Continental Organization Beyond Africa," *Global Governance*, vol. 19, no. 3 (2013): 425–41. Assesses the extent to which the AU has influence on key issues on the agenda of global governance, and suggests ways that the AU could further that influence.

Useful web sites

www.achpr.org/
   This is the homepage of the African Commission on Human and Peoples' Rights
www.africa-eu-partnership.org/
   This is the homepage of the Europe-Africa Partnership
aprm-au.org/
   This is the homepage of the African Peer Review Mechanism
www.au.int/
   This is the homepage of the African Union
www.au.int/en/organs/cj
   This is the link to the African Court on Human and Peoples' Rights
www.nepad.org/
   This is the homepage of the New Partnership for Africa's Development
www.pan-africanparliament.org/
   This is the homepage of the Pan-African Parliament
www.peaceau.org/en/
   This is the homepage of the AU Peace and Security Department
www.securitycouncilreport.org/monthly-forecast/2014-12/un-au_partnership_on_peace_operations.php
   This is the homepage of the UN-AU Partnership on Peace Operations

Index

Routledge Global Institutions Series

Routledge Global Institutions Series 213

**4 The UN General Assembly
(2005)**
*by M. J. Peterson (University
of Massachusetts, Amherst)*

**3 United Nations Global
Conferences (2005)**
*by Michael G. Schechter
(Michigan State University)*

**2 The UN Secretary-General
and Secretariat (2005)**
*by Leon Gordenker
(Princeton University)*

**1 The United Nations and
Human Rights (2005)**
A guide for a new era
*by Julie A. Mertus (American
University)*

Books currently under contract include:

The Regional Development Banks
Lending with a regional flavor
by Jonathan R. Strand (University of Nevada)

Millennium Development Goals (MDGs)
For a people-centered development agenda?
by Sakiko Fukada-Parr (The New School)

The Bank for International Settlements
The politics of global financial supervision in the age of high finance
by Kevin Ozgercin (SUNY College at Old Westbury)

International Migration
by Khalid Koser (Geneva Centre for Security Policy)

Human Development
by Richard Ponzio

The International Monetary Fund (2nd edition)
Politics of conditional lending
by James Raymond Vreeland (Georgetown University)

The UN Global Compact
by Catia Gregoratti (Lund University)

Institutions for Women's Rights
*by Charlotte Patton (York College, CUNY) and Carolyn Stephenson
(University of Hawaii)*

International Aid
by Paul Mosley (University of Sheffield)

Global Consumer Policy
by Karsten Ronit (University of Copenhagen)

The Changing Political Map of Global Governance
by Anthony Payne (University of Sheffield) and Stephen Robert Buzdugan (Manchester Metropolitan University)

Coping with Nuclear Weapons
by W. Pal Sidhu

Global Governance and China
The dragon's learning curve
edited by Scott Kennedy (Indiana University)

The Politics of Global Economic Surveillance
by Martin S. Edwards (Seton Hall University)

Mercy and Mercenaries
Humanitarian agencies and private security companies
by Peter Hoffman

Regional Organizations in the Middle East
by James Worrall (University of Leeds)

Reforming the UN Development System
The Politics of Incrementalism
by Silke Weinlich (Duisburg-Essen University)

The United Nations as a Knowledge Organization
by Nanette Svenson (Tulane University)

The International Criminal Court
The politics and practice of prosecuting atrocity crimes
by Martin Mennecke (University of Copenhagen)

BRICS
by João Pontes Nogueira (Catholic University, Rio de Janeiro) and Monica Herz (Catholic University, Rio de Janeiro)

Expert Knowledge in Global Trade
edited by Erin Hannah (University of Western Ontario), James Scott (University of Manchester), and Silke Trommer (Murdoch University)

The European Union (2nd edition)
Clive Archer (Manchester Metropolitan University)

Protecting the Internally Displaced
Rhetoric and reality
Phil Orchard (University of Queensland)

The Arctic Council
Within the far north
Douglas C. Nord (Umea University)

For further information regarding the series, please contact:

Nicola Parkin, Editor, Politics and International Studies
Taylor & Francis
2 Park Square, Milton Park, Abingdon
Oxford OX14 4RN, UK
nicola.parkin@tandf.co.uk
www.routledge.com

Made in the USA
Monee, IL
21 January 2025

10484438R00134